One Man STAND

One Man STAND

Short Stories for the Military Enthusiast

P. R. Hirsh

MARINER PUBLISHING

Buena Vista, VA

3 5 7 9 10 8 6 4 2

Library of Congress Control Number: 2025902759

One Man Stand
P. R. Hirsh

p. cm.

1. History: Military—Weapons
2. Fiction: Historical—20th Century—World War I
3. History: Military—Strategy

I. Hirsh, P. R., 1962– II. Title.

ISBN 13: 979-8-9863592-2-9 (softcover : alk. paper)
ISBN 13: 979-8-9863592-3-6 (ebook)

Design and Layout by Karen Bowen

Mariner Publishing
An imprint of

Mariner Media, Inc.
131 West 21st Street
Buena Vista, VA 24416
Tel: 540-264-0021
www.marinermedia.com

Printed in the United States of America

This book is printed on acid-free paper meeting the requirements of the American Standard for Permanence of Paper for Printed Library Materials.

This book is dedicated to the loving memory of

Lieutenant Eugene Folks, USMC

*"I'll lay down my sword and shield.
Down by the riverside
and I ain't gonna study war no more."*
                    —Plantation Melodies, 1918

Contents

Part 1

Edward III, The Black Prince whose victory at Crecy was largely made through use of the long bow.

1

Bloody Constraint

"You may not be interested in war, but war is interested in you."

—Leon Trotsky

I am a responsible war buff. No matter what the era, I *try to* separate military glory from the marshal abyss that lies beneath, but this insight does not come naturally. Like most Americans born in the late 1950s, for most of my life, I looked at war as something akin to a football game. We do like to keep score. Bill Murry famously said in his military comedy *Stripes* (1981) that, "We are ten and one!" War, however, saps my objectivity. I tend to reduce most battles to a simple list of high-minded ideals centered on discipline, duty, honor, and courage.[1] Now that I am in my old age, I have come to realize that I have spent too much time examining the very tip of the spear and not enough on understanding where soldiers get those pointy sticks in the first place.

As I analyze various firefights and pitched battles on land, sea, and air, I am impressed with the fact that warfare has always been a matter of finance. Sure, wars may spark over a dastardly infraction, but it is the *business* of war that puts troops in the field. So it was with the Hundred Years War between England and France, which raged with varying degrees of intensity between 1337 and 1453. English

---

1. Another *Stripes* reference. Ironically for an anti-military film, Sargeant Hulka delivers the perfect list of soldierly attributes.

3

kings invaded France hoping to capture enemy nobles who could be ransomed for astronomical amounts of money. Captured lands were sold off or given as compensation for loyalty to the crown. The newly conquered peasantry was bled, raped, starved, stripped of all possessions, and then raped some more. British citizens were ferried over to replace the locals who were chased off to the nether regions of France.

The French would eventually catch a rare military break with the appearance of presumably heaven-sent and iconic Joan of Arc (1412–

Joan of Arc dressed to kill.

1431). As a young teen, she engendered a religious and nationalistic wave that revived French military confidence during the crucial siege of Orléans. She was present for a few epic battles and given much credit for French success. Then the French wave broke, and they reverted to their usual military slump. Joan's ardent supporters began to whisper…

"You know what I think, Jacques? I think she craaaazy."

Joan was captured and tried by the British who found her guilty of heresy. She was burned at the stake in 1431 for, among her other offenses, wearing men's clothes. This may have been the first French crime against fashion.

Meanwhile, back home in London, New Castle, Bristol, Nottingham, and various other scrofulous dung holes, the English people loved their monarchs with a similar reverence. After all, kings were thought to be heaven-sent, somehow. Royal authority was based in a divine right. When the king declared war, His people accepted the decision as God's will, and they worked flat out until they either heard the church bells peal their victory or, more likely, they died from an infected hangnail. Their unified purpose built a national identity, or more correctly put, it made their brand.

Straight to the Point

Let us begin the study of weapons with the simple English arrow. Making a long bowman's missile was no small thing. The arrow is literally a striking example of the early need for standardization. Few other items were mass-produced at that time. Entire industries evolved to manufacture each individual part of an arrow. There were fletchers, shaft makers, and arrowhead or bodkin forgers. Each human-driven factory produced one thing dependably well.

Virtually no original bows or arrows remain from the Hundred Years' War period, but one trove of ancient British bow weapons was recovered from a most unlikely locker. In 1545, while in battle with the French, Henry the Eighth's overloaded flagship, the *Mary Rose*, was mishandled as she came about to fire a broadside from her massive guns. It is thought that the extra weight of her newest weapons lowered the ship's waterline. She listed rather more than usual in the maneuver and managed to take on water through her open lower gun ports. This promptly sank her in the Solent near the Isle of White. Other reports suggest that the *Mary Rose* was holed by gunfire near the waterline and sank. Many unsuccessful attempts were made to raise her, but she was stuck fast. Her guns were occasionally brought up from the relatively shallow forty-foot grave well into the 1830s. The wreck settled in deep mud which largely preserved the site for modern archeologists who finally raised what was left of the ship at fantastic expense in 1982. They recovered a treasure trove of artifacts including bows and scores of arrows. These came in two lengths. The famous "cloth-yard shaft" was, in fact, about thirty-two inches long. Shorter arrows may have been intended for accurate close-up work, whereas the longer arrows had greater weight for longer range.

Archers made up about eighty percent of King Henry the Fifth's forces. He had a mighty pool from which to find the best men. English archers learned their trade from a very young age. Commoners were required to practice with their bows regularly. In battle, an archer might average five to perhaps as many as eight shots per minute. When pressed to the wall, they could fire ten or even twelve. A typical battle might see the archer loft twenty to fifty arrows over a considerable amount of time.

John Keegan states in *The Face of Battle* (1976) that we are not sure how archers were controlled in combat. Henry's archers are depicted on film as more of a mob than a military formation. We do believe that they were well spread out with the men standing behind long, sharpened forward-leaning stakes that could easily impale a horse and throw off its armored rider. Certainly, their indirect volley fire was organized. Somebody had to conduct the orchestra, but how did he make his orders heard? Did they use flag signals? Were there leaders of archers on each wing? If so, did they somehow coordinate their volleys? Did lead archers call out range? And while we are at it, who brought additional arrows forward for those thousands of men? The climax moment at Agincourt occurred when the archers dropped their bows and entered the fray with hand weapons. Who made that call? Did a noble give an order to charge the French men-at-arms or was this a case of infectious heroism?

While the longbow is the most famous weapon of the Hundred Years' War, and highly effective at the beginning of the conflict, a remarkable evolution in weapons technology took place over the course of that one-hundred-and-sixteen-year debacle that would end the bow-weapon's dominance. That is, until the deadly arrow was re-encountered in the hands of Native Americans who took a dim view of European expansion. The bow-weapon's silence, relative effective range, and above all, rate of fire, were vastly superior to clumsy and unreliable early firearms that were meant for volley work on a European battlefield. Matchlock weapons were more bluff than bash, but if one's enemy is unfamiliar with any form of chemistry, the weapon might frighten its way to victory. Many worthless weapons do.

Weaponology is a twofold concept. There is the offensive capability of the device, and then there is the all-important defensive reaction against it. This is obvious with tanks, which keep getting bigger and heavier as anti-tank weapons increase their penetration. During the Hundred Years' War, plate-armored knights on armored horses were the tanks of their day. The noble's armor rendered him immune to a commoner's improvised weapons. Advances in metallurgy improved armor protection to the point of rendering arrows, and even crossbow bolts, useless against plate armor. Iron bodkin points cannot easily penetrate even a thin steel plate. The tip tends to collapse on impact, and a glancing hit does no damage. A new weapon was needed.

Penetration wasn't the only problem. The arrow's demise was also a matter of training and logistics. Archers required years of practice to be effective, but a musketeer could be trained to fire his weapon in days. Compared to lead musket balls, arrows were expensive and, taken in sum, difficult to transport. Gun powder had its safety issues, but it was easy to ship. Most importantly, the early musket ball was just barely capable of penetrating plate armor at close range. Even a deflected shot could knock a man off his feet or kill his horse. Plus, one has to admit, guns are just more fun. He who has them possesses an irresistible advantage.

Muskets were still a long way off in Henry the Fifth's era, but ever-improving cannons were used during the Hundred Years' War. They were primitive and suited only for siege work, but it was obvious that artillery was the answer to all battlefield problems.[2] Early on, just getting a cannon set up took considerable time and effort. The rate of fire was unimpressive, and they occasionally exploded, but when King Henry wanted to knock out a bastion or punch through a castle wall, he called for his experienced cannoneers. The final battles saw the French use cannons at Castillon against English troops in the field quite effectively. In terms of casualties inflicted, this battle was Agincourt in reverse. The British just kept coming despite the obvious futility of their assault. Historians wrote that every French cannonball fired killed at least six Englishmen. At the outset of the Hundred Years' War, artillery was virtually unknown, but by its close, concentrated artillery would decide the ultimate victor.

At that time in history, a serious English invasion of France numbered ten to fifteen thousand troops. Henry could call on only twelve thousand men in 1415, but he did manage to bring over thousands of horses to give his armored men-at-arms mobility and to drag his provisions, arrows, artillery, and siege weapons from one fortified French town to the next. It is hard to know if the English counted noncombatants acting in some form of official support in their muster. By the time of the Battle of Agincourt, Henry's army was seriously depleted by the siege at Harfleur where raging shigella bacillus caused widespread dysentery disease. Non-existent camp sanitation contaminated food and water. This was a military fact of life and death at that time as, amazingly, they did not consider crapping where they ate to be a problem. Indeed, Henry must have eaten a shit sandwich in the late

---

2. Thanks to World War Two British Field Marshall William Slim for that euphemism.

spring or early summer of 1422. The bloody flux would kill him by August 31st.[3]

I have seen many figures that claim the French fielded massive armies of thirty thousand men or more at Agincourt. I question these statistics. The French figures may include noncombatants and even camp followers in their totals. The logistics of supporting such a huge force, or simply organizing this massive body to deliberate effect, would have been unmanageably difficult at that time in history. The optimistic number in my mind is twenty thousand, though Keegan believes the French to have numbered closer to twenty-five. Let us suppose here that the French numbered fifteen thousand troops. This was still double Henry's strength. Worse still, they were healthy, well fed, and rested. They shined themselves up and waited for Henry to advance on their well-prepared line.

In comparison, Henry led a haggard band, but they were hardened men, and the English archers, many of them Welsh, were a dependable "force multiplier" when the French threw down. Other factors that bolstered Henry's strength include English faith in leadership, their *esprit de corps*, and above all, their defensive posture including the all-important long stakes. This option essentially doubles one's strength. Neither side had a technological advantage at Agincourt. The famous longbow was old-school and would rapidly lose ground against firearms technology. Bow-weapons were used for many more decades, but Agincourt was one of the last of the famous bow fights.

3.　While most sources cite dysentery as the cause of Henry the Fifth's death, this should be seen as a general description for several possible illnesses. When he first fell ill, he was out of action for several weeks, but over time, he seemed to rally. He had the benefit of the best nutrition and fluids. If his doctors didn't bleed him too much, he could recover from dysentery. He briefly appeared on the battlefield in full armor, but this act sapped what little strength he had left to give. He might have suffered heat stroke. Henry likely experienced a relapse of his former illness and was never ambulatory thereafter. He took weeks to die. He was only thirty-five. www.britannica.com/biography/Henry-V-king-of-England lists the cause of Henry's death as "Camp Fever" or Typhus.

Steel armors, mostly, kept nobles safe from bolts and arrows. They no longer needed to carry a shield and could use two handed weapons like halberds and pics in place of a sword or axe.

Other force multipliers in this fight were related to terrain, weather, and organization. Henry used the ground effectively. His force was well deployed. The weather, though harsh, favored him. The French did not realize that they were at the mud's mercy.

The battle of Agincourt began as a staring match. Henry had to dig up stakes and advance to extreme bow range to harass the French into action.

The French maneuvered their forces on the actual field in large rectangular formations that they called *bataille*. Shakespeare used the term "battles" as a substitute. No two *bataille* were the same size, so it is difficult to say how many men-at-arms made up each formation, but they numbered in the thousands. Remember, only the men at the front of the formation could strike at their enemy, and even these men had limited freedom of movement because they were so tightly packed together. They attacked Henry's center in echelon, so only one battle group could engage the British at a time. They were also unable to spread their *bataille* abreast to envelop Henry's entire stand.

The French army was visually stunning and came complete with crossbowmen and romping heavy cavalry that tried to drive off the English archers before the battle proper was joined. Thanks largely to the sharpened stakes that screened these archers, they failed rather badly in the attempt, and their disorganized withdrawal took their crazed retreating war horses right through their own advancing troops. Henry should have run or surrendered at the sight of that mighty force, but the French proved at Agincourt that a large body of men tightly packed together on a sodden battlefield was both a danger to itself and unable to inflict serious damage to the enemy. The English monarch likely watched with glee as the retiring French cavalry ran down their own men.

Shakespeare *did not* record Henry saying, "Now my brave brothers, I confess before God and my retinue, that in the face of this vast enemy I didst grapple with a weaker thought. But as I watch cowardly French hooves stamp out our French foe, I am touched by Saint Crispin who tells me, fear not, brave king, for thou art on a roll."

Henry's men-at-arms fought extremely well, but Agincourt was really an archer's battle from start to finish. Stationed primarily on Henry's flanks behind the previously mentioned abatis of sharpened wood stakes, they stood a little forward on the flanks and so funneled the advancing French straight into the noble-rich British center. They poured fire on the French men-at-arms and cavalry both from long range and point-blank. Close range fire was largely enfilade. The armored French troops were heavily peppered and occasionally mortally struck. Horses, however, were not armored on their flanks and were cut down almost immediately.

*English longbows behind sharpened stakes
won the day at Agincourt in 1415.*

One has to wonder how many arrows were loosed at Agincourt. The English ran their magazine dry. How many arrows did Henry have? I have seen references to three hundred thousand carried in dozens of wagons. However, this number may represent a topping off of another supply. It is difficult to gauge if this was considered to be adequate for the entire campaign or if his stocks were replenished over time.

The Arrow Storm Cometh

Five thousand archers firing a leisurely five shots a minute launch twenty-five thousand arrows every sixty seconds. They could squirt three hundred thousand arrows in less than fifteen minutes of continuous firing. Many arrows were recovered after a battle and great effort was put into restoring once-fired missiles by fletchers who accompanied the army, but the recovery rate was likely quite low.

Between 1359 and 1360, 1.3 million arrows were delivered to the Tower of London. Hundreds of thousands, perhaps millions of arrows, were stockpiled in other armories elsewhere in England. This procurement went on year after year. A great deal depended on domesticated fowl. Only swans and geese have feathers long enough to be used by the Worshipful Company of Fletchers, founded in 1371. Every goose in England had feathers plucked, gathered, and sent off for arrow production. A special fletcher's glue with insect-repellent qualities was developed so that arrows could be stored long-term. These cached arrows were carefully maintained and turned every so often to make sure they did not warp. Henry had plenty of high-quality ammo.

The arrowheads were held in place with glue or press fit, which distinguished a hunting arrow from a single-use military arrow. The hunter's point was usually a broadhead and likely had a cross pin through the shaft to keep the two together when the arrow was pulled from the deer's chest. To prevent the immediate reuse of the arrow, the military version leaves its bodkin point inside the target. In order to get an arrowhead out of a body, it had to be pushed through. Yeah, think about that a second. If a soldier takes an arrow hit below his collar bone, it has to be pushed through his shoulder blade to get it out. More likely, it would be left inside the victim, who either endured the subsequent complications and lived, or not.

At the Battle of Shrewsbury in 1403, the sixteen-year-old future king of England, Henry the Fifth himself, was struck *in the face* by one such arrow, and it burrowed in deep just below his left eye. It is thought that the arrow might have been a ricochet as a hit from straight on would likely have gone through his skull and killed him outright.

I have seen several presentations and read many more about the amazing surgery that followed. They differ in the fine details, though I would assume that their facts are from the same sources. First, there is actually some disagreement about which side of Henry's face took the hit, though the left side is favored. The real issue, however, is a dispute over the angle of impact. There are two camps. One group says that the prince presented at England's only Emergency Room with a projectile that transversed his sinus. The point actually could be touched in Henry's right nostril. Other experts believe that the arrow penetrated straight into his face a full six inches with the tip much farther back toward Henry's brain or base of his skull. Six inches, though? Really?

I asked my father, the doctor, about such a wound, and his response was similar to my own instinct on the matter. "Six inches? Man! That's deep. Measure that on your own face with a ballpoint pen which is about six inches long. That arrow point would just have to wind up touching his spine or penetrate his skull. If it did go that deep, and if it did go straight back into his face, it was a miracle he lived ten minutes, let alone days."

We believe the sinus hit would be far more survivable than a bodkin ending up anywhere near his brain, spine, or the blood vessels and nerve bundles that make life worthwhile. Supposedly, Henry continued to fight for some time with the arrow sticking out, which to me would indicate, if true, that the hit was to the sinus and not the deeper skull. Whatever the situation, it would soon become infected if it were not removed, and even then, the likelihood of complications was insanely high. The young prince was very likely, royal toast. The English would say, "Oh bad luck!"

Saving Face

The wound was beyond battlefield medical science, and Henry was moved fifty miles to Kenilworth castle and the care of John Bradmore, who had been a physician with Henry's retinue since 1399. Bradmore took a long look at the wound and said something to the effect of, "Dude, I think I can get that out. Let me jet off to the blacksmith's shop to whip up a special tool just for the occasion. The monks here will sing their greatest hits to you continuously, and we are going to sedate you with special teas and the like. I will visit you periodically to cause pain, but unlike every other physician in England, the pain I cause actually heals."

The monks sang for four days straight. That's how long it took to make the complex device. I'll bet Henry was begging for a sea shanty. A few of the monks got so sick of singing that they left the band.

Bradmore's craftsmanship was well known. I have seen sources that claim the good doctor was previously arrested for counterfeiting royal coins and only released from prison to save Henry. Whatever his past, remember that Bradmore had to do the extraction by feel alone. I am left to wonder how they handled suction to clear the wound channel other than to have someone actually hoover it out perhaps with glass or metal straw? Who got that job? Once inserted into the still-open wound, the unique instrument fit in the arrowhead socket and, using a screw-like tensioner, he hoped to grab the bodkin. The device is known to this day as the Bradmore Screw. It is one of the earliest purely medical devices ever devised and a worthy *Jeopardy* answer.

Henry's wound management was just as remarkable as the surgery itself. While considerable time passed before the extraction could be attempted, Bradmore tended to Henry's wound with a poultice of his own concoction. This kept the puncture sealed, but he packed the wound with honey-soaked linen that he referred to in his notes as "tents." This allowed him to keep the point of impact open until he was ready to make the big grab.

The actual procedure must have been truly horrific. In order for the device to work, Bradmore had to push it with considerable force.

I'll bet they had twenty guys sitting on Henry to hold him perfectly still. Picture that ballpoint pen being pushed into your face, slowly, all of it. Bradmore wrote that he failed in his first attempt. Blood created a suction that caused the device to slip. The wound was sucked out, and the second attempt succeeded. Researchers who prefer the hit to the sinus theory report that Bradmore was assisted in a second try by pushing the bodkin point in the prince's nose backward toward the tool. That, I believe.

Henry's innovative physician wrote that it took considerable wiggling and a little help from God to get the bodkin free. I'll bet the screaming was unforgettable. I can picture the tool coming out, soaked in blood and goo, and there for all to see was *the* most consequential bodkin of all time. Somebody must have kept that artifact after the surgery. I wonder if it still exists. I want to put it on my key chain.

The level of relief for everyone concerned must have been remarkable. Spectators at the event were impressed by Henry's endurance. The ugly scar it left also helped his warrior image. He was painted in profile for his royal portrait thereafter, though again, historians differ as to how severe the scar might actually have been. The wound was rinsed with white wine and packed with a poultice of barley flour, honey, and "terebentine," which were thought to prevent infection. After twenty days, it healed nicely. Henry was so grateful to his doctor that he paid Bradmore an annual salary of ten Marks a year for the rest of his life.

The real hero in this story is the creativity that was harnessed to heal instead of kill. The entire affair was emblematic of the budding Renaissance.

Henry's surgery marks a dramatic change in how a wounded soldier might be saved. The ambulance system, aid stations, surgeries, and recovery hospitals would not appear until 1862. Doctor Jonathan Letterman set up this system for the Army of the Potomac. Medical science and war are uncomfortably intertwined. Surgeons get a lot of practice after a battle. Discoveries are made. Techniques are perfected that over the eons save millions of lives. News of Bradmore's maxillo-facial surgery success must have spread like wildfire. I am left to wonder if this event helped to awaken medical sciences.

Bradmore authored *The Philomena* which documented the surgery, but it was not published until after his death. He wrote in Latin, and the book was translated many years later into what at that time passed for English. Thus, he was not around to clarify the meaning of his descriptions. For example, he refers to right and left, but it is often unclear if he means that of the patient or his actual perspective. I suspect that Latin's medical verbiage and subsequent problems with translation of the text have somewhat obscured what truly transpired with Henry's case.

Certainly, the prince's stoic performance must have been idealized. History cannot record that the future king cried out for his wet nurse. It is possible that he was not lucid or even conscious when they operated on him. Even so, saving Henry's life by pulling that arrowhead changed France and greater Europe forever. It seems only fitting that someone was screaming.

It wasn't just arrows and arrowhead extractors that British hands were making. They built every ship, forged all the cannons, and chiseled every gun stone *by hand*. Artisans were in demand. I'll bet a quality suit of armor was tough to find and very expensive when you did. Blacksmiths, skilled tradesmen, and children worked around the clock all over Europe. Apprentices learned their trades and dreamed of a day when they might own their own shops. There was hammering aplenty at Armors 'R Us and The Armor Hut. So much, in fact, that people began to innovate.

The early chemists mixed the gunpowder, and the early biologists on thousands of small farms fought the Little Ice Age and tried to provide food for the army. Every tinker and teamster made a fortune in times of war. There was grift and graft of every sort. With every passing year and decade, the weapons makers and provisioners learned how to wage a war just a little bit better. Eventually they looked around and realized that they had become an industrial complex that needed wars to survive.

Superweapons at Sea

Somewhere along the proverbial line, the weapons makers became indispensable. I imagine this was first apparent in naval warfare where specialized knowledge and experience were crucial. Nation states realized that letting their war industries atrophy was dangerous, even suicidal. Naval craft, aircraft, and tanks require constant modernization. President Eisenhower was literally right on the actual money when he warned of the rising power and influence of the Military Industrial Complex. It is always there, holding the keys to our missiles, aircraft, and totally cool tanks. It looks so trim and powerful as it patiently waits for the excuse to be of service.

Throughout history, war's horrors have precipitated rational and significant pushback against the weaponeers. Anti-war politicians have been known to curtail military spending in an attempt to stall or stop looming arms races. Before the advent of weapons of mass destruction, the great powers worried about a balance of battleships at sea. The Washington Naval Treaty of 1922 capped battleship main guns at sixteen-inch bores. At that time, the naval rifle was the world's most deadly weapon.

Imagine cannons that shoot high explosive shells that weigh more than a ton at targets twenty-plus miles away. The shell's initial velocity is about the same as a deer rifle bullet, 2,500 feet per second. The time of flight to maximum range is well over one minute. The gunner could drink a cup of coffee, do a cross word, check his horoscope, or light up a smoke while waiting to observe the splash through a powerful telescope. By the mid-1920s, radio-carrying observation planes launched from shipboard catapults could spot for the battleship's gunners far more effectively.

Battleships might motor up to an enemy shore and open fire on a capital or port. "The Star-Spangled Banner" is an account of one such fight during the War of 1812 when the British attacked Fort McHenry at the mouth of Baltimore Harbor. By the turn of the twentieth century, battleship technology was near its zenith. Seafaring nations never knew when a whole slew of these monsters might row in from over the horizon and challenge the home fleet to shoot it out! There were relatively few large battleship-oriented slug fests before the aircraft carrier and oceangoing submarine rendered battlewagons obsolete. The Japanese and Russians fought each other in several naval actions, the last of which was at Tsushima in 1905. The Germans and British fought a huge action at Jutland in 1916.

The United States executed just such a move at the outset of the Spanish-American War in May 1898. A raiding force of four American protected cruisers, two gunboats, a revenue cutter, and a few transport ships attacked a pathetic Spanish armada which sheltered under the cover of fortress guns in Manila Bay. The Americans expected that this squadron would steam to the Caribbean to assist Spanish forces in Cuba, so it had to be obliterated. After reviewing the Spanish order of battle, and the pathetic half-stripped nature of their fleet, I doubt the

Spanish could have captured a rowboat crewed by belligerent monkeys, let alone challenge the American fleet in its home waters. But, when you get an opportunity to exercise your guns, well, how do you pass that up?

You don't. The Battle of Manila Bay is known for one famous quote. The commander of the US fleet, Commodore Dewey, issued the famous order, "You may fire when you are ready, Gridley."[4]

What followed was not a shining moment for the American Navy. American gunnery was said to be abysmal, but even still, her cruisers shot the hell out of the Spanish who didn't manage to kill a single American sailor in return. Ok, several men were wounded when a tarp caught fire, and one American sailor had a heart attack. The Spanish claimed that American casualties were far higher than what Dewey let on. Only about two percent of American shots fired hit their targets, but the weight of hits was more than decisive. The Spanish would say, *Bastante! Nada mas!*[5]

Dewey's communications were poor and serve to show how the smallest factors change the course of mighty events. At one point he ceased fire and moved off, supposedly to allow his men to eat breakfast. In fact, a miswritten message erroneously caused command to think that they were running out of ammunition for their five-inch guns which were the predominant American weapons in the fight. The sudden appearance of biscuits and coffee was a face-saving gesture for the crews as the ammunition issue was sorted. The real message said that they had fired only fifteen shells per gun. The error gave the Spanish fleet a desperately needed respite. They took the opportunity to withdraw and scuttle their ships in shallow water. Interestingly, they took their guns' breach blocks ashore perhaps to discourage salvage by their enemies.

---

4. Gridley was suffering from dysentery and likely also liver cancer at this time. He left the service shortly after the battle and was given a hero's farewell by the entire fleet. He would pass away several weeks later on June 5th before his ship could return to the United States. Admiral Dewey briefly sought the presidency in 1900 but dropped out to support William McKinley.
5. Enough! No more!

Battleships were all the rage there for a while. They could chase anything afloat, from merchantmen to ocean liners. They could blockade ports and shepherd fleets of invaders. This was the real worry. Whoever controlled the sea had a grip on world commerce, and battleships were seen by world leaders as an essential investment.

The 1922 treaty set allowable naval tonnage, and totals differed by nation. The United States and England each were allotted 525,000 tons. The Japanese were assigned 310,000 tons. The French and Italians were allowed a mere 178,000. It took less than a decade for the major players to break with the treaty, and more importantly, technological development never lost a step during the time that the treaty was in effect. Forbidden battleships were repurposed to aircraft carriers whose air power was lethal to everything afloat and at greater range than ever. Carrier-launched bombers could level targets deep behind an enemy coastline or destroy an entire fleet before opposing surface ships ever saw each other. This would first occur at the Battle of the Coral Sea on May 5–7, 1942.

The 1922 naval treaty did little to stem the much-feared arms race at sea. Oceangoing submarine production proceeded swimmingly. Nazi wolf packs ruled the North Atlantic by 1940. By the end of the Second World War, submarines could stay submerged and charge their batteries using a snorkel. They attacked with wire guided and acoustic homing torpedoes. The Japanese even built the I-400 series which carried three torpedo bombing strike aircraft with folding wings in a tubelike hanger beneath the conning tower. With a length of four hundred feet, it was the largest submarine in the world at that time. They planned to use this type against the locks at the Panama Canal.

Naval warfare changed quickly between 1918 and 1939, but the Second World War began with obsolete weapons on the front lines. Some of these, like the Brewster Buffalo fighter would be chased from the Pacific Theatre by the newest weapons including the Japanese Mitsubishi A6M Zero fighter. Other second-rate aircraft fared much better and pulled off impressive strikes that set the tenor for what was to come.

Imagine a British carrier-borne torpedo plane pilot named something like Reginold or Barry, from Shropshire perhaps, who is not more than twenty years old in November 1940. This lad finds his fuel in a blend of patriotic and personal rage and wants nothing more than to send an enemy cruiser to the bottom of Taranto Harbor. His Swordfish torpedo plane lacks speed, armor protection, defensive firepower, and maneuverability. He calls his aircraft The Stringbag, but truth be known, she is beloved. Barry understands that if his enormous

Barry the British Swordfish pilot and his stringbag.

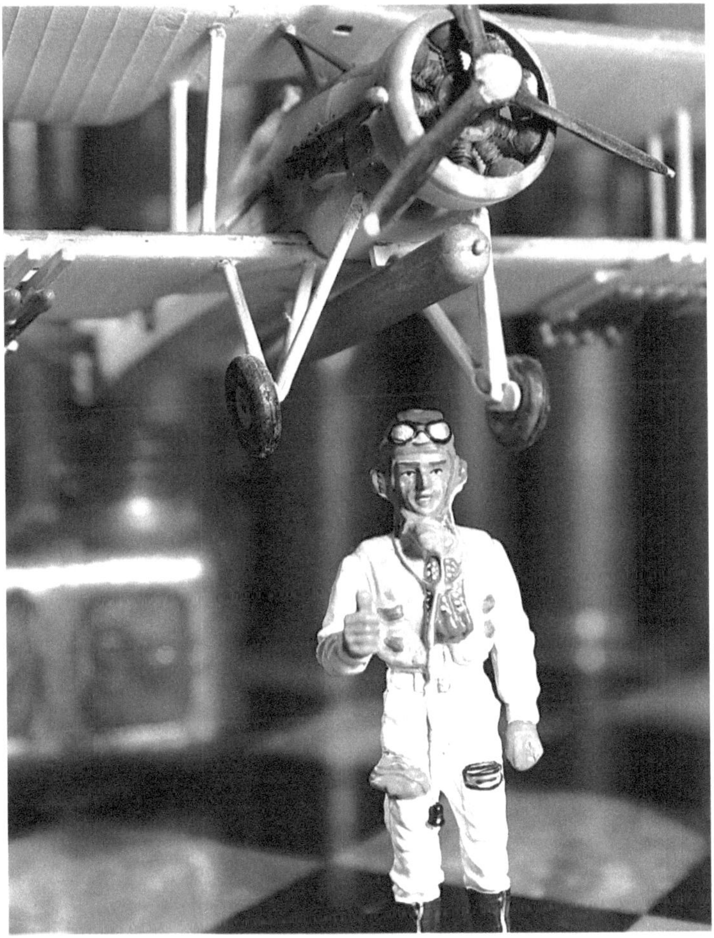

biplane is spotted by an enemy aircraft, even a lumbering flying boat, he and his crew are cooked meat. Anti-aircraft gunners should have had an easy time downing the massive biplane, but it was so low and slow that they tended to over-lead in their aim which caused them to miss in front of the target. If this is true, it has to be the only time in military history when lingering in front of the enemy was a good idea.

The Swordfish was already obsolete when it went into service in the mid-1930s, but ironically, this design sank more tonnage than any other torpedo plane and was used throughout the war. In fact, someone a lot like young Barry dropped a lucky Swordfish-delivered torpedo that wrecked the *Bismarck*'s rudder. This forced the famous battleship to steam in circles and prevented its escape from British surface ships that were in hot pursuit. The Royal Navy caught up to their fifty thousand long ton prey on May 27th, 1941. The Nazi battleship was ensnared, but rather than surrender, she made the naval equivalent of a one-man stand.

The *Bismarck*'s demise had a serious revenge factor to it. Only three days earlier, on May 24, 1941, the British people took a punch in the gut when the HMS *Hood* was sunk by *Bismarck*'s guns at the Battle of the Denmark Straight. Worse still, the Germans made that confrontation look easy. The *Hood* just detonated. The plume over the disaster could be seen for miles. It has been speculated that a design flaw left her magazines vulnerable to *Bismarck*'s plunging fifteen-inch shells, a lesson they should have learned after the First World War's Battle of Jutland. Whatever the exact reason for the *Hood*'s loss, its final moment was spectacular in all the wrong ways.

Two British battleships, the *King George the V* and the *Rodney*, utterly pummeled *Bismarck* with their big rifles. They were assisted by cruisers and destroyers. It took a relative handful of shots to destroy the *Hood*. Almost three thousand large caliber shells were fired at *Bismarck*, and it is believed that somewhere around four hundred hit. It took hours of blasting, several coup de grâce torpedoes, and ultimately, a German scuttle to send the *Bismarck* to the bottom. The wreck has been found and studied.

One hundred fourteen German sailors were pulled from the water before a possible U-boat sighting ended the rescue mission. Only three British sailors survived the *Hood*.

The reader no doubt has noticed my sensitivity to battlefield irony. The fabulously advanced *Bismarck*'s fate was sealed by a lucky shot from a fabric-covered airframe. If the Swordfish were a soldier, he would charge into battle behind a geriatric's walker. The seeds that would draw the United States into World War Two were planted by Barry's Swordfish. On the night of November 11, 1940, twenty Royal Navy torpedo planes attacked the Italian military harbor at Taranto. They did significant damage for light losses, and it can be argued that the attack changed the balance of power in the Mediterranean Sea. The key weapons were the aircraft carrier and the torpedo plane. The attack impressed the Japanese naval attaché stationed in Berlin who visited the Italian disaster area. His report was the genesis of the plan to attack Pearl Harbor. The actions of that young British pilot and his squadron mates changed military history by showing America's future enemies exactly how to strike a fleet at anchor with naval airpower.

New Rules for the Arms Bazaar

Less than ten years before World War Two began in Europe, President Hoover spoke of the need to reduce the "overwhelming burden of armaments which now lies upon the toilers of the world."[6] First, if ever there was a word to describe the industrial revolution at that point in history, it is "toilers." Hoover wanted to abolish the manufacture of tanks, poison gas, bombing planes, and large cannons. Meanwhile, the Soviets and the Germans were just beginning to get their arms industries back up and running. The Germans found that circumventing the Treaty of Versailles was a simple matter of semantics and geographical location. They managed all sorts of interesting developments with "mail plane" and "racing plane" projects. Early

---

6. *War and Anti-war Survival at the Dawn of the 21st Century*, Alvin and Heidi Toffler, 1993, p. 15.

Nazi panzer designs showed no armaments and were listed as "agricultural equipment." The Swiss assisted with small-arms designs. The Germans even worked secretly with the Soviets on armored vehicles and tactics at the Kazan Tank School in the Ural Mountains.

Henry Ford said in late 1928 that people were too smart to have another large-scale war. I wonder what Ford would say about current American eighth-grade test scores in reading and math. Ford was a brilliant engineer and business manager, but like most people, he did not grasp the destabilizing effects of constantly evolving military technology. Ford saw a world where the United States and Great Britain maintained the peace. Geopolitically, the world was relatively stable at that time. The colonial power structure was still in place. The Soviet Union was a fledgling state largely looking inward. Hitler was a journeyman politician in a beaten nation. The Japanese would not invade China until 1931. The stock market had yet to crash, and Ford was selling cars and trucks hand over fist. Peace felt permanent during the Roaring Twenties.

As predictions go, Ford's vision of a peaceful world was a huge whiff. Oddly enough, financial status does not deliver expertise on every subject, though for some unknown reason average folks think it must. Rather the opposite is likely to be true as wealth and political insulation tend to go together. The best training in the military realities includes having served in the armed forces, but the advent of a volunteer army, rather than conscripted force, keeps that number of experts down. As subjects of conversation and debate go, the modern public is in no way prepared to drill down on warfare.

Understanding armed conflict well enough to predict outcomes, or at least see trends, requires nuanced historical knowledge beyond whatever passes for history class on the secondary level and even college. Names, dates, and outcomes need to flow like a river when the debate is on. Military historians should be experts in geography, especially where contentious borders and areas rich with natural resources are concerned. They should also be intellectually objective and resistant to any and all types of political and race-based propaganda. The military analyst needs to understand how various forms of government function, especially in times of war. He or she must grasp the different religious tenets, particularly where they clash. The best military historians have a firm grasp of economics and complete fluency in military terminology. These skills, along with a scientific appreciation for how weapons work, make the astute student of warfare stand out among the armchair warriors and anti-war activists.

People with military insight do "battle math" where they weigh firepower and the mission with lives in the balance. They look at past and present squabbles in the same numerical light. I would posit that this is the most consequential of all abstract calculations. The sum or quotient might pull a trigger or raise a white flag. The formula scales up from man-versus-man to nation-versus-nation in a snap.

Teach the Children Well

War is no game, but play can teach us much about battle. The military analyst should play chess, backgammon, and above all, the board game *Risk*, which was first released by Parker Brothers in 1959. Chess teaches a player to think ahead and anticipate reactions to many different possible avenues of attack or defense. Backgammon teaches us how to win despite the need to face pure chance. *Risk*, however, is the real teacher. A single game can take many hours. The players talk shit and manipulate each other constantly. Alliances are made and broken. There are double crosses, brutal betrayals, waves of victory and defeat, and then, world domination by a single color! I like to play Red, the traditional color of tyranny, and I rarely ever lose.

The famous British comedian Eddie Izzard joked that Hitler never played *Risk* as a kid. Had he done so, he never would have invaded the Soviet Union, and our entire planet would be a different place. I'm not saying there would be no Walmart, but almost. Sure, in the game, Russian territory looks so profitable. Winning and holding onto that massive landmass gives you seven extra armies at the start of every Go, but it is too large to defend and one of the other players always breaks you before you can get that game-winning payoff. Look at the trouble the former Soviets are having holding on to Ukraine. Putin needs Ukraine to reunite the former USSR, but the other players are frustrating his plans. *Risk* actually mirrors the world quite well.

So young Hitler plays *Risk* and learns his lesson about Russia. A few decades later, he is large and in charge of Germany. He stomps various smaller states, takes half of Poland and then quits. In the game he would take his card and pass the dice. He could then make nice for a few turns while he built up on his home base.

That would have been the smart move. Hitler kept going because he wasn't truly interested in victory. He just liked causing havoc. Experts on twisted psyches like his say Hitler's narcissism fed on human misery. Motivated by aversion and loathing, Hitler could no more pause his gluttony for creating order than fly to the moon. Taking France and Belgium bled German resources badly. He squandered 140 divisions of troops, aircraft, and tanks in Operation Barbarossa, the invasion of the Soviet Union in June 1941. A year and a half later he would lose 282,000 men at Stalingrad. Hitler threw away massive assets on North Africa as well. Then came the largest tank battle ever at Kursk where the Nazis lost a thousand tanks, and the Soviets smelled blood. And on top of all that he wasted vast resources in the Final Solution just when he knew that he needed everything he could muster for his battered and depleted war machine.

I have to wonder, what if Hitler got ahold of his mental illness and listened to his generals early on? They were amazed that the little corporal bluffed his way along so successfully, and they were ready to overthrow him in a coup at the first sign of failure. The Europeans kept giving in, and Hitler's overextension would not be apparent until the battles of Stalingrad and the Second El-Alamein. By that time, Hitler's grasp on the Army was total.

Thank God Hitler never played *Risk*. He did not understand how to play the long game. Avoiding conflict in 1939 would have saved the German economy from a wartime footing and allowed a great deal of wealth to accrue. German industry is a formidable economic driver. Their population would have had a few more years for the next batch of cannon fodder to grow. Alliances with other nations might have solidified, and with technology transfer from Nazi Germany, the Italians and Japanese would have entered WWII with significantly better training and firepower. Imagine Italian troops in Tiger tanks instead of their ridiculous tankettes.

Imagine what would have happened if Hitler's design teams had time to perfect the next generation of weapons before the war and mass-produce them in vast numbers. I mean, come on…technology is kind of the German's thing. Adolf's blitzkrieg a la 1945 or later could possibly have taken all of Europe in one big sweep. The question is, would the Allies, especially the United States, have kept up with Nazi technological advances? It would seem unlikely unless a war with Japan gave the United States the impetus to rearm.

Hitler would have made every effort to hide military progress and lull the Americans, French, and British into five or six years of slack military spending. The Great Powers would think defensively. The French would hide behind the Maginot Line. The British would curl up on the other side of the English Channel with a cat and a cup of tea, and the USA would say that the Atlantic Ocean makes military spending on things like fighter planes and tanks look wasteful. Would they have embarked on the A-bomb project absent any obvious signs of a looming war? The United States Army ranked 19th in the world, behind even Italy, when World War Two began. This would likely not have changed much by 1945.

Stalin's influence is another spoiler here. He was in no position to invade Europe after Hitler, his ally, took half of Poland. They might have tussled over the decision to split that territory, but Uncle Joe had a great deal of modernizing to do himself, and the Germans were financing it with their trade.

So in the "Hitler took a pass universe," peace and blue skies made every day between 1939 and 1945 feel like a holiday from fear. People sang only happy songs, and everyone got a puppy. The Nazis worked like ants to build underground factories during that idyllic absence in hostility to produce jet- and rocket-powered fighter planes that could accept or refuse combat at will. They developed synthetic fuels. Hitler's engineers produced a surface-to-air missile called the Rheintochter which was capable of taking down a strategic bomber and wire-guided, air-launched, anti-ship missiles. Even more consequential to convoys trying to reach England from North America, the Kriegsmarine-fielded schnorkel-equipped, deep diving submarines armed with advanced torpedoes that would sink every other cargo ship bound for England or Arch Angel. Their radars would be better. Their code machine would be even more complex. Axis infantry would carry an assault rifle when most other nations still issued a bolt action. They would wear the perfect camouflage and pack handy anti-tank weapons in their luggage. Imagine the Nazis starting the war with the ME-262 and Tiger II instead of ending that way. Worst of all these possibilities is the unstoppable V2 missile and perhaps an atomic bomb to go with it, the ultimate cherry on top.

If Hitler had paused earlier, a lull in the fighting would mean that he could not hide his Final Solution. I am sure that antisemitism would be noticed by the world press. German Jews might have emigrated to Israel and bolstered that state-to-be long before the United Nations made its mandate. No doubt Hitler would have committed the same atrocities post-1945.

The implications and lessons behind "what if" thinking are lost on most people. Americans are no longer classically educated. It takes too long, and a great many students just don't have the ability to think for themselves. Ask your average American public or private high school graduate to tell you three things about his or her nation. These days, it is entirely likely that the first example will decry our racist history. The second example will show the nation to be hopelessly sexist, and the third will deal with some form of environmental destruction that actually makes the United States a danger to everyone else. You won't hear, "We won World War Two, baby! Capitalism saved the world. Booyah!"

America was badass and proud of it in 1950. We had the balls to actually use the atomic bomb, twice. Clearly, the whole world saw that the USA was not screwing around. Our aviation industry was dope at the end of the war. A B-29 might drop an A-bomb anywhere. The peace we won with our bombers, however, was an illusion. During the Cold War Era, from the end of World War Two right up to 1990 or so, there were more than one hundred and fifty civil wars and other conflicts that took the lives of 7.2 million soldiers. There is no way to calculate the civilian dead, wounded, and dispossessed. Estimates vary, but thirty to fifty million people seems a *very* conservative number. The soldier casualty rate alone is close to the total number killed in World War One.

Since the turn of the twenty-first century, and after 9/11 in particular, another eight hundred thousand to a million people have been killed or wounded in the war on terror.[7] I just checked for an update, and there are still 140 military hot spots as I write this sentence in 2024. So, apparently, the happy fact that there was a bloodless Cold War between the East and West is misleading. Nations and alliances saber-rattled and produced weapons that were farmed out to various lesser players who were only too happy to fight as proxies for the heavy hitters who dared not have a direct confrontation. This tired workaround is now so transparent that its inoculating effects are no longer proof against a larger, perhaps world-ending confrontation over the Ukraine.

The most decisive of our high-tech weapons must be operated by American personnel, as it would be insane to hand over our premiere weapons systems to people who will sell them on the black market in a heartbeat. This use of advisors has been standard procedure for decades. Soviet-supplied experts manned most of North Vietnam, Egypt, and Syria's anti-aircraft systems. They even sent pilots to try and cow the Israelis in air-to-air combat. They were not successful. American technology and Israeli grit are a formidable combination.

Modern warfare has become a complex social, political, and kinesthetic phenomenon. The news media decides how we are supposed

---

7.   www.brown.edu/news/2021-09-01/costsofwar.

to feel about a conflict. They push poll, deepfake, censor, and manufacture news as needed to keep the conflict going. Military targets are weighed for their political and strategic value. War is not often declared. Congress need not be involved. A great deal depends on the terminology and nomenclature used to frame the fight. For example, The Korean *Conflict* was not a war. Those troops fighting in that struggle did so under a United Nations mandate, and that political body did not have the authority to declare a war. So, the West faced a very messy *security problem.*

I wonder about the efforts of the president's press secretary, Stephen Early, to explain that one.

Imagine what he would say to our current White House press pool.

Reporter: "Soooo, Stephen, could this Korean situation lead to World War Three?"

Stephen Early: "No! Hah! Not if we just use our heads to think about this…you know…correctly. It's comical. This is not even close to a war. I mean, yes, well, sure, that showboat MacArthur does make this *look like* a 'war.'" Early's air-quotes gesture around the word "war" drew a chuckle from the reporters in the press pool. "We asked him to cut down on the tanks and blasting and such, but you know old Doug. He went on a rant about needing a dozen atomic bombs to stop the Chinese, but we held him down to an endless supply of napalm instead, because, as I said so clearly, this is not a war. Again, let me

The Korean Conflict featured the Soviet's best weapons.
The MIG 15, T-34/85 tank, and PPSH 41 submachine gun.

stress that. Clearly. Congress has *not said* this is a war. Until they do, it can't be, and it isn't. President Truman called this situation a police action. I have not heard a better description. It's a local problem. The South Koreans dialed 9-1-1, and the United Nations responded with police from sixteen countries."

All told, more than three million people died in what has come to be called The Forgotten War, a conflict that technically is still ongoing to this day. The United States would lose about 54,000 policemen killed and another 103,000 wounded in that domestic disturbance. The South Koreans lost 140,000 and took a half million wounded. The North Koreans lost 300,000 men killed in action, over 90,000 missing in action, and 230,000 wounded. Their civilian losses were very heavy as well. The Chinese lost over 180,000 dead and 25,000 missing in action, and they had to care for more than 300,000 wounded. Even with financial assistance from the Soviets, the Chinese damaged themselves economically as well. They spent anywhere from thirty-five to more than forty percent of their total budget for years 1950 through 1953 on the war. They owed the Soviets more than a billion dollars when the armistice was signed. These numbers sound small today, but in their time, they were significant and a drag on national progress.

The combined military weight of the Chinese and North Koreans backed by the Soviet bloc proved that primitive tactics and sheer weight of numbers could battle the West's best expeditionary force to a standstill. But, the cost of this virtual draw was so high that pushing for outright victory was pointless.

The staggering waste of both human potential and actual lucre is impossible to miss when we see pictures from space of the Korean peninsula taken at night. Below the DMZ, lights are everywhere. Roads are obvious. Ports are well lit as they never sleep. To the north, the exact opposite is strikingly apparent. The capital is somewhat lit and a few military bases on the coasts, but that's it. With help from the West, the South Koreans recovered from the war and kicked ass. The North was unable to break free of its dark and militaristic mindset and remains one of the most God awful places on earth. I'd rather run naked through Newark at midnight than spend five minutes in North Korea.

Back to Basics

All of this brings us back once again to the Hundred Years' War. Battle was once a highly prescribed operation. Rules of war were taken seriously. Nothing about the scrap was subtle. Aggrieved nations sent delegations to potential adversaries to say plainly, "Hey, you're pissing us off. This means war. That's what's up."

Henry really knew how to make a point. According to Shakespeare, the French insulted him by sending a batch of tennis balls as a gift. The implication was that the young king was a child not to be feared. Henry dictated a curt reply and sent it by armored messenger. Call it an early example of express mail.

In *Henry the Fifth* (1599), Thomas Beaufort, referred to as Exter in the script, is admitted to see the French king with a rather curt message from young Henry, who demands the French crown. The French King asks what will occur if he refuses Henry's demands for surrender. Exeter replies, "Bloody constraint."

> Bloody constraint, for if you hide the crown
> Even in your hearts, there will he rake for it.
> Therefore in fierce tempest is he coming,
> In thunder and in earthquake like a Jove,
> That, if requiring fail, he will compel,
> And bids you, in the bowels of the Lord,
> Deliver up the crown and to take mercy
> On the poor souls for whom this hungry war
> Opens his vasty jaws[8]

---

8. *Henry V,* Act 2, Scene 4.

Politicians and royals can rage against conflict, but bloody constraint is an eternal reality. War is only held in check when the potential adversary truly fears a response to his aggression. Nations need to be a little dangerous if they are to be respected and peace maintained. Military virtues have to be valued no matter how politically incorrect they may be.

Everyone should sign off on this basic reality: The soldier's job is to bring hellfire to the enemy's door, kick it in, and stomp on everybody who doesn't instantly surrender—and maybe not even then. That would depend on who started it and how. Osama bin Laden's fate leaps to mind. Collateral damage is on the enemy's head for picking the fight in the first place.

That is a cold and calculating point of view in a world where militaries allow soldiers to publish videos of themselves doing little dances and posing in nonmilitary attire. When Putin pictures American troopers, I want him to see legions of some guy named Leeroy who is six feet, four inches tall, weighs two hundred and forty pounds, and runs marathons with his German Shepard terrorist-sniffing dog named Daisy. That is what deterrence looks like. Soldiers giving eye makeup tutorials on TikTok invite attack. How could they not?

Let us not forget that every soldier's life matters. They are not fungible. The military is not a commodity from which one takes a slice or two as needed. Eliminating this attitude begins with teaching the right books and stories in English class. These should include, *All Quiet on the Western Front*, *The Red Badge of Courage*, *A Farewell to Arms*, and one other story that I taught on the eighth-grade level.

The Drummer Boy of Shiloh, by Ray Bradbury, was supported in our textbook with the addition of a now-famous letter sent by President Lincoln to Mrs. Bixby after he learned that she lost all five of her sons in Civil War battle. It is beautifully written and the basis of the *Saving Private Ryan* story. Lincoln says that he hopes:

The Heavenly Father will assuage your bereavement and leave you only the cherished memory of the loved and lost, and the solemn pride that must be yours to have laid so costly a sacrifice upon the Altar of Freedom.

I warned my students that the "Bixby Lesson," for sure, would cause me to get a little misty. Did you catch that "Altar of Freedom" part? It bears saying again that I am easily moved by courage, duty, honor, and, above all else, personal sacrifice in the name of brotherhood. I fully understand the horrors soldiers face, and their willingness to stand and take it overwhelms my sense of admiration. I am also in awe of all those on the Home Front who face sleepless nights and endless worry for their children and loved ones serving in harm's way. Mrs. Bixby has my deepest sympathy.[9]

Sadly, nobody reads anymore. We learn everything from watching screens. As a child, I learned all there was to know about war from watching war movies that were made between 1930 and 1970. I also never missed TV shows like *Combat!* with Vic Morrow. For the record, most older war movies are pretty awful. The special effects are often poor, and the action sequences do not suspend our disbelief. The very worst war movie ever made was John Wayne's *The Green Berets* (1968). There is just no excuse for this film, but it does have a young George Takei in it. The best war film at that time was probably *The Longest Day* (1962), otherwise known as The Longest Movie. These pictures and their star power reinforced a belief that Americans were faithful and superhuman warriors.

War flick scripts often seem to follow a standard plot line. First, we see the civilians join up despite the mother's plea to stay on the farm. The boot camp sequence is always brutal with a fire-breathing drill sergeant who knows the real score.

---

9. All those years ago, I only knew what the eighth-grade textbook provided about the Bixby Letter. I now know that the original letter has been lost to history. It has also been suggested that President Lincoln's personal secretary, John Hay, wrote the letter. Mrs. Bixby likely lost "only" three of her sons, not all five. Interviews with her descendants indicate that Mrs. Bixby's political allegiance may not have been with the North.

The Platoon

The cast of stereotypes is predictable. One of the enlistees has an emotional breakdown in basic training, but ultimately, in the thick of a losing fight, this timid recruit decides that he has had enough! The sergeant who gave him constant shit for being a coward breaks under the strain, himself. The men are strung out and pinned down with nobody to lead them. The radio takes a bullet. The medic can't reach the wounded as they bleed out. The music swells as the last man one would ever expect dashes forward into the face of intense machine gun and mortar fire.

He uses his bayonet to feel his way forward as he belly crawls right through a minefield. He pauses for just a moment by his dead buddy's body to retrieve the satchel charge. Then he crawls under the bullets to a point right next to the bunker aperture. The deafening muzzle blast from the MG-42 sweeps back and forth. Our hero pulls the pin but coolly waits just a moment before he tosses the bomb into the bunker. BOOM! He silences the deadly machine gun. Spectacular! Nothing left in there but German jelly. His brothers cheer, but as this man among men dashes for safety, a sniper nails him. Zap! The camera cuts to his platoon sergeant's heart-wrenching reaction and a solo violin.

The comedian in the platoon just couldn't help himself and set the world record for pushups in basic training. His timing problems cost him dearly. During a lull in a mortar barrage, he defiantly shouts a one-liner about German girls doing it for a chocolate bar. His buddies laugh, but the Nazi audience responds with a mortar round right in his fox hole.

Of course, the guitar player who knocks out an amazing Flamenco instrumental in the first act, loses a hand. The conscientious objector medic is forced to kill a Nazi who was about to spray the helpless wounded men under his care. He stands over the writhing Nazi trooper with the smoking .45 in his shaking hands. He looks at the pistol, and for a moment it appears he will throw it away. Instead, he fires another round. He lowers the hammer and sticks the gun is his belt.

One of the wounded men grabs the medic by the arm says, "Thanks, Marty. You did the right thing."

Marty adjusts the bandages and sighs, "That was his idea not mine."

The star of the show, the loner, finds out that despite his self-doubts, he is a born leader of men. He survives with a picturesque wound and medal to match, but, wow, it was a near thing. Based on the musical score, we were sure he was dead there for a minute. The newly armed medic takes his pulse expecting to confirm his passing. He yells some version of, "Oh my God! He's still alive! Bring me some plasma! Goddamit, don't you quit on me! You're gonna make it. Come on! We gotta move this man!"

Boy, oh boy. All I can say is, under these circumstances, it's good to be an American.

At first, the platoon of strangers cannot march, shoot straight, or pass a barracks inspection, but after the crucible, these civilians are forged into razor-sharp weapons. The training sequence sucks us in, and we are bonded with the boys. We share their pride and believe in their mission. Yes, never forget—the mission comes first.

There once was a time when I could watch war movies with enough steel in my heart to get through what I knew was coming, but now that my sons are grown, I keep thinking that these soldiers were really just kids, quite possibly mine. How the hell does anyone send a child off to war? People do. So when I watch war movies these days, well, I always cry a little when the kid gets hit. OK? There it is. Call it the Bixby Factor. I admit it. A lot depends on the irony in play. When the writer, director, and actors strike dramatic gold, tears just streak down my cheeks.

It's a funny thing. A script can kill off every last good guy in any other kind of film, and I just yawn. Yeah, burn'm up, squish'm, bury them alive. Better yet, feed them to a huge shark that lives for vendetta. War pictures are different. I keep thinking that the hero was some father's son. All those years of playing catch, fishing together, learning to drive, the father-son talks, the hug goodbye…Jesus. What a God-awful waste. I would never get over it. Not even close.

I grew up in an era when just about every man I knew had served and likely lost family in combat, and yet, like most kids, I could not comprehend the level of violence they had endured. I chalk this up to the highly sanitized film and television of that time. Theatrical military violence has changed since the 1960s. Old-school war movies, especially those shot in black and white, are almost bloodless. I was reared on movies like Gregory Peck's *Porkchop Hill* (1959), which might as well have been rated "G." Other childhood favorites include *The Devil's Brigade* (1968) and the simply awful *Battle of the Bulge* (1965) which was so inaccurate that Dwight Eisenhower had a fit and called out the studio for rewriting history. I watched these movies over and over without any appreciation for how historically inaccurate and hokey they were. When one of the good guys took a bullet, I said, oh well. He died for his country. How noble. If you have to die, that's not the worst way to go, right?

Modern war movies often take an emotional toll on the audience. Make sure your PTSD is under control before watching *Hamberger Hill* (1987) or *Platoon* (1986). *American Sniper* (2014) was so powerful that the entire audience sat through the credits before they solemnly and silently left the theatre. It was a dignified moment, and I didn't want to sully Chris Kyle's memory by callously leaving before every last frame was shown. People were changed. I recall how the audience was completely overwhelmed by *Glory* (1989), where emancipated Black troops laid down their lives in the name of freedom. People were sobbing and hugging each other when the lights came back up. The catharsis was unreal.

Rather than turn me away from history, these depressing films prompted me to do something almost lost in our culture today: They made me crack a history book. To this day, I read very few novels. My Christmas books this year from my favorite used bookstore were *Henry the Fifth: Scourge of God* by Desmond Seward (1987) and *Boxer Rebellion* by Henry Keown-Boyd (1991).

Reading history just about always ruins a war movie. Directors tend to deliver apocryphal renditions of true events in the name of entertainment. This is fine. I get it. The audience needs to be engaged, but the public is likely to be woefully ignorant. They need a better disclaimer before the first scene: *This story is based on true events* just doesn't cut it anymore. I want a freaking percentage. If I were directing the World War Two tank versus tank movie, *Fury* (2014), right after the last of the opening credits, a black screen would come up, and the music would fade to a single snare drum.

Black screen. Fade in to bird's-eye view of a tank battle that ended some time before. There are smoking wrecks everywhere. Bodies litter the ground. Writing appears center screen:

(Fade in) **The story you are about to see is weak.** (Fade out)
(Fade in) **But the tanks are real and super cool.** (Fade out)
(Fade in) **Plus, Brad Pitt is in it, so...** (Fade out)

People believe that whatever they see on screen is The Gospel, and so I say God help Henry the Fifth's memory if people rely on Timothee Chalamet's version of the monarch in *The King* (2019). Of course, this revision of events and the creation of sometimes completely fictitious "historical composite" characters is nothing new. Most of us believe that everything Shakespeare wrote was historically correct. Seward's book on Henry the Fifth cured that one for me. Henry was a monster, but in those times, everyone was.

*Lee A. Archer, America's only African American ace
shown with the ME-262 and P-51 Mustang.*

Red Tails (2012) is another film where the need to add drama caused a ripple or two in history. Even with its flaws, it is a very important movie. The Tuskegee Airmen are famous for fighting segregation, low expectations, and the Germans. Their rise to equality is story enough without embellishments. Some of the tall claims about these Black airmen are ancient. *The Chicago Defender* published an article on March 24th, 1945, that claimed the Red Tails never lost a bomber under their protection. This was erroneous, but people wanted to believe it was true. Statistically, it *almost* was.

The Red Tails lost approximately twenty-five of the bombers they escorted to enemy aircraft. That is actually an impressive statistic. Certainly, some Allied planes were lost to a combination of insults, and one wonders how the cause of each loss was determined. Some say this remarkable success rate against German and Italian fighters was because the Red Tails stuck unusually close to the B-17s and B-24s under their care. Other fighter escort squadrons ranged further out in front of the bombers in an attempt to head off the enemy. This often worked, but it was also true that those Mustangs might not be around when the Germans snuck up on a bomber formation.

The 332 Fighter Group downed 112 enemy planes, but there were no aces in their ranks. Not one. The highest score at the war's end, four kills, was held by several pilots including Lee Archer.[10] It has been suggested that pilots were rotated out of the squadron before they could make ace. To be fair, however, by the time the Red Tails were in the thick of it, the Luftwaffe had very few interceptors left to stop the huge bomber formations that came by both day and night, and the Allies could sortie about a zillion fighters on every big effort. Opportunity for air-to-air kills were few and far between. After the Germans pulled out of Italy, they concentrated their fighter plane strength over Germany, and the Mediterranean-area-based Red Tails went four months without a single air-to-air kill.

Several pilots in the 332nd pulled off impressive triple-kills in a single engagement and were decorated for their achievements. The Red Tails destroyed 150 aircraft on the ground along with numerous trains and other tasty targets, including an Italian torpedo boat[11] and more than forty other boats and barges. They were part of a vast air armada that flew one of the longest escort missions of the war. During a strike on Berlin, the Red Tails engaged German ME-262 jet fighters. Three

---

10. Confirming air-to-air victories took considerable time. Many pilots had to wait months for their totals to be confirmed. Lee A. Archer's victory total has been *amended*. First, another half-kill was awarded after the war. He shared credit for this kill with his wingman. However, after careful analysis made more than seventy years after the fact, the wingman's hits were deemed to be of no importance in the outcome of the fight. Archer had already smashed his enemy's wing and the ME-109 was going down. Thus, Archer made ace after all. Lee Archer is the only Black fighter pilot ace in American military history, and his name is well worth remembering. The History Channel offers a computer-generated reenactment of Archer's ace-winning kills that differs somewhat from the documentation I have seen. The narrator sounds as if Archer's status was conferred during the war.

11. In the movie version of this event, that torpedo boat becomes an impressive destroyer, the only one in history sunk by fifty caliber fire. It looks spectacular on film but stands as an example of small theatrical decisions that frame our historical perceptions.

kills were claimed, and as far as I can tell, they have been confirmed. Other squadrons on that mission shot down ME-262s as well. While valorous, the action was not somehow unique. Their list of awards for valor and unit citations is lengthy. In addition to many other medals for valor, they earned ninety-six Distinguished Flying Crosses. Sixty-six Tuskegee Airmen were lost in combat. Thirty-two were captured and made POWs. The Nazi looked at the Tuskegee pilots as subhuman and treated them very badly.

My stand-in for Chuck Yeager and the war-winning P-51 Mustang fighter.

Yearning for Yeager

So of all the famous fighting men, who was the best soldier? I would nominate Major Dick Winters of *Band of Brothers* fame whose achievements are well documented. He was a paratrooper, and that ought to move a man to the front of the line. He is an obvious choice, and the small-unit tactics he used so well are still studied at West Point. If medals show one's metal, Audie Murphy's possible claim is bulletproof. These men won many of their nation's highest honors, and I cannot fault them in any way, but what of the career man who was badass in several theatres over many decades? I refer to any soldier who starts off in the ranks and ends up in leadership. Men like Chesty Puller, the most decorated Marine—who served as a private, NCO, and finally, a lieutenant general—fit this bill. I look at a soldier's entire career, and from my perspective, the perfect combatant was Chuck Yeager. He started off as an enlisted aviation mechanic and ended up a general. Metaphorically, he was a jousting knight who quite literally surfed the wave of military tech for his entire career.

I am struck by the fact that many, even most fighter pilots, never saw an enemy aircraft, let alone a gaggle of them. Chuck Yeager flew sixty-four missions over Europe and scored most of his thirteen kills on two occasions. He downed five planes in a single engagement, which made him an "ace in a day." Two of these were unusual "manouvre" kills. Apparently, an enemy pilot panicked when he saw Yeager behind him and slid right into another ME-109 in the formation, which took them both out. Chalk up two kills for Chuck without firing a shot! In another dogfight, Yeager downed four Focke-Wulf FW-190 fighters.

Chuck Yeager is the quintessential military fighter pilot, test pilot, and squadron leader. He fought with a wingman watching his tail, and his duels were really squadron-sized events, so for the purposes of this book, his stands were not of the one-man variety, but damn, it's close. I have to wonder if actors playing similar roles study his swagger. Scott Bakula, who played Captain Archer of *Star Trek Enterprise* semi-fame, was told by the show's creator that his version of a starship captain was to be half Chuck Yeager and the other half Han Solo.

Yeager stayed in the service after the war as a test pilot and was one of three men sent to evaluate the MIG-15 brought over by a defector from North Korea in 1953. He is famous for being the first test pilot to break the sound barrier on October the 14th, 1947. He had two broken ribs at the time that he did not disclose. His story was featured in *The Right Stuff* (1983). A few years later, Yeager was assigned to lead the Air Force's Aerospace Research Pilot School, which was a pipeline to placement on the NASA roster. New space exploration technology came on fast, and testing much of it fell on Yeager's department. He personally checked out a specially converted, rocket-boosted NF-104A Star Fighter that was used to train astronauts in the use of retro rocket systems. All he had to do was get the experimental aircraft up to the edge of space to give it a proper…whirl.

The aircraft climbed to over 108,000 feet, but a tail control surface failure caused the ship to pitch up, and in the thinnest of atmosphere, it went into a flat spin and fell to earth. Yeager tried everything to regain control, including deploying his landing drag chute, but nothing worked, and he was forced to punch out at seven thousand feet. His face was badly burned by the ejection seat rocket pack, but he was one tough hombre, and when the rescue team finally reached the crash site, they found him walking home with his parachute over his shoulder.

This was not Yeager's longest jaunt. Early on in his war, after being shot down over France, Yeager worked with the French Resistance for some time until he hiked over the Pyrenees Mountains with a badly wounded comrade to escape the Nazis. He was temporarily interned in Spain, but he was repatriated to England and allowed to resume his fighter pilot mission after pitching a fit about retirement from combat. It was feared that if he were shot down again, his knowledge about the French resistance might be forced from him. Once France was back under Allied control this was no longer an issue, and Chuck got the keys to his P-51D back.

Over the course of his long career which ended in the mid-1970s, Yeager earned a Bronze Star for the escape from France. He would go on to score a Silver Star with bronze oak leaf cluster, the Legion of Merit, the Distinguished Flying Cross, a Purple Heart, the Air Medal with more Oak Leaves, and ultimately the Presidential Medal of Freedom—to name a few. He also wore numerous champaign ribbons including the Armed Forces Expeditionary Medal and the Vietnam Service Medal with two stars. There are many other awards and citations that I could mention, but I would be remiss if I did not point out my favorite. Yeager won the Air Force Expert Marksman Medal.

It is easy to overlook Yeager's post-World War Two combat career, which included tours in Europe flying F-86H and F-100 Super Sabres with NATO forces. He flew more than 120 missions over Vietnam as leader of the 405th Tactical Fighter Wing operating out of the Philippines. He trained Pakistani Air Force pilots and observed the air war between Pakistan and India. He even flew rescue missions to recover downed Pakistani pilots. After the military, he did well in business and advertising. In the end, he used a Sharpie pen to scribble his name on all sorts of things for a pricey fee.

The only strike against Yeager that I have found concerns an accusation of racism from the only African American applicant to the astronaut training program at that time. I have no idea if this is in any way true. I do know that many Black aviators gravitated to the new United States Air Force where, unlike the Navy, they were given fair promotion. We also know that President Kennedy was very keen to see some diversity on the launch pad. Ed Dwight was the obvious choice. He was a test pilot, but he had no combat experience. Dwight was bitter about what he described as Yeager's displeasure over having a Black pilot assigned to the astronaut program. Some years after the fact he accused Yeager of calling on his men to give him a social cold shoulder and compel his transfer. I could not find other information on this hurtful detail, though knowing the times, it seems *possible*.[12] Yeager is so genial in interviews that such an infraction seems impossible. I found no firsthand accounts or testimonials to support this claim.

---

12. Ed Dwight was in line to be the first Black astronaut. History had other ideas. NSPR (mynspr.org).

Ultimately, Dwight was not selected to be part of NASA and retired from the Air Force in 1966. Yeager would later say that objectively the record showed that Dwight was a good pilot but not good enough to be an astronaut. Yeager may have resented the press attention that Dwight garnered perhaps for nonmilitary considerations. That would not sit well with a pragmatic West Virginian who wasn't focused on a changing national identity as part of his mission. Dwight went on to become a famous artist and was made an honorary Space Force officer. He is also the oldest person to have achieved suborbital flight. On May 19, 2024, he beat out Bill Shatner for that honor when he flew aboard Blue Origin's NS-25.

Yeager was a quotation machine. My favorites highlight his bravado. These include: "The first time I ever saw a jet, I shot it down." He did so on November 6, 1944, as the enemy jet was landing. The ME-262 was not equipped with airbrakes and had no choice but to slowly throttle down as it approached the airfield. This was likely the easiest kill of Yeager's career and certainly the one at lowest altitude. Once an ME-262 was up to speed, they were very difficult to catch unless they banked or turned steeply which bled off energy. German pilots found that throttle adjustments could flame out their engines, so they stayed at high speed once they achieved combat altitude. This was smart defensively, but Nazi fliers found that gunnery at high closing speeds was surprisingly difficult, even against large and slow-moving bomber aircraft. A single burst from their four 30 m/m cannons could be fatal if it landed on a B-17's flight deck or the wing root behind the cockpit of a B-24, but they had less than two seconds to line up their sights and fire.

Chuck could be fortune cookie philosophical. "At the moment of truth, there are either reasons or results." My all-time favorite sounds great but means nothing. It is classic fighter pilot speak. "Rules are made for people who aren't willing to make up their own." It sounds so brave and antisocial too! His very best quote was as a guest on *The David Letterman Show* where he said something to the effect that breaking the sound barrier was great, but it will never replace sex.

In interviews, Yeager said that his exceptional eyesight gave him a distinct advantage in a dogfight. He could spot the enemy long before they could see him. Perhaps equally important, he was raised in a hunting culture. He had a woodsman's instincts and knew how to stay "up sun" to stalk the target. Yeager attributes the Allies' enviable air superiority to the P-51 Mustang's great range and superior speed, but he also insists that other technology in the cockpit played equally important parts.

By mid-1944, all Allied fighters coming off the production lines were equipped with lead-computing K-14 gyro gunsights that made deflection shooting much easier. The pilot had a twist handle on the throttle that adjusted the diameter of the ring he saw projected on the glass gunsight panel. It was a simple matter to match the wingspan of the target to the size of the ring. This automatically sets the correct range to target. Pressurized G-suits were another important bit of innovative kit. These allowed American pilots to pull tighter circles than the enemy without blacking out. Yeager also gives high praise to the choice of six .50 caliber machine guns over cannon armament as he claims better penetration and more internal damage was caused by .50 caliber armor-piercing incendiary ammunition.

The Unwinnable Fight

Yeager's lectures about the science of war, tactics, and training help us to identify combat's important common denominators. He also seems to appreciate luck and experienced his fair share. I do not dismiss this factor at all, but it is easy to forget other important themes in the fight once we focus too closely on chance.

The reader will note that I give credit where it is due to the baddies, particularly with regard to their technology. I also discuss their attitudes, idealism, and grit. While it is impossible to respect the fascists, evil military genius must be studied. As it happens, some of the good guys turned out to be real monsters as well. As I said, King Henry the Fifth was unbelievably brutal to his enemies and even, at times, to his allies and helpless hostages. If the political or tactical winds demanded their sacrifice, he knocked them off by the baker's dozen. Shakespeare washed Henry clean, and now we associate him with the famous and most military of expressions, "We band of brothers."[13]

The three stories that follow are all based on true events and technology. They serve as a portrait of the one-man stand. We begin here with Audie Murphy's Medal of Honor moment. I have filled in the German side of this incident. We then move on to a Vietnam experience, and last, we have the pure historical fiction story of a British pilot's obsession with downing zeppelins during World War One. I blend technical detail and historical exposition in an effort to discuss not just the essence of the fight but also, to put it bluntly, the questionable sanity of the weaponeers versus the heft of the warrior's stones.

---

13. Act 4, Scene 3.

2

The War Dance

"I am a soldier. I fight where I am told, and I win where I fight."

—George Patton

*French infantry armed with the revolutionary
Chauchat squad automatic weapon.*

Just like cars and architecture, soldiers have a nationalistic look. Consider the average French infantryman of the pre-World War One era in his disastrously colorful sky-blue uniform or the British Tommy and his pie pan Brodie helmet. Israeli soldiers all need haircuts. Japanese soldiers were viciously caricatured as bucktoothed and nearsighted. No soldier on earth is more distinctive than the samurai. World War Two German SS troops look like they could man Darth Vader's Death Star. But what of the American soldier, World War Two's famous G.I. Joe?

Well, according to legend, he was a bit of a mutt, but tall, square-jawed, and physically fit from being so darn athletic. He could sing, swing dance with Betty Lou, break a wild horse, and shoot a gun over his shoulder using a mirror to aim. He could take a punch or deliver one. Generally, he fought a fair fight, but if someone picked up a pool cue, he could up the ante. Americans come in different brands, such as whisky or milk drinkers. Also available are city boy or redneck models. Once the boot camp process broke them down and built them back again, they looked smart in their uniforms and were a joy to watch on the parade ground as they marched in tight and precise formation.

The American soldier has always been lavishly equipped, especially when it comes to small arms. Unlike his enemies, for most of World War Two, he had a general issue semiautomatic M-1 Garand rifle that was both accurate and worked reliably under all combat conditions. This was a huge advantage and spread the firepower between all of the riflemen. Unlike the bolt action armed soldier who had to take his eyes off the target between shots to cycle his rifle's bolt, any rifleman armed with a self-loading rifle could bear down on a target until he connected. The round it fired was useful on everything from soldiers to airplanes. In comparison, the Nazi small arms philosophy was to concentrate most of the squad's firepower on a single general purpose, belt-fed weapon that the other men supported as ammo bearers and security.

American officers, cooks, drivers, mortar men, and even members of the band carried the impressive M-1 carbine for personal defense. Just before the end of the war, the M-2 select fire version of the dainty carbine was introduced. For all intents and purposes, this was a slightly underpowered modern assault rifle, arguably one of the world's first. These rifles would eventually replace the Thompson and M-3 submachine guns that were plentiful but rather heavy. A G.I.'s .45 automatic gave him comfort and stopping power. Many found their way home in G.I. duffle bags. My Uncle Gene, to whom this book is dedicated, left my father his .45 that he carried on Okinawa. His palm print is worn into the slide. It has talisman status in our family lore.

In comparison to other armed forces, the American uniform was comfortable, durable, and thanks to the quartermaster, easily replaceable. The G.I. had excellent boots and socks aplenty. He could fashion his web gear to suit his needs. On the battlefield, the average American trooper quickly degenerated into a slovenly character devoted to bearing his burden as comfortably as possible. No matter how they looked or smelled, American soldiers at the front were fed excellent, nutritious food from highly organized and well supplied truck-borne kitchens that stayed close to the action. Even cold rations were scientifically designed to pack thousands of calories into conveniently sized cans that a soldier could stash anywhere.

The real G.I. likely never played football on the high school team. He didn't ride in the rodeo or dance with Fred and Ginger in a black-and-white movie. He was happy with a C-average in high school. He worked at the car plant and liked to go bowling. He never shot a gun or rode a horse. Yet, somehow, the American soldier kicked tail in every theater of war. Sure, he had every industrial advantage imaginable, but technology alone is not enough to win wars. If it were, the Taliban, the North Koreans, and the North Vietnamese would all have been routed. G.I. Joe's success was founded on emotional boundaries that he could count upon to keep him relatively sane under extreme stress.

The average G.I. knew in his bones that he was fighting for freedom, and Americans are trained in utero that liberty is a cause worth dying for. (It always will be.) Like so many men in his generation, just looking at the Stars and Stripes was a considerable comfort. He felt free to utterly despise his enemy. Once the death camps were liberated, it was pretty damn obvious just how bad that enemy was too. A soldier could take great pride in the righteousness of his battlefield wrath—no matter what he did. He likely did some pretty horrid stuff. There was no need to hold back in that fight. Everyone back home agreed. After the war, the guys could joke about their war crimes at cocktail parties. While this is shocking, I see it as a form of group therapy with Jim Beam standing in for Prozac. Back then, you could even tell graphic war stories to the neighborhood kids while smoking a Marlboro. Those were the days.

The value placed on each man's life is what makes the American military mighty. American industry encouraged its military leaders to knock on mysterious doors with artillery shells instead of men. Engineers at defense plants back home actually listened to feedback from

the field. Little changes saved lives, like spring-loading the crew hatches on a Sherman tank. This allowed men to quickly exit the vehicle if it caught fire. An average of one crewman was killed per tank loss. This nearly doubled when tanks brewed up, so manufacturers looked at the problem and delivered a quick fix. Designers in totalitarian regimes would never concern themselves with saving that .8 percent of a man.

The G.I. knew that if he were wounded, he would be cared for as if he were the president's son. The Allies offered their troops impressive battlefield medicine, and thanks to their mechanization, they were often able to get their wounded to a field hospital quite quickly. The advent of the Bell H-13 Sioux would get wounded Korean Conflict soldiers to M*A*S*H* hospitals in under an hour. The response time during the Vietnam War was even better.

During peacetime, the Army medical system employed about 1,200 doctors. By 1944, there were fifty thousand doctors in the European theatre. Eighty-three of them were women. Fifty-two thousand nurses were commissioned as officers. There were fifteen thousand dentists and even two thousand veterinarians who saw to horses and livestock. Deaths from infectious diseases dropped from shocking highs to amazing lows. Pneumonia deaths fell from twenty-four percent to six percent. Where 1 man in 700 died from malaria at the start of the war, this would drop to 1 man in 14,000 by the war's end. (Thanks DDT!) The doctor's arsenal of blood plasma, morphine, and the combination of sulfa drugs and penicillin administered in copious quantities gave the wounded or sick Allied soldier an excellent chance of recovery so that he might return to the front and be killed outright.

The Allies stockpiled eight hundred thousand pints of plasma and six hundred thousand doses of penicillin for to the D-Day invasion. They readied ninety-eight thousand beds for the wounded in England with eight thousand doctors and ten thousand nurses standing by. If needed, they could expand their services to almost two hundred thousand patients at all levels of care.

Of all the medical statistics generated by combat and disease, it is the American record of fighting illness on the battlefield that impresses me most. Remember how many soldiers died throughout military history from disease. This, as we have seen, includes kings. The Dauphin of France, who opposed Henry during his reign, also died of dysentery disease. Of the 918,300 men treated for disease by the United States Army during the Second World War, thanks to miracle drugs, only 585 died.

If the G.I. fell in battle, life insurance would soften the blow, as if that were possible, and buy the family farm back from the bank. He believed in the edge that was given to him by the Arsenal of Democracy. The American military-industrial complex put weapons in his hands that were obviously very expensive. The folks back home did not care one wit about the bill. Society was changing rapidly to meet wartime demands. Rosie the Riveter was changing women's rights forever by working a double shift on the B-29 production line. More than three billion dollars were spent in its development and production making this plane one of the most expensive weapons systems ever devised. Eggheads at Los Alamos labored around the clock and spent two billion more dollars to develop an atomic weapon for these planes to drop.

Japanese and Nazi soldiers were definitely outspent, but they were not prone to surrender. Some pressed Axis troops fought with guns to their heads. The Nazis raised forces in captured countries that were not made of the same metal as German iron youth. Other Axis troops fought fanatically because they knew that they were dead anyway. Nobody wanted to surrender to the Soviets. A great many men must have lost family in the bombing raids that went on around the clock. That might make a fellow a little vengeful. Early on, the Germans had a patriotism of their own, but the Third Reich terrorized and propagandized its way to power. It used anger, envy, bigotry, and outright violence to justify its existence and silence any and all opposition.

I have to believe that in the end, most German soldiers saw through the fascism and wanted nothing more than to surrender to the Americans, French, or British, but their fanatical officer corps was suicidally dedicated to their military code. The Japanese officer class behaved the same way. Rather than surrender, the proud men of these beaten military cultures chose to die as "good soldiers" in a "lost cause," and their souls be damned.

Audie Murphy does not mention many specifics about his opponents in *To Hell and Back*. They seem like silhouettes in his retelling. The Nazis he faced in the Colmar Pocket in Alsace, France, were all but played out, but they still managed to cobble together an effective force from the remnants of depleted units. It is difficult to know for certain which officers specifically made a play for Murphy's men. Generalleutnant Hans Degen commanded the Second Mountain Division and may well have provided the two companies of infantry that attacked Murphy on January 26, 1945. Also present was Lieutenant Colonel Johannes Marahrens, who led what remained of the 708th Volksgrenadiers, and under him, Oberleutnant Sommer commanded the 106th Panzer Regiment. He likely led the detachment of six tank destroyers that emerged from Holtzwihr that famous afternoon.

The Nazi's fuel and artillery ammunition were limited, so they planned their attack only after a thorough post-midnight scouting of the American positions.

German Army Staff Meeting
Holtzwihr, France, January 25, 1945

The German feldwebel (sergeant) reported on his reconnaissance, "They have a few tanks just sitting on the road. One forward and the other further back. As you can see, they block our path, but obviously, not for long." He pointed to a spot on the map. "There is a machine gun position here. I believe this area is their command post. We did not see any prepared emplacements. No mines or wire. The ground is frozen solid. They appear to be only a few platoons. Possibly less. Most of what we saw were men moving about to keep their feet from freezing. This is the right spot to ram through."

"How close did you get this time?"

The feldwebel raised his hands. "What is this? About a meter."

Sommers lit a cigarette and sighed tiredly as he addressed his staff. "I am surprised they didn't smell you. We shall split the tanks into two groups of three on the left and right of this hedgerow running down the middle of the field. Stay on the road as long as possible before we fan out. If all goes well, we will encircle what is left of these Americans. There is a great deal of open ground to cross. Even at a dead run, it will take five minutes to reach the woods. We are all tired, but your men must move at the double.

"The barrage will not last long. Sweep forward as soon as the shelling begins and eliminate any anti-tank weapons and artillery spotters that remain. We shall destroy the American armor and then proceed through the woods along the road. We will deliver a spoiling attack against whatever we find in our path.

"Understood?" The officers nodded. "Questions?" There were none, but the officers traded glances.

Sommers read the room and dug deep to find his last ounce of optimism. "I know this looks too easy. It very well may be a trap, but the Americans are rarely that imaginative. They do not have to be. We have no idea what lies beyond the woods. There will almost certainly be more tanks. At least the weather favors us. Their airplanes will be useless."

One of the junior officers decided to say what everyone else was thinking. "We trust the weather. It isn't the jabos that worry us, Oberleutnant."

"What then?"

They said together, "Artillery."

"Then be quick across the field.

"We will attack as soon as the panzers are ready. I expect that will be shortly after dawn."

The weary troops discussed code words and checked their watches. None of them were optimistic about their armor being ready by first light. In fact, it would be noon before all were operational. It took even more time to bring them forward. Sommers understood the issues but threatened his mechanics anyway. This did nothing to speed up repairs.

The last old hand in the unit was particularly close with his commander. "I am told several of our Jagdpanthers are in poor condition. We can only count on six? Is that so?"

"Maybe six. One is just barely worth the effort. We shall put it up front to take the brunt of any anti-tank guns. They worked on it all last night, but without heavy equipment, they cannot dismount the main gun, so the transmission issues are still bothersome. One of the mechanics dropped a spanner through a deck hatch, and they had to take the entire rear deck off to get it back. When we evacuate, those tools will be my first priority. I suspect we will lose all six Jagdpanthers today. I will throw the maintenance crews into the line as riflemen. There, you see, reinforcements have come indeed."

"If we live through this, and are captured, do you think they will send us to America as prisoners of war? I could use a holiday to gain a few pounds."

"I was talking about this with one of my tank commanders." He looked about and lowered his voice. "I hear Colorado is nice. Like Bavaria in winter. I would take care who hears you. I told this other officer the same I shall tell you. A jest can get you shot. Worse still, they will want to know who told you that same joke. Before you know it, there are three bodies on the floor and a Gestapo man with a hard-on has had a good day. No more travel jokes. Understood? Tell your men to treat any Americans who surrender with respect. It's a sound investment if you follow my meaning."

Cold Feet
Holtzwihr France, January 1945

Giant slayers often arrive in ironically small packages. Audie Murphy was an undersized soldier who won a staggering number of medals for valor, including the Medal of Honor, the Legion of Merit, the Distinguished Service Cross, two Silver and Bronze Stars, the Purple Heart with several oak leaves (meaning several woundings), and a whole smear of others from both his United States, France, and even one award from Belgium. It took him a little over a year to earn the lot and all between bouts of recurring malaria and gangrene. He stood just over five feet, five inches tall and weighed 112 pounds wringing wet with a brick in each pocket when he enlisted in the United States Army shortly after Pearl Harbor. A loaded M-1 rifle was almost ten percent of his weight. He was rejected by the Marine Corps for being too short. Today, he is a larger-than-life American icon.

Anyone who reads Murphy's account of his one-man stand will see how inaccurate the movie recreation is. Murphy reenacted the events himself, so he ought to know, but there were severe limits to what could be shown on film, especially by late 1950s Hollywood standards. They scaled the whole scene way back. For starters, the studio could only muster five American (M-41) tanks instead of the actual six German vehicles. Murphy shoots it out with the Germans while standing on a Sherman tank, not a tank destroyer. Yes, that makes a difference. There is no snow on the ground and too few enemy troops. The set is too short, and the Germans begin their advance practically at point-blank range. The worst issue stems from how time is condensed from nearly an hour of combat to about five minutes.

It was two o'clock in the afternoon when Lieutenant Murphy looked across his front and realized that his forty under-equipped and desperately tired men were about to be overrun by six tanks and more than two companies of infantrymen wearing white snow capes. He ducked instinctively as enemy shells precisely took out his machine gun team and other officers. Murphy correctly reasoned that there was just no way his riflemen could stop what was coming. He ordered his depleted command back into the woods to find better defensive positions. He remained behind to face the charge alone. Well, sort of alone. Alone American style. He had a phone.

Murphy later described how he mastered his initial near panic. He experienced the sensation countless times before. He knew that once the battle was joined, "The nerves will relax, the heart stops its thumping. The brain will turn to animal cunning. The job is directly before us: destroy and survive."

Audie lacked much in the way of heavy support, but there were two tank destroyers at the scene. They were dangerously exposed, and

Murphy told their commanders to get off the road and under better cover long before the Nazis struck. The tankers feared bogging down and demurred. Once the fighting began, they didn't last long. Even with special armor-piercing ammunition, their guns were nearly useless against the well-sloped and thick Jagdpanther frontal armor. Say what you will about the complexities of German tanks, and you would be right, but by 1944, they had finally mastered the simple sloped glacis plate. Murphy said that he saw the M-10's anti-tank rounds bounce off the Nazi armor, so they must have gotten off a few shots before they were neutralized. Perhaps they did more damage than we know.

One of the M-10s backed into a ditch and mired itself at such an angle that its guns could not be depressed enough to shoot the enemy. Like Henry the Eighth's battleship the *Mary Rose*, they essentially took themselves out of the fight. That takes some skill. These tank crewmen abandoned their machine. The other M-10 took a hit during the initial artillery barrage and was partially on fire, but its turret-mounted .50 caliber machine gun was still operative, and the engine deck was not engulfed in flames. This was the weapon Audie used so famously. That particular M-2 might well be the most glorious .50 caliber ever built. One has to wonder where it is today.

Murphy fought basically single-handedly using an M-1 carbine, the smallest rifle-type small arm issued at that time, and a .50 caliber machine gun, which was the largest rifled weapon a soldier might fire. In his book, he describes his opening burst with the .50 caliber as "Sweet music. Three Krauts stagger and crumple in the snow."[14] He did the most damage with a field telephone as he expertly called mortars and howitzer rounds down on the German infantry. The enemy tanks held short of Murphy's position and waited for their mountain troops to move ahead, but they were too busy being blown to pieces by shell fragments and .50 caliber bullets to do their assigned job.

Audie had a couple of things going for him. First, ironically, the burning tank destroyer he was standing on was expected to explode

---

14. Murphy, *To Hell and Back*, p. 241.

spectacularly at any moment. It blocked the road where the woods began. This created a no-go zone and a thick smoke screen that helped to conceal Audie's position. The wind gusted from moment to moment, allowing the combatants to glimpse each other, but by the main, Murphy benefitted from the thick smoke. Second, Murphy had world-class communication going on with truly professional and well-supplied artillerists. He would not have lasted long if that slender phone line had been cut. Third, he stood on the tank destroyer's engine deck behind the turret. This elevated his position just enough to improve his observation considerably. The turret also offered some excellent cover from small arms fire. He was not a big guy to begin with and crouched behind that enormous M-2 machine gun, he was a challenging target. Though the tank was on fire, he did note that, for the first time in days, his feet were warm. Though this last detail seems trivial, it speaks volumes about state of mind. Murphy spent most of his time at the mercy of the harsh winter weather. He writes of waking up with his hair frozen to the ground. Was it warm feet that kept him up there?

Murphy manned one of the all-time deadliest weapons ever devised, the Browning-designed M-2 heavy machine gun. The open-top turret on the M-10 tank destroyer gave him fast access to .50 caliber ammunition which was racked within arm's reach. He only mentions reloading the big gun once, but it seems likely that he went through several boxes of shells. His fire was more or less constant.

Some weapons make it easier to win a Medal of Honor than others. They both energize the combatants and neutralize their targets. Alvin York, of World War One fame, used a super accurate 1917 Enfield rifle and a 1911 Colt .45.[15] Played by Gary Cooper in the 1941 retelling of that day, York showed his genius for shooting was nothing compared

---

15. "York" uses two different Luger pistols in the movie version of this Medal of Honor moment. This is likely due to the fact that 1911 Colt .45 pistols do not work well with theatrical blanks. If the viewer looks closely, many .45 auto pistols shown on screen in older films are actually 9 m/m Spanish Star Model B pistols that look remarkably close to the 1911.

to his ability to read the battlespace, maneuver between threats and position himself to do real damage. York got the drop on a German trench line and began to methodically pot the enemy from the rear forward so as not to spook his next target. After shooting a dozen men, a German officer offered to surrender everyone under his command if York would just stop firing. He captured 132 prisoners and a slew of machine guns.

John Basilone plugged the line with a forty-pound .30 caliber water-cooled machine gun during a desperate defense at Guadalcanal. He also resorted to a .45 and even a machete before it was all over. He was one of only three men to survive that action, which actually went on for several days. At one point, he had to fire the weapon free of its tripod. He cradled the superheated gun and continued to blast away, an act that gave him third-degree burns, but he ignored the pain and sprayed belt after belt that kept the Japanese at bay during a critical phase in the battle. Basilone could have taken the rest of the war off to sell war bonds, but he returned to action in time for the battle of Iwo Jima, where he was killed in action on February 19, 1945. He received the Navy Cross posthumously for his actions that day.

Audie Murphy had the best weapon possible for his situation. The .50 caliber M-2 has a throaty boom to it. The muzzle blast is exhilarating. The rounds it fires are five times heavier than an M-1 rifle bullet. It has tremendous penetration against fortified targets. It stands out against the other rifle-caliber machine guns on the battlefield. Tank mounts or tripods absorb the recoil and balance the weapon. Shooting it feels effortless and instantly promotes the operator to badass status.

Murphy had him some gun.

This is where we have to talk about luck. I will say it plainly. Audie was awful damn lucky. How to describe it? At first, I compared this fight to a high-stakes poker game. Murphy was the wild card. He was all in. Somehow, that didn't strike the right level of lucky. Poker players can lose all their chips and still hit the buffet before the floor show. This was no casino game. Finally, I think I hit the right note with this: Lieutenant Audie Murphy did a full-on Native American war dance in a pit full of pissed-off rattlesnakes—for an hour—and didn't get bit. Not even close.

This picture shows the open turret M-10 tank, machine gun, and soldier in correct scale. Audie Murphy fired that machine gun while standing in the position shown.

The Burning Tank

People who know Audie's story believe that he was the only hero in this fight. He stood his ground and weathered the onslaught alone. I submit that the burning tank destroyer on which he stood was an equally heroic partner. In its way, that brave dying tank destroyer held the line. You may recall that it was the one destined to explode at the start of this fracas. We know that it was struck by German tank rounds at least twice after Murphy climbed aboard, but by some military miracle, it didn't explode. Murphy decided to keep on dancing right where he was. No other soldier on earth would have taken that bet. The supporting infantry and German artillery must have fired a zillion rounds in his direction, but they could not kill him either. Murphy's final artillery adjustment brought rounds down right on top of his position. He literally said he didn't care about killing himself, and yet, nope. The explosions cut the phone line, and fragments punched holes in the map he had in his hands, but not one tiny piece of shrapnel touched the young Lieutenant.

Murphy refers to the American armored vehicles in this fight simply as tank destroyers (TDs). They were likely of the M-10 variety. Like all TDs on the Allied side, it did not boast much armor protection. Its glacis plate was sloped at 55 degrees, which helped somewhat, but it was only 38 m/m thick to begin with. Like most tank destroyers of this era, the fighting compartment or turret was open topped so that the crew had better visibility. On the downside, they were vulnerable to airburst artillery and infantry attack.

The M-10 was designed to snipe enemy tanks rather than shoot it out toe-to-toe with heavy armor. Maneuverability and a heavy gun were thought to be adequate compensation for armor plating that was proof against rifle bullets and shell fragments, but little more. The M-10's offensive performance lacked as well. While it was more than adequate to deal with early war Nazi armored vehicles, even at point-blank range, the three-inch main gun had trouble penetrating a Tiger I or Panther's front plate.

The Jagdpanther's PaK 43 gun, on the other hand, was so powerful that the hits Murphy experienced should have ripped the M-10 apart. The Nazi tank gun could penetrate nearly eight inches of armor at one thousand yards. No Allied tank's frontal armor could withstand such a hit. The 88 m/m anti-tank rounds were fused to explode after smacking armor of 30 m/m or more. The M-10's armor was not much better from the front, and the flank measured only 25 m/m. There was racked ammunition everywhere and fuel to burn. So long as the enemy Jagdpanther was coming straight on, in this tank destroyer versus tank destroyer battle, the M-10 was outclassed in every way. Had the M-10s taken better cover or prepared to fire from a flanking position, the fight would have turned out differently, and we would be singing the praises of the American Tank Destroyer Program.

Murphy describes the first hit to the tank he was standing on with the simple word, "Crash!" It is the absence of any other description of an explosion that makes me think that this shell passed straight through the vehicle without hitting stored ammunition. The second hit is described as a flash *and an explosion*. Murphy was knocked off his feet and startled for a moment, but he was otherwise unhurt. By all rights, the M-10 should have been demolished with this second hit. It is possible that the shot was deflected, perhaps by a hit to the gun mantlet or a hit to the lower hull. It must not have hit ammunition which lined the turret walls and hull. Thank goodness Murphy was standing on the engine deck and not inside the turret ring when that shell went off.

However thick the armor, it was supremely ballsy play and memorably medal-worthy.

Murphy did not emerge completely unscathed. Descriptions of his post-action condition differ, but all agree he reopened a previous surgery in his hip area. He refused to leave the field and reorganized his men to face another attack. He likely killed well over fifty Germans in that action with small arms alone. He reported firing on a dozen men who crept up on him in a drainage ditch. The smoke blew clear as they prepared to spring their attack. Murphy swung the massive .50 around and literally chopped them up at point-blank range. There's an image that's tough to get out of your head.

In the film, Murphy gives artillerists coordinates and then abandons the phone. However, before he tosses the receiver, he offers some glib dialogue.

"How close are they?" asks the fire coordinator.

"Just hold the phone, and I'll let you talk to them," comes the immortal reply.

The German perspective must have been very confused, and often, in battle, this is enough to win the day. I am sure that they believed themselves to be up against a far larger force than one little Jack armed with a field telephone and a huge machine gun. The M-10 tank destroyers were both knocked out, but that didn't mean that others were not hidden nearby. Murphy's artillery support was impressive, enough to give any tank commander second thoughts.

German tankers wore black uniforms with pink piping. My stand in for Schiff commanded the Jagdpanther behind him.

The German Assault outside Holtzwihr, France: Lead Jagdpanther Number 131, January 26, 1945

Leutnant Wolfgang Schiff commanded the lead Jagdpanther in the column and took the brunt of American tank fire. Though only twenty years old, he was an experienced officer and artillerist with many Sherman, Cromwell, M-10, and Churchill kills to his credit. Ideally, he deployed his heavy tank destroyer in a static, well-hidden position where he could take maximum advantage of his gun's long-range lethality. Such deployments were rare. Close fighting in French hedgerows very nearly cost him his life when Shermans and British infantry swarmed his position. He abandoned his tank and ran like a dog. Not very dignified. A rapid counterattack recovered the Jagdpanther, but not before the enemy urinated in his open hatch.

Schiff did not approve of the current plan. Tanks and infantry did not simply roll straight through an American artillery barrage and expect to be effective on the other side.

A 76 m/m anti-tank gun hit gouged the glacis plate between the diver's vision block and the gun mantlet. This rang the bell but did not penetrate. A second round hit the lower front, where the armor was sixty millimeters thick. This shot managed to poke a ten-millimeter hole in the Jagdpanther's hide. A three-ounce piece of metal struck the labyrinth of parts behind the plate. This caused a fluid leak, which quickly began to smolder. The driver choked and reported that shifting gears was difficult as the transmission began to overheat.

A fan was supposed to evacuate any fouled air in the fighting compartment, but it had long since ceased working. Schiff opened his hatch to vent the smoke, but airburst artillery forced him to close it and reach for his gas mask. Though he had a throat-activated microphone, the mask muddied his orders.

Interlocking explosions from the incoming American 105 m/m howitzer rounds straddled the Nazi tank destroyers. Schiff's Jagdpanther was spattered with fragments that destroyed external stores, cracked periscope vision blocks, and could play the devil with his tracks and running gear. The crew flinched but remained determined.

Outside, the German infantry was feeling less than elite. The vast, open field offered the troops no cover. The first company advanced in a ragged skirmish line, and they came on well while their artillery was firing in support. When the American guns chimed in, it took only minutes to kill most of them. The next company bravely made its dash, but they ran into the same wall and were scattered. The last platoons were the most experienced, and they decided not to make a move until the artillery ceased.

The Nazi tanks kept up their slow approach toward the woods. Eventually they would cross the entire field. The tankers anticipated a massive explosion from the burning M-10, but none was forthcoming. They gave the pyre plenty of room.

"Driver, advance!" Schiff ordered. The Jagdpanther crawled forward at walking speed.

"Gunner, target the burning tank destroyer again. Driver, straight down the road! Gunner, on the move, fire!" The 88 m/m recoiled, and the loader swung another round toward the breech. "Damn! It's still blocking the road. Unbelievable. How did you miss? Settle down, it sits in the shadows, farther back than it looks. I think we are the only tank who can even see it."

Schiff's seventeen-year-old gunner, Carl Benz, trained for less than two weeks before being ordered to the front. He studied the complex sights and shell trajectories with a schoolboy's enthusiasm. He practiced leading targets in the simulator and did acceptably well with his limited allotment of training shells. He was not required to wear a gas mask while doing so. He discovered to his dismay that "his" mask was filthy, and he had great difficulty seeing anything clearly through the sooty lenses. The tank sight's chevrons and stadia were blurred and useless to him.

Carl began his war as a gunner in a Panzer Mark IV. He got in a few licks before a Sherman shot off their left front sprocket. Their motionless tank was peppered but, amazingly, the entire crew escaped. He was posted as a gunner in a Panther tank, but it broke down before he got a chance to fire a shot. The Jagdpanther was his third tank in the past week. Having never served or trained in a turretless vehicle, he was not prepared for the limited traverse of the main gun. The successful Jagdpanther gunner worked in tandem with the driver, who sat immediately in front of him. They shared a roof hatch at the back of the fighting compartment that was difficult to reach in an emergency.

Carl barely knew any of the crew, and he had never worked with the driver of any tank, but then losses were so high that this lack of team cohesion was expected. Normally, in a tank with a turret such as the Mark IV or Panther, a gunner would wait to either feel the loader slap his shoulder or shout "ready" on the intercom before he touched the trigger. The original Jagdpanther design called for two loaders who stood at the rear of the fighting compartment. This was reduced to one man who wore no headset or throat microphone as the attendant cables got in his way. The loader found that the gunner's shoulder was just out of easy reach and so he could only shout his readiness. A gunner specifically trained on the Jagdpanther knew to glance back at the loader, just to be sure he was clear of the recoiling breach before he touched off a shell.

Even wearing headsets, the noise inside the tank destroyer was distracting. The sound of anti-tank and shrapnel hits, the tracks creaking, the engine's whine, the radio operator spraying away with the M-34 machine gun, and the driver's cussing loudly right in front of him all made it difficult to hear commands. Finally, Carl aligned the gun on the burning M-10, but every yard they crawled moved the crosshairs. The gas masks made everyone sound the same. He did not see the loader's fumble that added a few seconds to the gun team's rhythm. He thought he heard his loader's voice give the all clear.

This projectile exited the barrel just as the road dipped six inches. It skipped off the packed surface to hit the M-10 quite low, but right on the nose. The round lost its stability when it struck earth and was beginning to yaw when it hit. Perhaps for this reason, it did not penetrate as deeply as it might have before detonating. Carl observed a flash from the open turret through his gunsight, and for a moment he thought the target was destroyed, but then the winking machine gun lanced through the smoke, and he heard the loader calling out for his blood.

Schiff knew why his loader was cussing. He looked back over the gun that bisected the compartment whose head bobbed in and out of view. Schiff had to remove his gas mask to yell, "Hans! Hans! How bad? Can you load?" The loader shook his head. He was fortunate to suffer only a fractured hand and wrist, but in effect, the PaK 43 was out of action.

Poorly trained crews were not the Jagdpanther's only issue. At best, it was a complex and finicky machine first delivered in early 1944. Just over four hundred were built in all, with most serving on the Eastern

Front. The first batch might best be described as the mechanically challenged Hitler Youth. They were completely unreliable and soaked up fuel and other resources that more traditional tanks desperately needed. About half received improved final drives and transmissions at the factory. Their dual exhausts had specially designed muzzles to hide revealing sparks and smoke caused by the engine at idle. When perfectly maintained, which was all but impossible under battlefield conditions, the last two hundred Jagdpanthers made were perhaps the best tank destroyers ever produced.

A great deal of the Jagdpanther's success depended on the driver's personal experience, and very few teenage Germans knew how to drive a car or farm tractor, let alone had the aptitude to drive a tank. Bad drivers likely killed as many Jagdpanthers as anti-tank gunners. Overworking the transmission or final drive was often mechanically fatal. The driver had to have an eye for matching the terrain to the six forward gears. Anything less than perfect harmony placed a great deal of strain on the dozens of complex components that drove the massive weapon. High torque turns were to be avoided, if at all possible, but the limited traverse of the gun required minute adjustments in heading that were the very definition of mechanical peril. Repairing transmission failures required removing the gun and mantle. This was best done at the factory, but overwhelming Allied control of the air made trips by rail a futile endeavor.

Lacking a turret, the Jagdpanther was relatively simple to manufacture. It had an excellent power-to-weight ratio, which made it fairly maneuverable across country. Wide tracks and torsion bar suspension helped it on soft ground. When fully armed for battle, the Jagdpanther carried fifty-seven rounds of improved 88 m/m ammunition. The projectiles themselves weighed twenty-three pounds and had a muzzle velocity of 3,400 feet per second, three hundred feet per second faster than a 55-grain M-193 M-16 rifle round used in Vietnam.

All tanks depend on a combination of maneuverability and armor for their survival. With a maximum speed of more than twenty-five miles per hour, the Jagdpanther was relatively speedy for its size.

However, reverse speeds were desperately slow, which rendered shoot-and-scoot tactics impractical. So long as the commander kept the enemy to his front and at a distance, he could expect the 80 to 100 m/m of sloped armor to offer protection against most Allied anti-tank weapons on the Western Front, but the British 17-pounder gun mounted in the Sherman Firefly was another matter. Any allied tank that mounted even the truly average 75 m/m gun could punch holes in the Jagdpanther's side armor where ammunition racks lined the walls. Allied tanks armed with a 76 m/m gun also had a limited supply of HVAP ammunition specifically made to deal with German heavy armor and so could try a head-on shot with what tank aficionados call, "a reasonable chance of success."

Schiff's tank lurched forward, running a few yards and then stalling for a moment before it began to crawl again. He knew from experience that his vehicle was not going to keep up with the other five. The driver swore loudly and protested that there was nothing he could do.

"Leutnant, we'll be lucky to make it another mile!"

"Another mile is all we shall need. Just get us through the woods."

"But the burning tank blocks our way through."

Schiff took stock of the situation. The intensity of enemy fire was overwhelming for the infantry support, but the tanks continued to struggle forward. Smoke inside the compartment was growing worse by the moment. Shell fragments carried away his radio antenna, rendering him both deaf and mute. He had no idea that the other tanks were letting him set the pace of the assault. With his loader down, the main gun was out of action. If he met enemy tanks, he couldn't even get up enough speed to ram.

Murphy methodically corrected artillery fire on the exposed infantry. The tanks were more difficult to stop though they wasted ammunition by firing blindly into the woods as they approached. The final domino to fall brought holes in the low cloud cover. Fighter-bombers could add their ordinance to the fight.

Schiff did the math. "Where is our infantry? Did any of them make it across at all? That damn burning tank! Goddamn it! If we could shoot, we could get through. Why won't it just explode? This is hopeless! Driver, reverse! Gunner, fire smoke! We're pulling back!"

The three surviving Jagdpanthers tried to disengage but kept their thick frontal armor toward the enemy as long as they could. The price of that protection was a bare crawl back toward safety. Once they came about, Schiff's driver caught a high gear sweet spot and managed twelve miles per hour. It took several long minutes to escape the shelling and make for cover in Holtzwihr. Only two tanks emerged. Schiff opened his hatch and took a look around for the first time since the fight began. The crew gulped fresh air. The loader had some trouble opening the heavy rear door with one hand. He crawled out onto the engine deck. The rest of the crew heard his alarm.

"Jabos!"

A pair of P-47D fighter bombers dropped through the gloom just as Schiff and the other tank destroyer reached a stone bridge on the main road into Holtzwihr. The American pilots were frustrated. Thick fog kept them from identifying targets, and they were wary of plowing into a church steeple or hillside. They spent half their fuel and lugged their five-inch-diameter rockets all over creation with nothing clearly German to shoot at. Then the clouds parted, and it seemed that God Himself wanted to smite a few Nazis.

Schiff screamed, "They have us! Everybody out!" and he was through the hatch. The loader rolled off the rear engine deck and took cover in a drainage ditch.

From the attacking pilot's point of view, this gun run was a layup. The Nazi tanks were caught in the open on a straight dirt road that led onto a single-lane stone bridge. Neither Jagdpanther had any anti-aircraft defense. German ground fire was desultory.

The lead P-47 pilot fired a burst from his guns to assist in aiming his rockets. He observed flashes on the leading tank. The rounds didn't do anything immediately fatal to the vehicle, but he put dozens of holes in the engine deck, exhaust system, and crew heater. Given the circumstances, a crew might abandon a tank with any sort of problem. Victory doesn't always require death, just a simple eviction. Or, you could blow it into a million pieces. He salvoed his rockets just as Schiff's Jagdpanther reached the bridge.

The World War Two era air-to-ground rocket was not the most accurate weapon system ever fielded, but the explosives delivered were the equivalent of a full broadside fired by a Navy destroyer. The rockets overshot the Jagdpanther but demolished the bridge it was about to cross. The tank driver managed to stop the vehicle before it went over the edge, but he could not reverse. With the tank commander gone, the driver wisely decided to bail out himself. He turned to tell Carl to get moving but found him gone already. Once on the ground, he saw the young gunner run out into the adjacent field where he was cut down by the relentless jabos.

The second P-47 circled the target area and lined up for his run. He was elated when his eight-gun burst caught and tumbled a fleeing tanker. He fired his rockets in two salvoes. The first narrowly missed the rear Jagdpanther but the explosions ripped its right track and took several wheels. The crew inside remained unhurt. Once the jabos flew off, these men took a vote and decided to drop their weapons, raise their hands and walk toward the American lines. The second set of rockets loosed were destined for greatness. One flew through the open rear hatch of Schiff's tank destroyer and detonated against the gun's breech. This set off the stored ammunition. The wreck was unrecognizable, and a small mushroom cloud rose hundreds of feet into the air. The P-47s circled the wreck. One did a barrel roll as they climbed away.

Schiff ran his hands over his body looking for holes but found none. He said, "My God. If I make it past my surrender, I am going to live through this war." He saw an American jeep with a long radio antenna coming up the road. He tossed his pistol on the ground and prepared his papers.

"The Americans will be here in a few moments. They will give you a shot of morphine for that arm."

"Wave to them. Let them see we are unarmed."

The jeep pulled up and stopped a few yards away. A young lieutenant with round glasses stepped out and pointed a grease gun at the men. Two other soldiers operated a radio and scanned ahead with binoculars. For a moment, the American looked as if he might pull the trigger and solve his custodial problem. Schiff pointed to the pistol some yards away. The American broke into a broad grin.

"Hey! Great. Thanks so much! Donka, Donka. I have been after onc of these. Wow. Great."

He picked up the Luger, checked to see that it was safe, and stuffed it in his web gear. "Oh man! Thank you, sir. This one is coming home with me. Hey, Frank, I know it's my turn to, you know, but these guys are alright. Not SS. I'm not gonna shoot'm. They might know something we can use." Frank shrugged and went back to his radio.

"Here, you want some cigarettes and chocolate bars for that pistol? You need water? Here, take some water. You speak any English? Goot. Goot. Wow, that arm looks painful there, buddy. We have some morphine around here someplace. The medics and the rest of the American Army will be here soon. My sergeant here will give your friend a shot, OK? Relax, Max, the war is over, and weirdly enough, you two are the big winners."

The Sargeant administered the morphine, and the loader relaxed with his back against the wheel of the jeep. The sergeant asked him questions in German as he frisked the wounded man.

The lieutenant pulled Schiff aside. "You know what is kinda funny? You are my friend. You are. Are you ready for a Lucky Strike?" He lit two cigarettes. "Take that. American tobacco for you from now on. You are in for an excellent time tonight and every other until Hitler gives it up. It'll be meat and potatoes, all you want for dinner, and bacon and eggs for breakfast. You will get a new uniform and shoes after the longest hot shower of your life. They'll get the bugs off you and fix what hurts, too."

"Why? Why do this for us? This is a…treck…a game."

"No. We don't gas our prisoners. That's right, we know all about that. If *you* were going to die, it would have been two minutes ago. But I just liked your look, and you gave me that swell pistol. I'll need your holster there. Hey, did you sign for it inside the flap? You did. Very nice. We make our prisoners of war regret taking us on by helping them gain weight. It's more of a 'we told you so' sort of thing. We want you to see how your leaders lied about us. You will go back home one day, hopefully soon, and we would like very much for you to be our friends instead of enemies. The real issue is Hitler and those mother fucking SS guys. You don't have to worry about them in the camp. We have a special hole for them. They will get a trial, then it is off to the hangman. But for you, an honest officer, hell, there might even be a movie tonight. It'll be a wild west cowboys and Indians picture or maybe a musical. You mind if I ask you a question? My friend here speaks perfect German if you need to speak more clearly. Have a look at this map. Where are the strong points in town?"

Twenty minutes later, Schiff spilled every last thing he knew about Holtzwihr to his saviors in the American reconnaissance platoon and the world's friendliest American intelligence officer. As predicted, the meal at the internment center was excellent. The bread was especially good. The cigarettes were beyond all description. He drank coffee with milk and ate a pumpkin pie. His bed was a cot, but the barracks was warm, and he had two blankets and a real pillow. Most of the guards were good natured and unarmed. They were actually snooping to find SS men hiding amidst the less guilty. Everyone was on his best behavior, and there were no fights or even shouting. Most men were in emotional shock and kept to themselves.

When the lights went out in the barracks that first night, before the snoring started, Schiff heard the sound of many men trying to stifle their tears. The man next to Schiff whispered, "I served in Russia for two years. Eight hours ago, I was an animal. Now I have to remember who I was before the war."

The Nazi assault faltered. The proverbial day was saved, and young Audie was still outwardly in one piece. One has to wonder if surviving these terrible moments might just have left him with an adrenalin addiction and a gambling habit that would plague him for the rest of his life. He clearly suffered from post-traumatic stress disorder, and he knew it. In fact, he was instrumental in helping other veterans get the mental health support they needed in a time when "real men" were expected to just handle it. Now, as my father would say, "I'm here to tell you" that admitting the need for help was heroic for its time and cements Audie's status with me.

Like many veterans, Murphy tried to self-medicate. He had trouble with alcohol and a sleeping pill addiction, which he famously beat cold turkey by locking himself in a hotel room for a week. He would die tragically in an airplane crash in 1971 after a successful postwar film career where he played passable though short-statured leading men mostly in the Western genre. He worked hard at his craft and studied acting seriously. He made more than forty movie and TV films including director John Huston's disastrous *The Red Badge of Courage* in 1951. His most famous and profitable film was, of course, *To Hell and Back* (1957) where he played himself. He wrote songs and did advertising as well, but he never promoted cigarettes or alcohol.

Murphy summed up his experience with a simple yet inciteful comment made to American reporters upon his return in 1945. He said, "Bravery is just determination to do a job that you know has to be done. I just fought to stay alive, like anyone else, I guess."

With this in mind, read on.

<h1 style="text-align:center">3</h1>

Of Mud and Bayonets

"I only regret that I have but one life to lose for my country."

—*Nathan Hale*

Southern Va, 1980

Though our family lost him to divorce, I was heavily influenced by
an uncle-type of guy who fought heroically in Vietnam at the height

of that interminable conflict. He didn't talk about the war other than to grudgingly admit that he did a tour in 1968. Like most returning veterans, he faced an angry and disillusioned homeland. Uniformed soldiers were rebuked in public, called "baby killers," and even spit upon by young people who had the money to attend college and dodge the draft. He threw his medals in the kitchen trash. It took decades for my uncle's angst to subside just enough to talk with me about combat. I relate to what he told me here. I quote him directly where I can clearly remember his words. Some of this is paraphrased, and as is customary in retelling sensitive stories, I have changed or omitted minor details to respect the warrior's privacy.

I'll just call him Cliff.

My uncle Cliff was something of a sergeant and could be a little gruff. He was impatient, particularly with children. Most of all, he was impossible to read. Good mood / bad mood? It was always a mystery. Words fail when I try to describe his demeanor. He liked Neil Young's music, if that helps. I don't remember him ever telling a joke or doing an impression. A casual acquaintance might well say that he seemed a bit grim.

Cliff's greatest asset was his amazing creativity, and he used his laser-like focus to build a very profitable business. I believe that his grueling experiences under fire taught him how to make a plan and tolerate risk. He was inquisitive and traveled the world to see its wonders for himself. He did the scuba diving thing in a big way. Next to myself, he was the single most materialistic person I have ever known. He built himself mansions to house massive saltwater fish tanks where expensive fish went to die. A six-car garage housed the newest Land Rover and Audi sports cars along with his personal bulldozer.

Cliff had a wild side, which explains his attraction for my aunt. For all his success, he was still something of a bad boy who rode the proverbial razor's edge. That being said, he watched his step. He was not the kind to drink and drive or get caught with an illegal substance. He liked fine smoke and going to concerts with his friends, but he protected his public persona from scandal. That included being tight-lipped about Vietnam.

Once I finally got Cliff to talk about the war, I realized that every last second of it was still with him. Most of his stories about his tour concerned the boredom of living on an airbase, getting the clap, smoking weed, the bad food, Agent Orange, and, above all, the oppressive heat and humidity. Even humorous stories boiled down to an obvious bond with his band of brothers, most of whom he lost in combat. Cliff had little to say about officers. The way he saw it, nobody below the rank of colonel really believed in the war.

Soldiers in the field understood how the South Vietnamese peasants were caught in a vicious crossfire. The locals were on the West's side by day and the East's by night. Their fighting-age sons were drafted by both teams. The American invaders tried to win "hearts and minds" by bringing Western medicine and protection to the very edge of the jungle, but the effort only fortified the Viet Cong. Cliff empathized with the locals and said that he never burned a hut. He watched others do it with everything from a zippo lighter to air-dropped napalm.

Make no mistake. There were very few good guys in any of this. North Vietnam was a militarized police state, but the South Vietnamese government was as corrupt as any failed state on earth. President Diem used truly ruthless tactics against political adversaries that played out badly on the evening news. Religious rivalries and government opposition in the South made for flamingly bad press, literally. In June 1963, a Buddhist monk publicly set himself ablaze to protest the policies of the Catholic-leaning government. Pictures of that supremely terrible statement made the front pages worldwide. President Kennedy well understood the power of the picture. I'll bet JFK took one look and said, "President Diem is in the chowdah now."

Promises were made to redress the Buddhist issues, but action did not follow. In fact, the government cracked down even harder on Buddhists, leading other monks to set themselves ablaze. By early November 1963, the CIA toppled the government in a futile attempt to pacify the religious passions that undermined the South's legitimacy.

Saigon's violent and suspicious politics seemed a sideshow to the military action taking place all over both North and South Vietnam. Year in and year out the American military high command consoled itself with illusory statistics about the war. They were dedicated to analytical and dispassionate ideals in an IBM or Rand Corporation kind of way, but they were anything but objective.

Oh, to be rubric-oriented and heavily armed in 1965. President Johnson was hip-deep in Southeast Asia and personally identified targets for air strikes. The popular metaphor of the time was to describe Vietnam as a falling domino. Not to worry though, as the mighty American military machine was going to put the damned Communists down once and for all. Early on, there was genuine optimism about the war. I mean, sure, the North did whoop up on the French, but knowing French military history, this was almost to be expected. The United States was a totally different opponent that waged a Space Age war against a near Stone Age opponent.

This war in Vietnam was akin to squishing a bug.

President Johnson's best military minds played a little fast and loose with body counts and assumed destruction caused by bombs or artillery shells lobbed blindly into the jungle or targets around Hanoi. Secretary of Defense McNamara's bean counters saw the number of villages cleared and weapons caches captured as solid evidence of steady progress. In truth, the Viet Cong were practically oozing infantry weapons. A lost cache or ten made no difference to them. They sat out our shelling in what could be described as underground fortresses and were back in control of the countryside three seconds after the Marines declared victory and took the first chopper home.

All of General Westmoreland's prime indicators indicated a looming total victory, and yet, oddly, these same bulletproof data points did not seem to wear the North Vietnamese Army down at all. This war just…was. Taking a hill did nothing to end the conflict. American military support and financial aid allowed the South Vietnamese government to stagger on when, by all rights, it should have imploded, but money alone could not win this war. The South

Vietnamese Army, the ARVN, though expensively equipped with the best weapons America could offer, was ineffective and rife with officers who knew that the South had no chance without continuous American support.

The North Vietnamese had many advantages, including proven talent on the bench. The first hero was genuine international celebrity Ho Chi Minh, and the second was the man of the hour, General Giap, whose convincing 1954 victory over the French at Dien Bien Phu surprised the world. These leaders were lavishly supplied with sophisticated technology and expertise from the Soviet Union and China. Soviet advisors built a surface-to-air missile ring around Hanoi that rivaled any anti-aircraft system in the world.

Fly the Friendly Skies of North Vietnam

American Navy, Marine Corps, and Air Force pilots had one hell of a time just getting their gas-guzzling technological marvels to the target. Each strike was a logistical nightmare involving scores of aircraft. At the base of every raid, multiple tanker planes loitered just outside North Vietnamese air space, waiting to fuel planes both going in and coming back out. Airborne controllers circling behind the battle space used powerful radars to warn of interlopers. There were also aircraft dedicated to jamming or shooting enemy radars commonly referred to as Wild Weasel missions. The bomb-laden strike aircraft were escorted by a rotating fleet of fighters spaced at several altitudes. After the strike, reconnaissance aircraft took pictures to assess the damage, and a whole slew of fixed and rotary-winged aircraft were often used to rescue downed pilots. At night, Air Force and Navy attack planes could fly beneath enemy radar coverage, but they faced an overabundance of "triple A" (anti-aircraft artillery) that ruled the low-level sky. Finally, Russian and Chinese-made MIG-17, MIG-19, and MIG-21 fighter planes were a constant danger, particularly to the strike aircraft as they dashed for home.

The North's interceptor pilots were well-trained by Soviet allies. While the North Vietnamese MIG-21 had heat-seeking missiles, the most common type used by the North was the MIG-17, which was only cannon-armed. Communist pilots worked hard to get a kill. For the first few years of the war, they gave darn near as well as they got. This was a mighty fall from grace as the American F-86 Sabre jet flying against the impressive Soviet MIG-15 over North Korea had a kill ratio of anywhere from 8 to 1 to as high as 13 to 1, depending on the source. Many of the American pilots benefitted from their World War Two experience. By 1965, however, American aviators were no longer trained in traditional air-to-air tactics because their miracle missiles could be fired well beyond visual range. It was more important to have straight-line speed and a powerful radar than a maneuverable aircraft. The now-famous Top Gun School did not yet exist. American pilots at that time were prepared to deliver battlefield atomic bombs or atomic "tipped" Falcon air-to-air missiles designed to take out an entire squadron of Soviet bombers with one radioactive shot. Hughes analog computers calculated the angles and release points for the weapons. The pilots were there to lift off and flare out on landing. They more or less supervised the fire control apparatus and collected the credit for kills that never occurred.

There was a time when American fighter pilots were the best in the world. After learning many lessons in the Vietnam School of Hard Knocks, American pilots could claim a kill/loss ratio of 3.8 to 1. Fighters flying MIGCAP topped out with a kill ratio of 15 to 1 in 1972–73. Today, the best fighter pilot honors would have to go to the Israelis. Though American pilots lost their dogfighting edge after Korea, post-Vietnam air strikes show that the United States is back and loaded for bear. The very idea of American airpower on the loose is still enough to cow most nations. This brings us somewhat obliquely to Teddy Roosevelt, who was the first president to take to the air. True, he was out of office at the time when, in 1910, he hopped a ride in Kinloch, Missouri. He was invigorated and said that it was one of the greatest experiences of his life.

Buffalo soldier circa 1898.
They were the real heroes at San Juan Hill.

Big sticks

Roosevelt knew nothing about airplanes when he famously said that we should, "Speak softly but carry a big stick." Of the thirty-one presidents who carried sticks into harm's way, which American leader had the deadliest weapon? Of course, Eisenhower commanded an entire army, but this doesn't count. I refer here to personal weapons. We know it wasn't Teddy Roosevelt and his revolver on what was advertised as San Juan Hill but was actually the adjacent Kettle Hill. I would be remiss if I did not mention at this point that five Medals of Honor were awarded to the "colored" Buffalo Soldiers of the 9th and 10th (dismounted) Cavalry and 24th and 25th infantry who were intermixed with the Rough Riders that day. Without their significant and inspiring heroism, San Juan Hill would not have been captured. This was the first infantry assault that was for all practical purposes, racially integrated and on foreign soil.

At first, Roosevelt gave credit where it was due, "No one can tell whether it was the Rough Riders or the [Black] men of the 9th [Cavalry] who came forward with the greater courage to offer their lives in the service of their country." This quote, however, does not jibe with later disparaging comments he later made about "colored troops" in his book about the war.[16]

Soon after Teddy became president, he invited Booker T. Washington to dine with him at the White House. This was a first and cost the new president considerable political capital. While Roosevelt's attitudes were not exemplary by modern standards, his experience at the battle at San Juan can be cited as perhaps cracking the door for military integration that would not happen in earnest until July 1948.

Captain Harry S. Truman was an artillerist in the First World War. I am assuming here that he must have pulled the trigger lanyard a few times. That's an impressive cudgel.

---

16. It was thought that "colored" troops had a natural resistance to tropical diseases, and they were often deployed to the Philippines. Three thousand of the seventeen thousand American troops deployed in Cuba were Buffalo soldiers. Black troops were led by white officers at that time, which caused some super understandable resentment. Black Jack Pershing led colored troops in this battle and would later command American forces in Europe during World War One.

The real winners of this contest are tied both in explosive force and the personal qualities that score hits on the enemy. Both George Herbert Walker Bush and John F. Kennedy were in the torpedo delivery business. The munitions they launched were identical. Bush air-dropped his from a Grumman Avenger strike aircraft, and Kennedy, more famously, fired his from *PT-109*.

Bush was among the youngest of all Navy pilots to serve in combat. He enlisted immediately after Pearl Harbor. Yale would have to wait. Bush was but twenty years old when he joined Torpedo Squadron 51. The Avenger aircraft that he flew had a three-man crew. It was the heaviest single engine aircraft at that time and vulnerable to everything

George H.W. Bush USN

from enemy ground fire to air interception. He operated from the USS *San Jacinto* and was shot down on a bombing run over the Japanese-held island of Chichi Jima. Though his engine was on fire, Bush still bore in and dropped his bombs on an enemy radio complex. He bailed out over the water and spent several hours on a life raft until he was rescued by a submarine, the USS *Finback*, which was on "lifeguard" patrol. This future president won several medals for valor, including the Distinguished Flying Cross.

The case for JFK is just as strong, if not a smidge more, and also includes a dramatic rescue. Kennedy's legend was made on a night operation in August 1943 when his Elco-made mahogany and plywood torpedo boat number 109 was rammed by Japanese destroyer Amagiri which was travelling at high speed and likely never even saw Kennedy's boat before hitting her. The Amagiri's captain would claim that the ramming was intentional.

Kennedy saved most of the crew, including one man with burns over seventy percent of his body. He towed this man on a raft as he swam. The crew floated on what remained of the PT boat's bow for almost twelve hours, but it began to sink, and they were forced to swim for practically barren Plum Pudding Island which, happily, was the only real estate not occupied by the Japanese in the area.

Someone had to guide in the rescue boat. Despite Kennedy's Addison's disease, which pained him immensely, and his having swallowed fuel-tainted sea water while rescuing a crewman, he dared shark attack and repeatedly swam at night out into the middle of the straights with a flashlight in an attempt to signal American forces. This was to no avail. The crew made several night swims to change islands and get closer to American patrols. Kennedy carved a message containing their whereabouts onto a coconut shell and passed it along to natives who got the husk to the PT-boat base at Rendova. A rescue was organized and succeeded in the nick of time. Kennedy underwent back surgery that sidelined him but received a richly deserved Purple Heart and the Navy and Marine Corps Medal for heroism under fire. Yes sir, both Kennedy and Bush deserve top billing.

Madness at Bunker Hill
Boston 1775

Mankind has always had a fascination with conflict, and so weapons figure prominently in our species' development. I suppose that the very first famous weapon was Samson's jawbone of an ass, which the Bible says he used to whack a thousand Philistines.[17] He had supernatural power behind his tool. The rest of us have to rely on our personal martial skills and whatever technology we can grab.

The dawn of modern warfare and global conflict is generally thought to be around 1480 when pikemen began to operate as organized troops meant to stop armored cavalry. Other historians say that the standard issue smoothbore musket is the marker to look for, but I think the bayonet was the real game changer between primitive and modern combat.

A bayonet implies martial professionalism and a grim willingness to get in there and run the other guy through. A bayonet charge must be delivered by a standardized, coherent formation of troops directed by highly trained officers who understand where and, more importantly, when to deliver the massed blow. This requires both sound military character and a great deal of parade-ground training to keep the men in tight formation while under fire.

---

17. Judges 15:15.

Picture what it would be like in the era before exploding shells to see solid cannon balls bounce back through the stacked ranks, cutting men in half and taking their legs for a hundred yards or more before running out of steam. The formation also endured musket volleys as they closed with the enemy. These could be withering, and soldiers often broke. Several assaults might be needed to win the day, as was the case at what we Americans call the Battle of Bunker Hill, which was actually fought on Breed's Hill. Yes, I know. It's complicated.

The Whites of Their Eyes

No official explanation exists as to why the Americans dug in on Breed's Hill. Bunker Hill appeared to be better a defensive position, as it was a bit more of a climb for enemy infantry, but Breed's Hill was adjacent to a stone wall and a split rail fence that extended the earthworks considerably and made the position difficult to flank. This also screened Bunker Hill, where a smattering of Colonial reinforcements occupied the heights.

The finest British infantry made multiple bayonet attacks on the hastily forged defenses, which, after a night of frantic digging, stood about six feet high and had a rampart for the soldiers to stand upon as they fired over the breastwork. The British waded through high grass that obscured rocks, fence rails, and the dead from previous assault. These obstacles played havoc with their line abreast and took the momentum from their advance. During the first two attempts to take the rebel position, British troops carried their heavy backpacks up the hill. While the "Don't shoot until you see the whites of their eyes" bit is very likely apocryphal, the defenders did hold their fire until the enemy was within thirty to forty yards.

While the ammunition lasted, the Rebels slung accurate lead. They might not have been professional soldiers, but they were recreational shooters and hunters with what I suspect were largely fowling pieces, basic smooth bore muskets, and a smattering of sporting rifles in the .36 to .50 caliber range. These rifles typically had a long sight radius and set triggers that enhanced performance dramatically, especially against British officers riding around on horseback just behind the line of regulars. The owners knew how their rifles performed over set distances, which helped them to keep their musket balls on target. They shot their rifles often and likely did not flinch with the sparking of the frizzen and flash in the pan. Other sources credit buck and ball loads for inflicting the legendary devastation. Had the young Americans been better supplied, they might have won the day. As it turned out, they were missing a key weapon that morning—the simple bayonet.

General Howe led the British troops in the center of the assault on Breed's Hill. He saw how effective fire from the Colonials had dispersed the advancing formations. History notes that the British did trade volleys with troops behind the rail fence. This was not enough to drive off the Americans, whose fire continued to be accurate and devastating.

Initial British naval cannon fire fell short of the earthworks. This more than any other error cost the British dearly. An accurate bombardment might have broken the inexperienced colonials. Effective rebel musket and rifle fire from the Charlestown area badly harassed General Howe's men as they tried to form their ranks. Incendiary artillery shells burned the town to drive off these snipers and provide a smoke screen for massing British troops who were told to rely on the bayonet to drive the enemy from their position. Fifteen hundred militia firing at the long red lines had other ideas, and the British were forced to retire and re-form for another attempt. In fact, the defenders drove off two determined attacks.

A third and final attempt was required to take Breed's Hill. It took several hours, but eventually, the British brought up more than four hundred fresh troops and artillery for the last assault. The redoubt was attacked from the front and flank simultaneously. Hand-to-hand fighting broke out inside the fort, but the British were in their element. No mercy was given. The rebels fought a brave, if not futile, rear action, which allowed for a fairly orderly retreat.

As the American survivors beat feet off of the peninsula, they encountered British skirmishers who were mistaken for a larger force. Panic ensued, but the fear of capture was not justified. The King's men were utterly knackered and unable to inflict further losses. They slinked off to Boston to await reinforcements from England and watch hundreds of wounded soldiers die or face amputation. The British were eventually driven off completely when, some months later, the rebels built an impressive earthworks on the Dorchester Heights above Boston that bristled with artillery brought all the way from Fort Ticonderoga on Lake Champlain by a twenty-five-year-old General Knox.

There were those in the fledgling American Army who disdained this young soldier and thought that other, more experienced men were slighted by the Knox appointment. General Washington wisely felt otherwise. Knox built sleds for the cannon and waited for snow. Some of the guns were quite massive. His men dragged them over three hundred miles of blustery mountain trails that spanned the length of Massachusetts. By January 1776, the *Guns of Navarone* moved to put a cannon to the head of the British Navy in the harbor below. General Howe planned an attack to dislodge the guns, but a heavy snowstorm changed his plans. A deal was struck wherein the British were allowed to leave Boston unscathed as long as they did not burn the city. They gathered up the loyalists and headed for Halifax.

The early battles of The American Revolution cost the British dearly and pushed King George III to declare what in those times amounted to total war. They suffered a staggering 226 killed and 828 wounded, taking Breed's Hill. Among these were twenty-seven officers killed and sixty-three wounded. The men who controlled the ranks in action were largely eliminated, which would have affected the force badly had they chosen to pursue another infantry battle. Add to these losses, another two hundred or more were killed and wounded during the previous skirmishes at Lexington and Concord. Few of the Revolutionary War's battles were as bloody as Bunker Hill.

The Americans lost about 450 men at Breed's Hill. Add in another one hundred killed or wounded in the running gunfight that occurred after the initial confrontation at Lexington Green, where eight colonial troops were killed and ten wounded in the war's first two vollies. As can be seen in these numbers, the locals stood up to the finest army in the world—twice—and inflicted two-to-one casualties on both occasions. Of course, they did it in their own, ungentlemanly way. I would suggest that this emphasis on rifle fire over the smoothbore musket was the birth of the American belief in the individual marksman. These early casualty figures boosted rebel confidence, but the battle at Breed's Hill was not a harassing action by roving bands of sharpshooters. It was a traditional European event where the bayonet made the King's point quite clear.

Many of the British casualties on the Breed's Hill assaults were no doubt inflicted by rifle-wielding colonists who previously used cover and other Indian tactics to harass the British as they marched back to Boston, but these rifles did not take bayonets, and being very delicate, they were not melee weapons. Without powder or shot, the rifle-armed colonist militia was essentially defenseless. The soldier armed with Brown Bess always had his bayonet, and his musket was as sturdy as Gibraltar. He could reload it three times a minute when he was really humming. Unlike rifles that required bullets molded for the specific weapon, the British soldier could also use his fallen comrade's musket balls.

The Minié Ball

By the time of the American Civil War, most troops were issued *rifled* muskets whose accuracy and range were substantially better than the smooth-bored weapons used by eighteenth-century soldiers. These rifles had rudimentary rear sights matched to a wide front blade/bayonet lug that was nearly immune to damage, and little changed from its first conception. The sights were basically worthless, but they did establish the right elevation over an established range, and soldiers finally had a reason to keep their eyes open when they pulled the trigger. The percussion cap replaced the flintlock in the 1830s. It offered near-instantaneous ignition of the powder charge and improved reliability under wet and windy conditions. Best of all, there was no distracting flash to cause a soldier to flinch just as the ball left the oversized bore. The munitions were no more deadly than one hundred years prior, but their delivery improved dramatically.

This percussion cap was revolutionary, but alas, beyond a few rounds fired in unison and on command, troops in training rarely fired their weapons in such a way as to learn real marksmanship. Unless they brought shooting skills to the party, their weapons sprayed and prayed at a rate of three rounds a minute and likely never hit a thing. The new firearms technology did nothing to cure human error or dispel the massive clouds of smoke that made shooting more guesswork than skill.

While the weapons matured, tactical formations were slow to change. Despite the introduction of the standard issue rifled musket, the need to hold a tight formation for communication and command remained. Troops still had to stand to reload their weapons. Meanwhile, other innovations in artillery, such as exploding shells, timed fuses, and canister shot, added to the carnage. Civil War single-day battle casualty rates were often higher than the sum total of soldiers killed in action during the American Revolution, the War of 1812, and the Mexican War combined. While the number of wounded is not included in this statistic, "only" 11,993 soldiers fell on these early American battlefields. Now consider the battle of Fredericksburg (1862), where a combined loss of more than eighteen thousand men didn't cause anyone to say that this war was like no other and had to end. Over forty-five thousand casualties (minimum) were incurred at Gettysburg on the first through third days of July 1863, and yet the war dragged on into 1865.

The use of rifles on the early modern battlefield was initially resisted by the officer class as a matter of self-preservation. They were the ones moving the chess pieces around. Who was a better target? Sniping officers was considered, at best, to be unsporting, and it did not often occur. Then an American sharpshooter named Timothy Murphy (1751–1818) used his rifle to shoot British General Simon Fraser right out of the saddle at Saratoga in 1777. Murphy was a member of the newly formed Morgan's Riflemen. It was a truly miraculous three-hundred-yard attempt only made possible by a rifled barrel. In truth, the record shows that three shots were required to zero in on the high-value target. The loss of leadership at this pivotal moment was said to be a turning point in the fight.

By the time of the American Civil War in 1861, both sides used the French-designed Minié Ball bullet that loaded fast but gripped the rifling well enough to impart tremendous spin. The stabilized bullet made 300-yard shots an occasional possibility. Claude-Étienne Minié can be credited with creating the link between the traditional round ball and the modern torpedo-shaped bullet with a rounded nose, not to be confused with the modern spitzer point. The average Minié bullet hopped along at a leisurely 950 feet per second. The trajectory was like a rainbow. Wind could easily blow the lead slug off target. The holdover needed to lob a bullet out to three hundred paces was several yards. The distance between the opposing firing lines opened up considerably. For the well-trained rifleman who understood how to use his sights, any human-sized target within one hundred and fifty yards was in serious peril.

At Fredericksburg in late December 1862, the South had a stout stone wall defense on Marye's Heights to give them cover as they poured lead into Union troops who marched uphill across open ground right into merciless rifle fire. The Confederates stood four ranks deep behind that wall. Union troops advanced to within fifty feet in some places. Their casualties were appalling, with many units losing more than fifty percent of their strength and nearly all of their officers. This was just another day in the war. The leaders on both sides fed entire divisions, even entire corps, into the most futile of attacks without a second's thought. Despite the new weapons, Union and Confederate generals still relied instinctively on Napoleonic tactics. Both sides believed in the bayonet and used what we have come to call the "human wave" assault.

Think of Pickett's Charge at Gettysburg in July 1863 as the most famous human wave attack in American history. Casualty figures vary somewhat. The Confederates lost somewhere around eight thousand men to all causes killed, wounded, captured, and missing in that gamble. Some records show that nearly half were captured. In comparison, the Union defenders took fifteen hundred dead and wounded, mostly from a massive Confederate artillery barrage that kicked off the fight and a brief but intense clash at the highwater point where the cream of Lee's army crested the wall and futilely threw itself on the Union center.

Stuart's Unknown Contribution

While Pickett was being mauled in front, there was a simultaneous Confederate cavalry attack in the Union rear that was miraculously stalled by Union artillery and cavalry. Infamous "boy general" Custer's troops participated in an intense cavalry versus cavalry engagement around Rummel's Farm with Stuart losing approximately 180 men to Custer's 220 dead or wounded. Custer was only twenty-four years old and is said to have screamed, "Come on, you Wolverines!" as he rallied a counterattack. With his blonde hair flowing and a red tie around his neck, Custer cut quite the iconic figure in his custom uniform. He fought well and had two horses shot from beneath him during the furious action.

The Confederate cavalry rode tired horses in their assault. Their mounts had no time to recover from the days of long, hard riding that took the riders completely around the entire Union Army. General Stuart only arrived at Gettysburg on the evening of the second day. His absence was ill-timed, and Lee complained that Stuart left him without detailed knowledge of where the enemy was concentrating. It is no doubt true to assert that with better reconnaissance Lee's opening moves in the battle to come would certainly have been different. Some blame Stuart's absence for the ultimate loss, but this is unfair in the extreme. Stuart was following orders that read like suggestions. He thought that he was permitted latitude to do what he did best, raid and forage.

Stuart took down a massive supply train and lugged away hundreds of wagons worth of much needed supplies. Excellent booty, but it slowed Stuart's return to the fold. I can understand why Stuart made his moves and thought himself well within his orders. After all, in Stuart's mind, General Lee still had cavalry brigades available for reconnaissance duties. These units were thought by some to be somewhat second rate, and Lee lacked confidence in their command staff, but they were cavalry and capable enough for the task at hand. When the battle flared, Lee wanted his old friend, Stuart, close at hand.

Lee famously and harshly rebuked Stuart when he finally turned up, but Lee also conceded in that meeting that Stuart remained the best cavalry officer he had ever known. Or at least that is how Martin Sheen plays it in *Gettysburg* (1993). Stuart's contribution on the last day was likely motivated by a need to regain some favor with his beloved leader. He used his cavalry as an anvil for Pickett's infantry hammer.

Obviously, cavalry fights proceed at a different pace than infantry engagements. Command and control suffer at speed, especially in a larger scrap. Worse still, the Confederates' conspicuous élan may have eclipsed their better judgement. Both Pickett and Stuart's men shared a suicidal dedication to their cause that held them together and kept them driving forward despite heavy casualties. Union cannons fired double-packed canister shot into oncoming enemy infantry in front and cavalry behind. The effects on Pickett are well known. Less famous were the gaps rent in the surging line of Stuart's best cavalry that filled right back in as they kept on coming.

The Union counter cavalry charge was epic. Eyewitnesses said that when the two forces crashed into each other it sounded like falling timber. Horses collided at full gallop. Many were knocked off their hooves with their riders crushed beneath them. Survivors remarked on how many cavaliers used their sabers in this mounted melee. People got sliced right and left. This has to be one of the last times in military history that swords were used by both sides on this scale.

Cavalry troops depend on handguns. The Colt 1860 .44 caliber revolver was the ideal weapon at that time. It was common for Confederate mounted troops to carry multiple revolvers, and many Union troops were just beginning to receive Spencer repeating carbines to replace their Sharps single shot weapons. The rate of fire between two similarly equipped cavalry forces would have been uniquely high. I wonder about the din. The revolver was the predominant weapon, and the ripple of massed handguns would render a different sound to the fight.

Joshua Chamberlain whose inspired leadership literally saved the United States at Gettysburg in 1863.

The Rhetoric Teacher Who Saved the Union

Then we have the other extreme. What do you do when the ammunition runs out? On the second day of Gettysburg, Colonel Joshua

Lawrence Chamberlain led a downhill bayonet charge from his position on the extreme left flank of Union forces on Little Round Top. The Confederates were desperate to work their way around the end of the Union line. The 15th and 47th Alabama regiments of Hood's division outnumbered the Maine boys by better than two-to-one as they came down from Big Round Top, into the saddle between the Tops, and then back uphill into hot fire. They made several determined assaults. Most of the action took place at close to point-blank range.

After an hour and more than fifteen thousand rounds of muzzleloader fire, the left wing of the 20th Maine was pushed from a ninety-degree right angle to something resembling a hair pin. Chamberlain did the math and went with the only option he had left. He ordered one of the most consequential bayonet charges in all of military history. The combination of surprise and momentum convincingly routed Hood's men and likely saved General Meade from utter catastrophe.

As I said in Chapter One when discussing Hitler, as a writer I try to avoid expressions like "would have" or "might have been." In this historical analysis, however, I cannot do without them, and their use fascinates me. See if you agree.

Had the Confederates achieved their objective and crushed Chamberlain's depleted unit, Little Round Top would have fallen, and the rest of the Union line would have suffered enfilade attack that would break or turn the entire left wing of the Union Army. Depending on the ferocity of this attack and its exploitation by Hood, Longstreet, and McLaws, General Meade might have been forced to retire in disorder or find himself surrounded. A great deal would depend of course on Early, Ewell, and Johnson and their attacks at the other end of fishhook-shaped Union line. If they linked up with Longstreet, the war in the East would likely be over. Under those circumstances, artillery and military supplies by necessity would be left behind. This would be a Dunkirk moment where the naked army escapes but is no condition to fight.

I cannot stress this next bit enough. Pickett's charge would not have occurred. Stuart's tardy arrival with a boatload of booty would have been remembered in history as perfectly timed manna from heaven. Lee would have had plenty of troops and the abundant supplies needed to execute an attack on Washington. That march might have taken a week. Those seven days would be well remembered in American history as the last days of The Union.

It would not have taken much to break through the little earthwork defenses, like Fort Marcy, that ringed the capital.[18] From there, heavy mortars could shell Washington with the Federal's own ammunition.

A great deal would depend on Lincoln's political reaction to a defeat at Gettysburg. A routing on Northern soil would demand a scapegoat. That was Lincoln's standard play even if he was justified in his frustrations with ineffectual fossils like General Scott or over cautious generals like George McClellan. The president might have sacked General Meade, but one wonders who Lincoln could appoint to lead the army in his stead. Grant was at Vicksburg at that time, and Lincoln was on the clock. This reality might have saved Meade. Leadership squabbles and a spooked army do not bode of an effective defense.

Even more importantly, if Little Round Top fell that day, a culturally significant plea for national unity would not have been made. Imagine an America that never heard the Gettysburg Address. This greatest of speeches has offered us guidance for the last one hundred and fifty years. President Lincoln might have had to resign, in which case he would have survived the war to be driven into deep depression by grief, his military failure, and the unyielding bipolar rage of his deeply troubled wife.

Or, Lincoln might have said, "Screw this war. My generals are all shit. Jefferson Davis, let's talk."

If this had come to pass, it is conceivable that slavery would not have ended in what was formerly the United States. One assumes that some other catalyst would have upended the Dixiecrats and wiped out this most dread of practices, but what form of rebellion that might have taken is beyond the scope of this passage. The balance of world power

---

18. Hillary Clinton's attorney, Vince Foster, was found dead of a self-inflicted gunshot in Fort Marcy Park during July 1993.

would have turned out differently and the example of the United States Constitution would likely be dashed as well. It is even conceivable that North and South as nation states may have backed different sides in future wars. What then?

All of this, of course, did not come to pass because a few hundred men from Maine fixed their lowly, primitive bayonets and literally saved the world from a dark future. So when someone asks you, "Is this the hill you want to die on?" Say, "Hell no, that hill would be Little Round Top just outside Gettysburg, Pennsylvania."

Going Smokeless

The American Civil War pushed military technological innovation at a frantic pace. Advances in artillery-fusing, breech-loading, and murderous new anti-personnel shells were not met with equally innovative infantry tactics, though by the end of the war earthwork fortifications began to resemble World War One trench systems but without barbed wire. By the end of the war, repeating rifles were becoming increasingly common. The Spencer infantry rifle with a bayonet lug on its thirty-inch barrel might well have become standard issue had the war dragged on. I do not see how the South could have withstood any force with that kind of firepower. The North purchased twelve thousand Spencer rifles and eighty thousand carbines plus fifty-eight million rounds of ammunition for the whopping price of 4.2 million dollars.

After the Civil War, the survivors took stock of what occurred and designed terrifying weapons to mow down human waves. The French introduced smokeless gunpowder in 1884, which greatly aided in the success of repeating weapons. Finally, snipers could remain hidden after firing a shot. The absence of dense firearm smoke allowed riflemen to truly aim their individual fire. Better rifle sights and marksmanship training followed, but it would be safe to say that the average rifleman was an uninspired shooter. The United Stares Marine Corps, on the other hand, made a fetish out of marksmanship.

Sadly for the repeating weapon-armed men on the firing line, battlefield communications were little better than those of the American

Civil War. Flag signals, flag standard bearers, and bugle calls were still used to guide an assault, and commanders had to tightly form the men to keep control of the formation. Prior to radio, telephone lines allowed for higher levels to communicate down to the company level, but once the men went over the top, they were almost impossible to control. A great deal depended on the professionalism of the noncommissioned and junior grade officers.

While the draftees practiced marching and the signalers learned their Morse code, the revolving barrels of the Gatling gun ushered in the stripper clip-fed Mauser rifle and belt-fed Maxim machine gun.[19] These weapons eventually gave rise to fighter planes and armored vehicles. During the First World War, human waves faced all these new terrors *and* poison gas. The assaulting waves may have opened up a bit, and the tempo of battle increased, but the new weapons were up to the challenge.

The Bayonet Soldiers On

The wasteful human wave continued in the next world conflict. The Japanese were famous for last resort "banzai" charges. The largest of these occurred on July 7, 1944, on the island of Saipan. Four thousand Japanese soldiers participated in the attack. These numbers include walking wounded and even civilians armed with nothing more than sharpened sticks. The battle lasted almost fifteen hours and cost over six hundred American lives. Very few Japanese troops survived. The officers all committed ritual suicide.

One banzai charge occurred on American soil. The battle of Attu, which took place in the Aleutian Islands on 11–30 May 1943, ended with American troops fending off a desperate Japanese final banzai

19. The Gatling gun would make a decisive contribution in the assault on San Juan Hill during the Spanish American War. On July 1, 1898, Lieutenant John H. Parker asked to advance his Gatling guns to the front so that he could suppress fire coming from the Spanish trench works. He was surprisingly successful. This was the first documented example of maneuver tactics combined with automatic fire.

attack. It broke through the American lines in several places. Rear area troops were badly mauled in hand-to-hand combat. Of course, the charge was futile, and less than thirty Japanese troops survived as captives.

The Japanese banzai charge is famously scary what with all those long bayonets and all the screaming, but the reality is, virtually none of the enemy were over five foot six inches tall. None of their rifles held more than five rounds if they had any bullets at all. They were likely half-starved. If I had to stare down one of these attacks, I would rather face it as an American machine gun crewman than a Japanese soldier.

As can be seen from all of the casualty figures I have mustered here, no matter where the fight occurs, we return yet again to military math. Japan, North Korea, and China are famous for the human wave tactic. They know how to do military calculations. These showed that wave after wave's worth of bodies thrown at their enemies would eventually win by attrition. The Korean Conflict featured a constant duel between Chinese lives and the United Nations' supply of 105 m/m artillery shells. The interlocking explosions of such an American-made barrage are impenetrable, and yet a rounding error's worth of enemy troops still got through to worry the most modern infantry in the world. Thanks to the Chinese human wave, Korea ended in a stalemate.

The last recorded official American bayonet charge took place in Korea on February 7, 1951, when Captain Lewis Millett led his troops in an uphill bayonet assault that swept the enemy from their commanding position. Of the fifty or more dead Chinese and North Korean troops found strewn around the trenches after the fight, over twenty died by American bayonet. Millett would receive the Medal of Honor for his actions that day. The site is now called Bayonet Hill.

British Commonwealth troops have been known to run a fellow through from time to time. On February 18th, 1967, "Diggers" of Australian Army performed a bayonet charge during desperate fighting in Phuoc Tuy Province, South Vietnam. The Falklands Champaign had its fair share of intense firefights and dramatic actions. On June 14, 1982, British troops, including Gurkhas, reported a predawn bayonet charge to drive the Argentines off Mount Tumbledown. These days, bayonets are an afterthought mostly used to check dead bodies and disperse unruly crowds of rioters. They also look great on parade.

Early Soviet human wave tactics were a little better than the Japanese version, but they quickly improved their lethality with some impressive small arms and tank technology. By the middle of 1943, they had it all figured out. First came the traditional aircraft and artillery preparations. They lost a lot of aircraft, but oh well, this is how they get things done in Russia. The Nazis went to great lengths to divert their enemy's preparatory fire with decoys or even empty frontline trenches that were hastily remanned post-Soviet blasting. They didn't have long to put their defenses back together. Ivan was coming.

They faced a true armored juggernaut that carried a human wave on its back.

Soviet tanks have no rubber wheel liners to lessen track noise. Even in snow and mud, the average Soviet tank's running gear announced its presence before firing a single shot. German veterans knew that sound too well and braced themselves with everything they had, from makeshift anti-tank weapons to well-emplaced tanks and artillery. Fanatical troops prepared to sacrifice themselves. Their families were dead or scattered anyway. They knew the T-34's blind spots and the best places to slap on a magnetic mine. Then, through the curtains of snow and smoke came waves of tank-riding infantry. Ivan found a way to limit his exposure to fragments and bullets by hitching a ride. This gave the Russian human wave real momentum.

The Nazis poured fire into the oncoming maw. They killed with nearly every shot. Smoking hulks of Soviet T-34s littered the battlefield. In some sectors, the Nazi defenders skillfully killed every Soviet soldier who came at them—for months on end. Ivan shook off the losses. His speedy tanks delivered intense suppressive fire and dismounted their riders within yards of the Nazi defenses. Soviet troops used their combined submachine guns to sweep out enemy positions and suppress anti-tank teams.

British PIAT anti-tank team and a
French Two-man tankette (not to scale).

Death at Close Range: Submachine
Guns and PIAT Launchers

If World War One taught firearms designers anything, it was that short-range suppressive fire makes all the difference in a trench fight. The proliferation of submachine gun prototypes between the wars shows a growing understanding of how to make reliable automatic weapons as inexpensively as possible. The British and the Japanese resisted adopting the submachine gun for quite some time. Imagine a Japanese banzai charge armed with even modest numbers of MP-40 submachine guns. Things might well have turned out differently. The basic American firearms suit was up to the naked blade banzai challenge, but United States Marine Corps losses would have been far higher had the Japanese embraced the submachine gun concept. As it was, they barely produced nine thousand Nambu Type 100 submachine guns before the end of the war. The British got over their aversion to the weapon and made 4.6 million Sten guns. The famously heavy and expensive American Thompson gun used early on in the war numbered 1.7 million. The Soviets made three thousand submachine guns a day. All told, they cranked out six million PPSh-41s in addition to several other models.

The Soviets armed entire battalions of tank riders with submachine guns. They crushed the depleted Nazi forces before them in a hail of 7.62 m/m submachine gun fire, but in so doing, they suffered perhaps a million combat casualties of their own in the last two or three months of the war. They ran through troops, tanks, and airplanes at a furious rate. In fact, they lost somewhere between eight and eleven million combat troops, forty-two thousand tanks, and 106,000 aircraft between June 1941 and the end of the Second World War in 1945. Russian civilian deaths bring this total to twenty million and likely a great deal higher. We will never know the true total. Let this information color any ideas you may have about casualties in the current war in Ukraine. The Russians are not casualty averse.

The Italians and Australians made the most interesting submachine guns of the war, but I confidently say that none of the weapons in general use was any better or worse than the others. Accuracy was not an issue. Weight and ease of manufacture were the prime considerations. Success or failure depended to a great degree on the magazine design. I have shot most of the common World War Two submachine guns, including the infamous Nazi MP-40. I have killed several derelict cars, a blender, refrigerators, computers, a Rubic's cube, and a dozen ash trays with these weapons. So my experience is extensive. I have to say that I prefer the PPs-43 and the Madsen. Both are supremely compact, lightweight, and dead reliable. My least favorite was the heavy Thompson whose exposed barrel reaches the temperature of the sun inside of two bursts. I wrapped my thumb over the barrel as I handed the empty weapon back to the instructor. I can still feel the sizzle.

Arnhem Bridge, September 1944

Even the best submachine gun is no match for a soldier armed with a radio or phone. Just ask Audie Murphy. World War Two saw amazing innovations in battlefield communications. Every American-made tank, plane, or ship had a voice transmission set. Troops on the line had mobile systems as well. The backpack-sized thirty-eight-pound SCR-300 is perhaps the most famous radio of the war, second only to the "walkie talkie." Famously, at the fight for Arnhem Bridge of *A Bridge Too Far* fame, communications between the badly strung out paratroopers utterly failed. The main issue had to do with the fact that the British "22 Set" radios were asked to operate at the limit of their range. Interestingly, the artillery communications net did work, and some messages were funneled through this system. Other sources say that the issue had more to do with the poor quality of British antennas. Those radios that did work were confounded by Holland's flat and obstacle-lined typography. The movie version of events uses the old,

"Sorry, General. Bad Luck. The radios were delivered with the wrong crystals," excuse. I would have shot somebody on the spot if this were true. I think this was just an expedient way to say that communications were out.

General Browning's Headquarters received only intermittent radio reports about the debacle happening in Arnhem. British officers fighting around the bridge had to physically search for each other while under fire to confer and plan strategy. I have found reference to two British paratroopers who swam the fast and freezing Nadir Rhine River both ways—at night—to communicate with Polish troops who were the last forces to join that ill-conceived party. I found only one name. Private Ernest Archer gets the award for best swimming in a combat zone.

Eight thousand British and Polish troops were killed or captured in their part of Operation Market Garden. Nobody heard their agony. They called for help. They got no answer. They had no way of knowing how long it would be before they could expect their tanks to arrive. The Red Devils tried to coordinate their defenses, but their forces were strewn for several miles between Oosterbeek and Arnhem Bridge. Johnny Frost's boys held one end of the bridge with about seven hundred men, but he was up against the combined remnants of two Nazi SS panzer divisions, the 9th and 10th.

The Nazis were well reinforced within twenty-four hours. The Germans even employed the new and formidable King Tiger tank (also known as the Tiger Royal) in house-to-house fighting. Several of these supremely powerful monsters were lost to pitiful British PIAT launcher anti-tank teams who fired their special warheads at suicidally close range.

Major Robert Cain of the 2nd South Staffords made notable use of a PIAT in defense of his position in Oosterbeek during Operation Market Garden. Survivors of that action lament that they ran out of PIAT ammunition and quipped that they might have stayed in Holland till Christmas if they only had more shells for the awkward spigot mortar. Due to the David versus Goliath qualities of the PIAT's battles, it was a medal winner for those who used it. By the end of the war it was obsolete, but it went on to be used by the Israelis whose meager anti-tank weapons were hard-pressed to deal with Syrian, French-made two-man tanks.

Consider all the massive tank battles of World War Two. Think about the Second Battle of El Alamein, Kursk, and the Battle of the Bulge where the fate of entire continents was carried on treads. Then we have the dramatic birth of one of the most consequential nations in world history, Israel. One would think that such an event would include a major tank battle or two. We have come to expect nothing less from the Middle East. Instead, the Israelis were nearly driven out by a few pre-World War Two tankettes manned by no doubt inexperienced crews. As tanks go, these qualified for the name, but you know you are on the ropes when rampaging Renault R-35s are apt to decide the fate of your nation.

The Israelis had no armored vehicles at this point. They had a few 20 m/m cannons that were ineffective against these light tanks head on, though certainly they were capable of shooting off their tracks or wrecking their suspension. Other than suicide teams, PIAT anti-tank weapons were the Israelis' only response to the R-35 tank's 43 m/m frontal armor. They did not have many of the ex-British weapons, and their ammunition was severely limited, but they proved pivotal at the battle for Degania Alef. In fact, the Haganah stomped on their enemies with what little they had and hung on through sheer chutzpah. In the hands of the Golan and Palmach platoons, the PIAT was decisive. Each time it stopped a pathetic French tank, Israel gained a little stature, a little confidence, and a better claim to the land they paid for with their blood more than a few times in history. This crude launcher deserves a special place in the Great Hall of Marshal Arms.

The PIAT bomb was very similar to the German panzerfaust and American bazooka rocket. They all used a "hollow charge" warhead that first instantly burned a small hole in armor up to 100 m/m thick, and second, shot a jet of flame through the aperture to kill the crew by setting off ammunition. Kinetic force was not needed. When the fuse worked and the hit was square on, a three-pound PIAT bomb could kill a thirty-ton tank. The Nazis used standoff armor skirts which offered protection against these new weapons and prolific Russian anti-tank rifles, but they were heavy and added considerable weight which degraded performance. They also made track and running gear maintenance much more difficult. This anti-tank warhead technology spelled the end of thick armor protection. Heavy tanks such as the Soviet JS series and the American M-103 gave way to Main Battle Tanks, which were lighter and more maneuverable, like the American M-48 Patton, Soviet T-54, and British Centurion. The British eventually developed advanced forms of armor that offered able defense against shaped charge shells. Of course, this, in turn, gave rise to the dartlike hypervelocity discarding sabot round made of depleted uranium. Good luck defending your track from that.

I cannot summon up a single moment where the Nazis did anything that was in any way laudable. They were *all* bad. Here are two weird things that did turn out well. Their rockets jump-started the space program, and they showed the rest of the world how to build a super highway. I know. That doesn't even put a dent in what they owe humanity. Occasionally, one hears a story about a lone Nazi or two who must have been pretending to be evil. There was one time when a German fighter pilot, Franz Stigler, escorted a damaged B-17 to safety. There was another brief moment of humanity during combat at Arnhem Bridge when a truce was called so that the wounded could be evacuated. The professionalism shown to the British paras by German officers was won in ghastly hand-to-hand combat. Medical supplies were stretched beyond the breaking point, but the medics on both sides essentially unified at St. Elizabeth Hospital and made remarkable efforts to save the wounded regardless of nationality. Leave it to the medics to show us the way.

I have stood on Arnhem bridge and tried to imagine the havoc. There was but one tiny plaque dedicated to this sacred ground. I got the impression that Europeans would largely like to forget the last two world wars. If that battle had occurred in the United States, the bridge would have a tourist trap museum with a gift shop and ironically named fast food in every direction. The Red Devil Grill and Paratrooper Café would get five stars in the travel guide. If it is your birthday at the Piat Diner, the servers gather round, put a red beret on your head and serve you a cupcake shaped like a PIAT bomb. They then sing *God Save the King*. The playground would include a Nazi tank that kids can climb on. Pilgrims like me would come by the busload to be emotionally moved by the story. Despite the schmaltzy atmosphere, the soldiers would be remembered. Mission accomplished.

Cliff Rides Again

Which brings us back, at last, to Cliff. Remember Cliff? This is a story about Cliff. As I stressed in Chapter One, history is replete with examples of how the democracies of the world value each and every life under their command. This softness is balanced out by their willingness to use technology on the battlefield that would make a psychopath blush. Our enemies know how casualty-averse we are, and they attempt to produce mass casualties wherever they can. It is always better, however, when fighting a democracy to take out a famous hero or an effective leader. Nothing pleased the North Vietnamese Army more than grabbing a downed pilot. For the United States and our allies, retrieving a fallen knight was a matter of national pride.

I need to back up just a little to talk about riflery in America. Come on down to Virginia, and I will show you country people who know how to shoot. We have plenty of live targets. Cliff and I shared a love of groundhog or woodchuck hunting on the family farm. They were everywhere. There were a few years when we popped over one hundred. We used all sorts of rifles, but the weapon he valued most was a cheesy Rossi .38 special with a six-inch barrel. Man! He knew how to shoot that thing and had great eyesight and excellent form with a handgun. I learned his grip, and it helped quite a bit with my pistol shooting. He taught me that "Long-range pistol shooting is all about judging elevation, and elevation is all in the pinky." I did not know how he honed his pistolry against human targets.

We rolled around the farm in the Willys jeep, looking for our prey. I had a .223 caliber Remington 788 bolt action with an 8 power Redfield scope. The close-range stuff fell to an Anschutz .22 magnum or Marlin 39A. We had sandbags to help with the really long shots, which were usually taken over the hood of the truck. Eventually, I showed up for a hunt with the original civilian SP-1 model of the Colt AR-15. This rifle was introduced for civilian sale in the mid-1960s. It was a pricy item at that time and commanded about five hundred bucks wholesale when ordered from middlemen who advertised in the *Shotgun News*. Today, Brownell's and other manufacturers are producing copies of the early versions of the M-16. An original Colt-made SP-1 model AR-15 can be had in excellent condition for around two grand at the time of this writing in mid-2024.

I scored heavy with the original version of the AR-15 rifle for many years. The fixed carrying handle contained the rear sight and a single hole for mounting the Colt-produced 3x optic. Back in the day, my original SP-1 version wore a 3–9 power Bushnell scope perched way up there on a B-Square carry handle scope mount. It felt a little awkward at first to have a chin weld instead of a cheek weld on the stock, but I will never forget how easy it was to snipe a soda can with that setup. I had myself a revelation when I first shot it off the bench at Clark's Guns shooting range outside Washington, DC, in Warrenton, Virginia. It was accurate as hell, and it never jammed. I took chuck after chuck with it using Federal Ammunition 55-grain soft points.

Naturally, the AR-15 was a powerful talisman for Uncle Cliff. "Oh boy, this takes me back. Jesus. It's just like the one I had." The more he shot my AR-15 rifle, the more he talked about the war. It was like a key, and I wondered how many other vets were so affected by handling their old, trusted weapons once again.

Eventually, some of Cliff's personal war stories dribbled out. Over the years, he added shockingly vivid details. We mostly talked while varminting with nobody else around who might judge him for what he did in the war. We had no PTSD vocabulary in those days. Cliff functioned just fine, but the look on his face when he told me of the battles, the uncharacteristic voice, and the subtle mime told me that the psychic wounds had not completely healed.

Nobody wanted to hear Vietnam stories anyway. Postwar, America's military star was a descendant. We were beaten in Southeast Asia and fought to a standstill in Korea before that. Our equipment was expensive and the effectiveness suspect. The Soviets were on the move in Afghanistan. We trembled at the thought of the thousands of tanks they could unleash in Europe. Our soldiers were riddled with poor morale and substance abuse issues. It was a lot to take in, and none of it was hopeful.

The M-16 Disaster

I'm a gun guy through and through, so I focused my doubts about our war machine on the M-16 rifle, which performed badly in Vietnam. Make no mistake, the earliest M-16 rifles looked like the perfect ticket.

It was issued on a small scale to ARVN special forces and airborne troops operating in South Vietnam during the Kennedy Administration. The results were spectacularly overblown for marketing purposes, though it was a uniquely suitable weapon for small-statured troops. The early guns were fed a proper diet of cleaner burning powder specifically designated for that weapon by the engineers at Armalite in Costa Mesa, California. The rifling on the early guns was set at one turn in fourteen inches, which barely stabilized the 55-grain bullet. The tumbling effect on impact was impressive. Later, rifles tamed the twist a bit to stabilize the bullet when the temperature dropped below freezing. This cost some lethality, but the M-16 could be used worldwide.

In 1965, the Colt M-16E1 was adopted for use in Vietnam without real troop trials. The introduction was mismanaged by the Defense Department, which, among other bad calls, decided not to spend the extra couple bucks per gun to chrome-line the barrels and chambers. Imagine that decision. The rifles were used in the world's most humid climate, and yet the wizards in Washington passed on preventative measures in common use with Soviet-supplied weapons.

The government also fouled up the ammunition by allowing a change in propellants to something the manufacturers had on hand rather than the expensive powder used in the original load. The rifle's designers would say that thanks to the government, their sexy new sports car of a rifle had to run on diesel fuel. The new load increased gas port and chamber pressures, which led to torn case rims. It raised the cyclic rate as well. The magazine spring could not keep up, which led to bolt-over base stoppages. The bolt velocity also increased which caused the bolt carrier to bounce backward oh so slightly on closing. This nasty malfunction takes the weapon out of battery. Even the carbon residue left behind was abrasive.

Without chrome plating to protect them, many rifles quickly developed pitted chambers, which was, in essence, a fatal condition. Call it carbine cancer of the chamber. Only a barrel transplant can save the weapon. To be fair to Colt and even the Secretary of Defense, it has to be said that the Armalite Firearms design team at Fairchild Aircraft overpromised the corrosion resistance of their space-age, lightweight materials. This may have been a factor in choosing not to chrome-plate critical areas.

The military tried to prevent the M-16's failure from becoming a public relations disaster, but word got out that the Army's wonder weapon was crap, and Congress got involved. There were hearings headed by Democrat Representative Ichord about serious issues with the rifle and what was being done about it. Newspapers reprinted agonizing firsthand accounts of how M-16 rifles catastrophically failed in combat. Letters from disillusioned troops were made part of the Federal Record. Amazingly, the weapon system was salvaged. The M-16 was the only developed option available at the time. Colt was too big to fail.

In the end, lazy and some say intellectually challenged conscripted troops took much of the blame for problems in the field. The M-16 might look all Buck Rogers, but it is, in fact, quite simple to strip and clean. I believe that the M-16 requires an IQ of 85 to operate more or less safely. The average enlisted man's IQ score was just over 95, and officers averaged 121. One wonders how smart the average procurement officer might be.

No individuals in government or with Colt Firearms were ever charged with malfeasance.

Oh sure, Colt fixed the M-16, but the process took a few years, and new parts were not retrofitted to rifles already in the field. There were dozens of modifications made that changed everything from the stock to the muzzle device. By the time of the Tet Offensive in 1968, most of the new recruits arriving in the country had the vastly improved M-16A1 version of the rifle. By 1970, everyone had the new weapon, and a thirty-round magazine was finally introduced as well. The M-16A1 was fully evolved and winning firefights. Colt Manufacturing made a mint as militaries around the world lined up to buy America's new assault rifle and answer to the Soviet AK-47.

The ultimate popularity of the M-16 surprises me. Weapons that make a bad debut often cannot shake their poor reputations. The M-16 was an initial logistics failure. Only the British L-85 Individual Weapon was worse, though like the M-16 it too matured into an effective, albeit insanely expensive rifle. One has to wonder if the M-16's pathetic debut was the result of deliberate sabotage. There were traditionalists in charge of the military procurement process who liked their issue weapons to be made of wood and steel not fiberglass and alloys. These manly weapons shot F-off-sized bullets that could kill a man at one thousand yards or even conceivably down an enemy aircraft. The "procurement swamp" did what it could to both drag military feet and skew testing.

When Colt's rifles began to fail in 1965, there were very few, if any, standard-issue cleaning kits in frontline hands. Some troops thought the rifle was self-cleaning, though they would have to realize that it wasn't, like—immediately. The M-16 gets dirty fast. The comic book manual was not out yet, either. Imagine it. The troops were given this incredible gift, and it got many of them killed simply because they did not understand the weapon's strengths and weaknesses. Even if they did deduce what they needed to do to get the M-16 to work, they lacked the tools and spare parts to do even basic maintenance. Add to this the fact that early guns were not sufficiently resistant to corrosive salt air and moisture, and the recipe for failure was complete.

The M-16 was criticized for the need to keep it clean and lubricated. This should be no sin. All military weapons should be clean and slick prior to operations. Weapons must be tested worldwide to know their true reliability which is affected by climate. Jungles and extreme cold call for different lubrication. By far, the worst environment for a firearm is a desert. Sand and dust magically concentrate in every vital area. Israeli troops clean their weapons before they eat whether they need it or not. The M-16 family of weapons have been widely used by the IDF in their sandy environment very successfully, even in preference to their own designs.

Once the M-16's design flaws were identified and dealt with, a well-maintained Armalite was discovered to be as reliable as any weapon in the field, including the highly overrated AK-47. Reliability of the M-4 version of the rifle used in Iraq was questioned. Eight in ten troops found their weapon to be satisfactory. A small number reported experiencing occasional malfunctions that momentarily took them out of the fight. A tiny fraction said that they experienced a malfunction that took them out of the fight entirely. Once again, a lack of maintenance was cited for most malfunctions.

Cliff's experience reveals the biggest fix of all. He was meticulously trained on the M-16 rifle in boot camp, and he had a quality general-issue cleaning kit that was stored in the butt stock. Colt finally got everything right on the production line, including everything necessary to make the rifle work with awful ammunition. Due to all the maintenance required and range time needed to create expert marksmen, it takes two weeks for raw recruits to master this rifle. An AK-47 can be handed off in less than half that time. Cliff mastered the rifle's needs, especially how to lubricate it, and shot expert on the Known Distance range. He was confident that he would not be the sort of soldier who panics and sprays away his ammunition.

It turns out that the most important factor in a soldier's rifle is the all-up weight of the weapon and ammunition. In World War Two, a rifleman might carry eighty rounds in his web gear and another forty-eight in a cloth bandoleer. That's pushing ten pounds. The heavy .30 caliber ammunition for the ten-plus-pound M-1 rifle demanded a great deal of stamina. The M-16A1 weighs less than eight pounds, and the bullets it fires are half the weight of the old thirty caliber. Today's soldiers carry seven to ten thirty-round magazines, one loaded in the rifle and the others in web gear on their chest plates. Most troops also carry bandoleers of ammunition on stripper guides to quickly reload their spent magazines. At a minimum, the modern rifle and ammunition loadout is more than twice the bang for the same World War Two buck.

Light, extremely accurate, and controllable in short bursts, the M-16 is an ideal jungle and street fighting weapon. It is both portable and relatively powerful. Cliff told me that he never had a moment's real trouble with his rifle. He knew several guys who used the AK-47 and swore by them, but as long as he kept his M-16 clean and oiled, it was great.

"Everyone had their own ideas about what kept the M-16 running like a top. I cleaned mine every time I fired it, and I oiled it every day. I kept the dust cover closed. I had a habit of ejecting a live round from the chamber every once in a while because I thought that they might swell and stick. I also used a different kind of lubricant that we got from home. My rifle jammed a few times, but only after extended firing in full automatic. Most problems were just a failure to pick up a round from the magazine, and that was, again, when we were firing in full automatic. Sometimes, we got a failure to eject, which results in a double feed. If you are lucky, all you have to do is pull the magazine, cycle the action a couple of times, and then reload. Sometimes, God just hates on you, and you get a case stuck in the chamber with a torn rim. That was the bad one. But you got that *mostly* with the older guns. The chrome-lined chambers fixed that pretty well. Everybody experienced a jam every once in a while, but we shot *a lot, a lot, a lot* of rounds on full auto and got the guns white hot and filthy dirty. The magazines caused problems too, and we marked the good ones for reuse."

Three Shootdowns

Cliff did tell me about a few of his hairier moments. Apparently, he arrived in Vietnam just in time for the infamous Tet Offensive, a nationwide battle that caused America's news anchorman, Walther Cronkite, to declare that we had lost the war. Though trained as a tank driver, Cliff volunteered to be a helicopter door gunner, one of the most dangerous jobs a soldier can have. In fact, he was downed three times. The urge to fly was a reaction to having an armored personnel carrier catch fire with him in it. Luckily, he was closest to the commander's hatch and got out with only minor injuries. Six other men were incinerated. Blow torch flames shot out the hatches before it exploded. Cliff volunteered for air gunnery the next day. He attended an abbreviated school that covered helicopter operations, maintenance of the weapons they used, and emergency procedures.

There was plenty of death defiance to be had in a Huey UH-1 helicopter. The first crash Cliff experienced was caused by a hydraulics system failure. Every warning light flashed, but the pilots never lost control. They were flying along at top speed when this happened, a factor which essentially saved them. Helicopter auto-rotation landing depends on forward momentum to work. They went down hard, but the Huey was salvageable. One of the pilots suffered a compressed spine injury, but they all basically walked away.

Some would blame poor preventative measures for this loss, but the crew chief and co-pilot checked all the systems during their preflight routine. Turns out, Murphy's Law kills just as fast as an enemy bullet. Cliff knew of several crews whose rotors failed and literally separated from the ship. This was caused when the massive nut that sat atop the rotors cracked. Cliff called this "the Jesus nut" because when it goes, the crew meets Jesus.

The second downing happened a few weeks later and was quite a bit more dramatic. They were among several scouts operating along a major river in support of Special Forces and Navy rivercraft when several VC on a grounded junk fired at them. It was a rare, rich target caught communist red-handed. Cliff fired on a dozen men or more frantically trying to unload supplies.

Cliff said, "You haven't lived until you see tracers coming straight for your nose only to have them veer off at the last possible instant. The first few hit the fuselage around me. The pilot banked and dove toward the river. I stupidly decided that was the moment to step out onto the skid so that I could rake the enemy as we passed over. I was late on the trigger, and Viet Cong fire hit the underside of the helicopter and the tail. We violently spun before the pilots recovered. At that moment, however, I was still standing on the skid."

No mortal could withstand the invisible forces of nature that pulled Cliff out of the aircraft. He would later find that his "monkey tail" safety belt failed because enemy fire put a neat hole right through the bulkhead buckle. Cliff plunged twenty feet into the river. He touched the bottom, but thank God, he didn't sink in. He was only in the drink for maybe five minutes before he got a lift from the navy patrol boat that they were escorting.

"I hit the water hard because I had some serious forward momentum. Thank goodness I wasn't wearing a flak jacket or even web gear at the time. We thought the protection dubious, so unless there was an inspection, we rarely wore body armor, but we did store vests under the seat as protection from ground fire. I wasn't wearing a life vest, and it was hard to tread water in combat boots. I grabbed a bobbing log and took in the show."

The Navy's river monitor boats were converted tank landing craft. In addition to several .30 and .50 caliber machine guns, they also mounted both flame throwers and heavy cannons in armored turrets. The one that arrived that morning blew the junk to smithereens with a single 105 m/m howitzer shell. This was followed by good cooking with napalm. Cliff's badly wounded Huey smacked down hard just outside a firebase, but nobody was injured in the forced landing. The helicopter was easily recovered and repaired. Cliff was reunited with his crew the same evening.

Then came the bad one.

Less than a month later, they unloaded a pallet of ammunition and water to what they thought was a cold staging area. It was their last run of the day, which, for once, had been completely uneventful. Just after lifting off, an RPG-type rocket killed both pilots and the crew chief who was crouching between and just behind them. They were still fairly low. The Huey bucked on without pilots in death throws that carried it a few hundred yards out into the rice paddies. It lost the will to fly and bellyflopped into the shallow water. The skids dug into the bottom and rolled the fuselage. The rotors slashed at the mud and broke, sending shards flying in all directions. The Huey wound up on its side. Fuel and smoke vented through fractures in the fuselage. The tail boom separated completely. This time, Cliff stayed strapped into his seat and came to a rest, looking skyward.

"I was the only survivor. After falling out of the ship that one time, I got real careful about tying in. The tether that took the weight on my M-60 had popped, so that day I hand-held my machine gun, and I just couldn't keep a grip on it when we splashed down. I had a pretty good cut on my left leg, and I was bruised quite a bit, but I didn't notice until afterward.

"The crew chief was gone. I thought he might be out there in the paddies, but he was found under the wreckage when the helicopter was retrieved. The pilot was half under blood-red water. He lost his right arm at the shoulder.

"I threw off my flight helmet and crawled back behind the copilot. I pulled the red lever that lowered his seat all the way back, but in this case, it opened like a door. He was on his side, just barely above the paddy water, and tough to pull out of there. He was a big guy for a helicopter pilot, and I knew he was dead, but I wasn't ready to admit it. I can still see the steaming hole in his flight helmet. I started to take his helmet off, but I heard the enemy yelling, and I thought I better defend my crew, both dead and alive.

"To make matters worse, I had no radio. The rocket zeroed them out permanently, so I didn't have to change their frequencies prior to capture. I fired a flare to let the rest of my brothers know that one of their own was still kicking. I had no way of knowing if the cavalry was coming. My flare attracted attention from the wrong side of the tracks."

Cliff described the situation as open season on helicopters. Well-trained and equipped North Vietnamese regulars used the downed ship as bait to lure more aircraft into their textbook local air defense system. After action reports on this incident would find that an estimated full company of Viet Cong and North Vietnamese Army troops manned a number of heavy anti-aircraft machine guns from concealed positions in the tree line; no doubt, individual riflemen fired skyward too, hoping that a golden BB would magically down one of America's premier weapons. Huey helicopters swirled like dragonflies, looking for an opportunity to rescue the downed crewman, but even for these brave and daring crews, there was just no way. The ground fire was too intense.

Both of the helicopter door guns were lost in the crash, but Cliff did have a sack of hand grenades, and miraculously, his M-16 rifle was still clipped in the cabin rifle rack. He also carried his personal Colt

Python revolver. Over the course of an hour, he used all these weapons to fend off several squads of infantry who rushed his ship.

Just like Audie Muphy in his Medal of Honor showdown, Cliff had a few things going for him in this lopsided fight. First, he was tough to overrun. The Vietnamese regulars faced a dash through shin-deep water over freshly planted rice paddy mud. Imagine what it would be like to pull each foot clean under fire. I liken what happened that day to the battle of Agincourt in 1415, where French knights in their thousands were literally tripped up by extreme mud that clung to their armored shoes.

Back to Agincourt

Like the British under King Henry the Fifth, Cliff was outnumbered, and his enemy was confident of victory. According to Shakespeare (who wasn't there), the French leader reportedly said before the attack, "A very little, little let us do, and all is done."[20] But being French, they were caught up in the emotion of the moment and didn't think about what would happen if they churned up the battlefield after a night of relentless, heavy rain. As described in Chapter One, they made a determined cavalry attack on Henry's flanking longbowmen prior to the main assault. Nothing whips up the earth like hundreds of overburdened war horses. Wooden stakes set by the archers to impale horses did their job, and the demoralized cavalry retired right through the advancing ranks of their own men-at-arms. This inflicted needless casualties and disrupted the formation by churning up the slippery ground all the more.

The Agincourt battlefield is long and wide with a very slight downhill grade. It is hemmed by woods and scattered buildings that make the field between a natural basin. It took a while for the fight to start in earnest, which gave the ground more time to fester. It was late morning by the time thousands of French knights stood shoulder-to-shoulder and advanced into literally deepening trouble.

---

20. *Henry The Fifth*, Act 4, Scene 2.

Typhoo Tea promotional material 1937.

There was intense hand-to-hand fighting along a narrow front where Henry's few nobles and men-at-arms were concentrated. The British gave ground slowly, but their line held. Every step they took backward likely improved their footing, whereas the advancing French had to wade through ever-increasing muck. The British took remarkably few casualties and stood up to the French first wave. Even Henry took part in actual combat. The French second echelon was harassed by arrows on both sides but kept up their advance in the center. They overcrowded the battlefield and caused a unique military catastrophe.

I am left to wonder which Frenchman fell over first. He alone is likely responsible for thousands of deaths. Perhaps he was struck by an arrow, but it is more likely that he simply took a step and was unable to pull his foot free of the mud. Perhaps he simply slipped as his shoes gave him no traction. As he fell, he knocked over the man next to him. The fellow behind him went down too. The calamity spread like tripped dominoes throughout the massive formation. In minutes, few men-at-arms were left standing, and the British archers, who had little in the way of fancy footwear, swept over the prostrate Frenchmen in an enfilade attack to take lives with a single accurate punch of a blade through the vision port or under the arm where the armor was often thin. Many a French knight drowned in six inches of water.

Captives were so plentiful that Henry did not have enough men to keep them secure. The King feared that these disheartened Frenchmen might find a second wind and arm themselves with weapons that were strewn on the ground just about everywhere. To Henry's front, the French were recovering, but the carnage of the battlefield was beyond ghastly. Men lay dead in heaps. Here and there, groups of French troops made futile, small-scale thrusts which the British parried. A full third of the French force remained unengaged, and for a time, they watched the beaten ground without making their intentions clear.

The situation was fluid. Henry faced a potential attack from both directions, and that would be the end of England Himself. So...the mathematical answer was to cut down the captives. What transpired next is open to speculation. It is impossible to know which chronicle to believe. Many French men-at-arms surrendered, believing that military law and precedence would guarantee their safety. Instead, they were herded into a barn and set ablaze. Others were torched in cottages. Imagine the cream of French nobility literally turned to dust. Prominent families were left without a single male heir. It would be a full century before the French nobility recovered. Henry's nobles eventually took a stand and refused to kill any more Agincourt captives. It was bad for business, and the French threat had passed.

The Longbow Perfected

The soldiers of the North Vietnamese Army struggled mightily to make progress across the rice paddy. They fired their weapons as they came, but Cliff ignored the danger.

"That was the first time I really used the '16. Most of the time I was just winging it with an M-60 machine gun as we flew around. Spray going in and spray coming out. I fired to keep their heads down as we zipped away. The day we got shot down in the rice paddies, the NVA tried to use that very tactic back on me, but they didn't suppress my fire. They were well protected, lying prone behind a raised dike wall not far from the tree line. They could take careful aim at me. Thank God, their accuracy was just dismal, and they didn't have a light machine gun or even AK-47 rifles. I don't think these guys were first-string. They were all shooting either really low into the wreck or over my head. A few rounds sucked the air as they passed close by, but I was on autopilot in that situation, and I just kept tracking targets and firing.

"My M-16 was brand new, and it worked well. It was correctly zeroed. The lack of recoil, the way the stock was in line with your shoulder, and my adrenaline all kept the muzzle down between shots. I had a sight picture in my mind that was dead on at one hundred yards and extremely fast to acquire. Just hold at six o'clock and a tiny bit low. Reloads were super smooth with the bolt latch. My rifle was an ass-kicker in that firefight.

"I was just trying to keep them back behind the berm. It seems obvious to say so, but the whole goddamn thing seemed like an amusement arcade shooting gallery. At one hundred yards or so, maybe a little more, we were close enough that I could see them quite clearly. It was late in the afternoon, and they were shooting into the sun. That helped me see them better and may have accounted for their terrible marksmanship. I don't know how many I hit, but I know I hit more than a few. Sometimes I could hear the hits. It's a unique sound that hunters know. I was shooting pretty slow, watching my ammo consumption. For a minute or two, the fire stopped. I thought maybe they were moving on. Then they got up and tried to rush me! I made them pay for my friends over that seventy-five yards of paddy water. I killed most of them. At least eight, maybe more. A couple turned around and went back and started up that long-range shit again."

Cliff ran through a half-dozen twenty-round magazines carried in his web gear and was reduced to using his revolver. "I scrounged around the cabin, looking for anything to keep up the fight. Both pilots had personal weapons, but they were mangled. One other rifle looked intact, but I couldn't reach it. I was pretty pissed at myself for not packing more rifle ammo. I attached my bayonet, and I was prepared to use it. I set it aside and drew my Colt Python.

"That was a sinking feeling because I was doing well with the rifle. In addition to the floaters in the rice paddy, I figured several more were piled up on the other side of the berm and all picked off with semi-auto fire. I didn't fire a single burst. It was all aimed. I guessed they noticed when my rifle quit. They tried another rush. More of them must have come up because, this time, they came in two waves and several yards apart to make my problem a whole lot worse. I fired six rounds at the first few men over the dike. I might have hit them, but they were stumbling in the paddy water, and I did not see who got back up. I carried spare revolver rounds in my right pants pocket. By the time I reloaded, they were only fifty yards away. I was just lucky to have a fresh six shots ready when they all ran their guns dry. I think they were armed with SKS rifles and Nagant bolt actions, which are hard weapons to reload on the move. They had their spike bayonets fixed and screamed like hell as they came at me.

"I had my six shots, and there were at least ten or more targets to worry about. I pictured puncture wounds in the near future. I wanted to make the most of my last shots. I took careful aim at the soldier closest to me and shot him in the chest. He looked very surprised. The kid behind him had a war face on. I shot at him, too, but I don't remember if I hit him. I must have, but I don't remember. I shot the last few shots purely instinctively. They were getting really close. I hit one guy at about ten yards, and it made him pause for a split second, but he just sorta shook it off, so I shot him in the face. There were more troops coming behind him, but they too were struggling and falling in the paddy. That left me with the grenades. I dropped the pistol and ducked down inside the wreckage.

"Everything around my area got real quiet. They stopped shooting. I could hear someone moving around, but I couldn't see anyone.

"I don't remember picking up the rifle, but it was in my hands when one of the enemy peeked over the edge. I was right underneath him, and I jabbed him under his jaw up to the muzzle of my rifle. Then

I pulled it back and he screamed. I heard him splash around. Other troops were yelling. I thought they had me. Without looking, I lobbed a hand grenade close aboard the wreck. I don't know how I didn't get hit with the fragments. I think that one killed a couple of them. I heard another blast which I had nothing to do with. I'm guessing somebody dropped a grenade before he could throw it.

"I'm glad I played baseball in school. I threw the rest of the grenades as fast as I could and hoped that the blasts would somehow break their spirit.

"Just when I thought that I ought to use the last grenade on myself rather than be captured, two things happened. Turns out there was an OV-10 Bronco spotting aircraft circling the battle area, and those guys orchestrated an airstrike to save me. Uncle Sam spent big bucks to get me outa there. A pair of F-100 Super Sabres screamed right over me about thirty feet up and dropped napalm on the anti-aircraft guns. I will never forget the wall of fire. I could feel the heat hundreds of yards away. Then, right on cue, practically before I could smell the smoke, a pair of 'Spads' [Douglas Skyraider attack aircraft] made a low firing pass that killed the NVA troops in front of me. Those eight 20 m/m cannons spewed shrapnel everywhere. The spray from each impact sent divots of rice paddy and Viet Cong ten feet into the air. A Huey followed the Navy planes and dropped a rope ladder that I wound my arm through well enough to be hoisted from the wreckage. I left everything and everyone behind. Once safely out of rifle range, they brought me onboard."

While Cliff was going nose to nose with the VC, American forces airlifted a full company of ARVN and United States Marines into the landing area. Even after the napalm strike, they were ambushed in the NVA bunker complex and forced to withdraw. This made bad press for the evening news, but Cliff's ordeal and survival were a high point in the day's events and the subject of much radio traffic as helicopter pilots who tried unsuccessfully to reach him reported his predicament and stalwart defense.

How pilots understood each other as their words ran together and over each other is beyond me.

"Taking fire! Taking fire! Watchthetreeline tothewest."

"Thatsonofabitchisputtinguponehellofafightdownthere."

"Roger. Wegottogetthatmanoutoftherepronto."

"Ahhh…That'saffirmativelet'sdosomethinaboutthat…ahhhh…god-damtriple-A downthere."

"It'shotterthanhelldownhere! Get the Spads in and… makeitalittlehotter."

"Roger. Hopehe'skeepinghisheaddown. Thisisgoingtobeabigone."

Once aboard the rescue helicopter, the crew chief/medic asked, "Is there anyone else alive? Do we need to go back?"

"The pilots, and I'm pretty sure the chief, were killed before we hit the ground. I tried to help, but they were all shot up, and the chief was gone."

Cliff told me that the helicopter ride to safety caused him to have what I think was a panic attack. I can only imagine what he went through. He was the only living casualty aboard. Several less fortunate men lifelessly crowded the deck at his feet. The irony of his lone survival must have been excruciating. First, there was the crew cooking in the M113 carrier, then the fall into the river, and now this. The single survivor thing never happened twice. While, by comparison, he was getting the royal treatment, his friends were dead. That realization ripped through his mind along with the permanently etched images of their bodies. He began to shake. It started as a little shiver, but within a minute, his hands trembled so badly that he couldn't hold a canteen. The sensation climbed his arms and took to his chin. His mouth was dry, and he couldn't swallow. A wave of nausea forced its way out. Cliff let his bile loose in a helmet.

"You done? You OK?" The medic asked as he put a dressing on Cliff's bleeding leg. "Then we don't need this." He handed the helmet to the door gunner, who dropped it in the strip stream.

Cliff remained grim. "It took me that whole ride, about twenty-five minutes, to get my shit together. I sat there with that medic. I think he thought I might just jump. He had a grip on me."

They flew along high enough to be free of anti-aircraft guns and other earthly troubles. In under a minute, Cliff went from pure combat, heat, humidity, and the putrid smell of Vietnam to the cool and clean heavens. The medic kept his arm around him and offered to take his hand. Cliff burrowed his shoulder into his brother but turned his face away.

"'Here, buddy. Shake my hand. Come on now. People are going to want to shake your hand. Let me be the first. Come on now. Easy, buddy.' He kept a hand on my leg, which was going about a hundred miles an hour.

"He said, 'You're a celebrity, at least for today. Hell, *Stars and Stripes* might write up your story.'"

"My story? That idea did not help me. I couldn't stop shaking. I got the shakes afterward sometimes, but not like that. Jesus. That was the worst.

"The medic was patching up my other wounds when I actually cried. It was just for a minute. That was the only time in that whole stinking mess that I did that. I think it was the adrenalin. I must have been riding that high for half an hour or so straight, right? Afterward, you're gonna shake a bit. Adrenalin keeps you alive. In retrospect, I am thankful for those shakes. Funny how that chemical saves you and then tortures you for the rest of your life. It's like it burns little pathways to your memory. Sights, the smell, even the taste…it's all still there."

Even after ten years, Cliff moaned when he told me about losing his brothers that day. His survivor's guilt was made all the worse when he won a silver star for his actions. His mother still had it, rescued from the trash; it was found in her bedside table after she passed away.

Just after dawn the following morning, American troops recovered the crashed machine and the bodies of its crew with a heavy lift helicopter. The Huey was a total write-off, but it was thought best to leave nothing for the enemy to use. The recovery team was wary of booby traps that would almost certainly have been placed in the wreck overnight.

Each team member had a specific task to complete as quickly as possible. The trooper assigned to recovering the dead crew had the most dangerous detail. The young corporal was supremely careful as he moved around inside the cabin. He looked over the space and bodies with an experienced eye. He knew that the enemy had been there as every last useful thing, including Cliff's M-16, was gone. They recovered the copilot's body after a careful inspection revealed a Russian-made hand grenade wedged between his back and the seat. Another trip line was attacked to Cliff's flight helmet. The pilot himself was badly entangled in the wreck and almost completely immersed in paddy water. He would stay where he was for the trip back to the airfield.

The corporal dealt with these traps and took every step like a chess master who thinks five moves ahead. He chose the wrong bit to hold his weight and fell over backward into the water. As he regained his feet, something solid and narrow stopped his foot, and he thought, for sure, that he was standing on a landmine. It was deeply planted in the goo, and short of sticking your hand in the muck, there was no way to know what it was. The trooper froze. His mind went fifty bad places all at the same time.

Cliff became quite animated when he told this remarkable part of the story. "So Bobby screams, 'Oh my God! I'm standing on a fucking land mine!' That's a tough one right there. That's as bad as it gets. There isn't much you can do except avoid them in the first place. They already found one booby trap. That marine was right to be worried."

The lieutenant swore, "Goddammit. Get ready to evacuate him."

The land mine scare cost the recovery team precious minutes on the ground as they debated how to proceed. They were hastened by harassing sniper fire that was of a better grade than the day before. The soldier on the landmine decided that his only chance was to somehow get ahold of it.

"So he sticks his hand down there and what happens? He comes up with an expensive Colt revolver, not a bouncing Betty. He had some sort of a stress-induced break with reality that made him believe with every fiber of his being that his survival depended on returning the revolver to the original owner. In an unusual act of paranoia or good character—you decide—Bobby went out of his way and actually did return the gun to me. He told the story and added that finding it was like playing Russian Roulette with his foot."

That revolver was used several more times but not in the sharpshooter role. Despite his best efforts, Cliff never got the action as clean as it was before its mud bath. It worked fine, but it had a grittiness where once Colt craftsmen honed the smoothest revolver made. Cliff found Vietnam untenable both on the ground and in the air, so he turned to the life of a tunnel rat and used the revolver's long barrel to poke at things in the dark that might poke back. That aspect of the war remained a locked door that I could not pry open. I asked him to tell me about the tunnels, and he just said, "Can't."

After a full tour and only days before heading home, Cliff sold the revolver to a friend for basically nothing. At the time, he'd had enough of guns and killing. As it turned out, he was fantastically good at generating a body count. Rather than pride, he felt anger and perhaps guilt as well, though what he told me about combat sounded like a fair fight.

This is a book about weapons, and we have to acknowledge that in this instance, the M-16A1 did very well in the hands of a twenty-year-old kid who had been shooting all manner of firearms since he was six. He manifested rare bravery and remained focused under fire. Like any good soldier, he was careful to keep his weapons clean and ready, but it was the factory changes that made the rifle effective. Here, we see why the perfected M-16 has lasted so long.

The admittedly small numbers of SKS and Nagant rifles used against Cliff's little Alamo were outclassed even by one determined man armed with a modern assault rifle. The NVA soldiers lacked the magazine capacity to cover their own charge across the rice paddy and depended on their bayonets. One is left to wonder if their rifles were properly zeroed or if the troops who used them understood how to set the range on their weapons. With the rifles' sights set to the "battle elevation," they may well have been shooting quite high at one hundred yards. The enemy's lack of training seems evident, and the simple soldier-proof rifle they used did not make up for this paucity.

The angel in this fight was the revolver. I suppose if there is a rifleman to your left and another to your right, the use of a pistol would not be an appreciable loss. But then we have this situation where the defender is alone with six in his wheel and a slow reload to look forward to. Yes, there is the accuracy, but with only six rounds, a soldier can't spray the bad guys as he gives them the slip. The revolver's limits are grave. It should also be noted that Cliff did not have .357 magnum ammunition for his weapon. Rather, he had Full Metal Jacket .38 specials. The lack of stopping power was an obvious issue.

Both sides employed some heavy hitter small arms and light cannons including the helo-killing "Dushka" 12.7 m/m and the Douglas Skyraider's Mark 12 20 m/m cannons that wiped out an entire North Vietnamese platoon in a single pass.

American pilots played a less-than-masterful game of cat and mouse with the North Vietnamese. The Arsenal of Democracy loosed millions of rockets and dropped thousands of bombs on North and South Vietnam. They denuded the jungle with Agent Orange. Mini guns, M-60s, and M-16s hosed away. Tens of thousands of rounds of small arms ammunition were needed to kill each and every NVA soldier. Howitzers obliterated, and napalm cleansed. Arch Light B-52 strikes turned the jungle into the surface of the moon. Somehow, it wasn't enough to win the war.

Meanwhile, the smallest player in all of Vietnam, old Cliff, had one hell of a private battle.

"I still think about it from time to time. That day and so many others, especially when I watch some stupid war movie. And looking back, I can say, honestly, I'm proud. It was savage. It was hell. The enemy made me mad, though. I was really pissed off. Half of the time, I was out of my mind over there, and a long time thereafter too. Hell, I'm still angry about it. Yeah… All that, but you know the one thing I wish about that fight? I should wish it didn't happen. But you know what I want even more? I just wish I brought more ammunition. I might have won the war by myself."

Part 2

Magic Beans

*War is cruelty. There is no use in trying to reform
it. The crueler it is, the sooner it will be over.*
          —William Tecumseh Sherman

Here's an old story with a useful villain. When Jack climbed his beanstalk, he had no idea what he might find in the clouds. He had his suspicions about gold and home invasion on his mind. Amazingly, he "found" some in a random giant's castle, but in the end, his Englishman's scent gave him away, and he barely got out alive. The giant taunted him with all that "Fee, Fie, Fo, Fum" dialogue. "I'll grind your bones to make my bread," seems kind of ho-hum threat-wise by modern standards, but that old giant was on the verge of something truly, memorably graphic. Had he gotten those massive hands on young Jack, there would most certainly have been some live dismembering and some memorably noisy chewing. The giant has no soul.

In the story's climax, Jack chops down the beanstalk with the giant in transit overhead. In the updated twenty-first-century version of the story, the monster lands on an Anglican church and is skewered by the steeple, killing him instantly. It was a huge mess. Jack had to use his newly found gold to pay off the locals who banned magic beans thereafter. They feared more giants moving into the neighborhood, and they didn't need the bad press.

For our part here in the story of weapons, we need to focus on the antagonist giant himself. He is an instructive fellow, both beastlike and supernatural. You can't hang out with a giant. Even when on their best behavior, they bicker, grumble, and threaten each other over everything. The average giant is worse than a cannibal, and he wins fights just by showing up…or at least *he should*. He's a giant. He's tough to miss, a safe bet, and yet, when the scrap is on, the giant invariably loses money. Think about the bets on old Goliath. A lot of shekels were lost that day.

The history of *military gigantism* lingers on in enormous Soviet-era submarines and power-projecting American aircraft carriers. One has to wonder if there is a beanstalk lesson here, and if so, when it will be learned. Obviously, gigantism in a military sense depends on the combatants. To an individual soldier, a tank is a giant. To another tanker, however, that armored vehicle is an equal. These days, a single missile can be a giant. A successful terrorist can claim the title, too. Ironically, a microbe can be the worst giant of all.

Weapons have two equally important effects on an enemy. First, they kill, hopefully in large numbers. Secondarily, they should generate military and societal paralysis through abject fear. Thus, the best weapons are so scary that they are never used. Size helps.

Bolts from Olympus

Zeppelins were the world's first super weapons. They were every bit as large as the mightiest battleship and capable of dropping bombs or poison gas from so high up that, at first, nobody could reach them to mount a defense. Zeppelins came along at a time when nobody, anywhere, ever saw anything manmade fly. An early airplane might take two people up to a thousand feet. In peacetime, a massive zeppelin could scoot fifty people around the world in a matter of days. That was a mind-boggling speed for the time. The military applications seemed endless, especially before fighter planes were developed and anti-aircraft gunnery was an unknown skill.

In reality, the average zeppelin was fragile beyond belief. Their crews must have been particularly suicidal as they relied on flammable hydrogen gas for lift. Only a fool would sign up for the ride, but when they first appeared over Paris and London early on in World War One, a desperate sense of vulnerability robbed people of their sleep.

Imagine being eight or nine years of age, old enough to be influenced by a picture on the cover of a newspaper or war bonds poster. No, the English Channel isn't going to save you, little Tommy. There's a bunch of evil Germans in the sky at night looking for your house. Sleep well!

The zeppelin's psychological impact was profound. It was also an excellent reconnaissance platform over the ocean where some Captain Nemo kind of guy could hang way up there and watch for mighty battleships on the horizon. It might even be used for quickly transporting critical supplies over safe territory. During battle, though, a single lucky incendiary bullet that weighs one third of an ounce might be enough to bring a seven-hundred-foot-long zeppelin crashing down. That's 150 grains of the bullet to bring down 177,000 kilograms of airship. Let's get even tighter: We're talking 1,180 kilos of damage per grain of projectile. Just as a mathematical bullet-to-damage ratio, this has to be a record.

All zeppelins died with the *Hindenburg* (LZ-129). Think about that single event in comparison to the multiple airship disasters that preceded this horrifying crash. In the United States, the dirigibles *Akron*, *Shenandoah*, and *Macon* all went down hard in bad weather with great loss of life, and they used safe helium instead of hydrogen for lift. Death by hydrogen fire would be horrible, but if a helium filled gas bag ruptured and the panicked crews inhaled the escaping gas as the dirigible went down, one is left to wonder what their final cries for salvation sounded like. All the other airship catastrophes weren't enough to end their dominance, but after the *Hindenburg* burned, people said, "I'll take the train to the boat, thanks."

The LZ 129 was a zeppelin of advanced design. It was the follow-on to the famously successful Graf Zeppelin. The explosion and fire were caught on film as the *Hindenburg* landed at Lakehurst, New Jersey, on May 6, 1937. The cause of the disaster is still something of an open question. Some experts have deeply explored the possibility of a sinister saboteur or two who had issues with the Nazi Party.

The *Hindenburg* was truly spectacular for its time, real Jules Verne kind of stuff, and the press couldn't get enough of it. This ultimate propaganda machine floated over Hitler rallies, playing music over massive loudspeakers and dropping leaflets. It pondered by in all the newsreels with its awful swastikas glaring from every fin. Blowing up the *Hindenburg* with all the cameras rolling would counter this propaganda in a flash. The loss did end Nazi lighter-than-air development, though various balloons remained in use throughout the coming war.

The motive for Zeppelin's murder was there for sure. Of course, we need to be practical and begrudgingly admit that it is also *probable* that a killer, errant static electric charge did the deed. The static theory is supported by scads of scientific and meteorological minutia. Of all the theories, this seems the most likely. It requires no thought of conspiracy. No *imagination*.

If the *Hindenburg* did release hydrogen in an effort to trim and land the ungainly giant at Lakehurst, it was primed for a bolt from the blue. That bolt might have been a rifle bullet fired from some distance away. The *Hindenburg* was the largest target of all time. One First World War balloon buster bullet could have done the job. There were threatening letters that promised this very scenario.

Zeppelins were not a new military technology in 1914. They were a logical development that began with observation balloons used as far back as the French Revolution and the American Civil War. Ferdinand von Zeppelin, inventor and primary designer of the ships that bear his name, was an official observer attached to the Army of the Potomac in 1863. He was particularly interested in the use of observation balloons for artillery-spotting and reconnaissance in general. While supremely useful, they were also vulnerable. The solution seemed obvious enough. They needed to fly free.

By the beginning of the First World War, observation balloons were everywhere along the front and were very high-value targets. Groups of balloons were also used to create aerial obstacles around important potential targets. They were connected by aprons of cables that might slash off an airplane's wing. It was still possible to fly between the strands, but they were difficult to see until a pilot was about to collide with one. They covered vital areas around London and Paris as well as on the battlefield. Specialist troops on the ground could crank down an observation balloon under fire, but this was a relatively slow process that practically guaranteed a cooked spotter. Later in the war, observers were issued primitive parachutes, which were stored ready to use in a large tube suspended from the observer's basket. Once the harness was on, all he had to do was jump to pull the chute. He had no control over his landing whatsoever.

It is impossible to know who had the original idea of using airships to bomb enemy installations. They could do so with near total impunity as early in the war; no aircraft had the ceiling needed to reach a zeppelin, let alone pump it full of enough full-metal jacket bullets to bring it down. Anti-aircraft artillery was in its infancy. There were only a few dozen anti-aircraft guns in all of the British Army, but the new anti-air gunners could not have asked for a larger or slower-moving target. Flying at night and using cloud cover, a zeppelin might slip through and scare the hell out of London, but for all that effort, they killed relatively few people. Approximately 560 British citizens were killed in zeppelin raids, and 1,400 were wounded. The damage to property was serious, but compared with what was happening in France, the effects were less than negligible.

Bombing from high altitudes ruined zeppelin marksmanship. This was mostly due to poor navigation that depended on spotty radio techniques and dead reconning. Neither side developed an effective bombsight during the First World War. Early aerial bombs were little more than repurposed artillery shells with leather used for fins. Cities, however, even smaller sections such as the London docks, were semi-feasible targets. The difficulty, however, was knowing exactly which city one was over in the first place. Finding smaller targets like aerodromes or factories was tough enough by day and virtually impossible by night.

Bad weather was the real worry. Cloud cover was a boon when hiding from anti-aircraft guns and searchlights. The bombardier might not agree, so an ingenious system was devised called various things, but "spy car" seems most apt. A gondola containing a telephone, powerful optics, and a brave observer was lowered on a strong steel cable from the mother ship. Shaped like a small zeppelin with a fin to make it fly straight, the device was far too small to be seen from the ground. This was highly effective and, for a time, gave the Germans an invisible bomber.

Londoners were galvanized by the zeppelin raids just as the Luftwaffe did during the Battle of Britain in 1940. Recruitment posters asked logically if a potential soldier preferred to face bullets or zeppelin bombs.

The Hollows Family, 1917

It seems to help our admiration if the bravest of men come from anonymous places like Audie Murphy's Kingston, Texas. Every once in a while, however, a Jack comes with a bit of glamor, as was the case with the focus of this story, a Major Xavier Hollows, Royal Flying Corps, assigned to command something of a distribution depot for newly arrived pilots and surviving aviators whose original squadrons were decimated while fighting on the Western Front in late 1917.

Major Hollow's father, the famously cantankerous and influential Lord Hollows—yes, one of those in the Coronet Gallery—was less than pleased with the "twists and gyrations" that his son used to get himself into actual combat. The family had plans for their firstborn and only boy. For example, his marriage was in the works though Xavier had not yet been told. There were plenty of things people in his position could do in uniform without risking the family's lineage. Xavier was just finishing a degree in engineering when the war started in 1914 and had not joined any branch of the military service, even the territorials. Those who knew Xavier well said that it was difficult to imagine him as a soldier, though a handsome one he would be.

It is only natural that soldiers get angry and have their brutal ways, but Xavier exuded no such emotion or inclination. He neither boxed nor wrestled in school, and he was none too fond of rugby either. He did well in the gentlemen's sports, which included crew, track and field, and tennis. He could drive a golf ball, but putting was beyond him. He took no interest in cricket, most un-British. He knew how to sail and navigate. He was good with animals, especially dogs. He kept rabbits as a small boy until he realized they were being harvested and fried for his supper. In a dead-of-night commando action, he freed the lot into the family flower gardens.

In the morning, he marched into his mother's breakfast and announced his crime.

Lady Hollows stifled her urge to laugh and hug her little protector of the weak and boy of action. Instead, she said quite calmly that he was very naughty and was to have no candy or cake for a week. His governess took him to London for a haircut and to shop for toys suitable for maturing boys. His haul included a working steam engine, tin toys, several sets of toy soldiers, and even a menagerie of exotic animals carved to scale in a wheeled zoo. When Xavier returned that evening, there were no stuffed animals in his playroom or on his bed. His favorite storybooks were gone as well. New and very challenging books took their place.

Xavier made a quick search of the gardens, which revealed no rabbits, but he did find an empty shotgun shell.

Normally, Xavier ate dinner with his governess and sometimes other household servants as well. He only dined with his parents when a day of leisure was in the offing or when family gatherings took place.

His post-London rabbit dinner came as a shock, but to his credit, the rabbit lover chose to dig in and fight back in the only way he could. He put down his fork and walked over to the pantry door. It swung open to reveal his mother and governess behaving oddly.

"Would you come sit with me, Mother? Thank you for all the new toys. I shall send father a note saying the same."

"Oh? Well, of course, dear boy."

Much to his mother's initial satisfaction, Xavier wolfed his bunny rabbit right down.

"Xavier, slow down. Chew."

"Can't, so hungry." He put down his fork as he chewed on his massive mouthful but rethought it and tried to stuff in some more. This proved futile, so he spit the works out on his plate. His mother looked quite alarmed. Xavier put down his fork and reached into his pocket. He tossed the empty shotgun shell on the table. He picked his fork back up and stabbed at his meat.

"Was this the one with white spots?"

He asked for seconds, but his mother said, "No. I do not want to see any more of that. You are making a point, are you not, young man? Well then. Is that not fascinating?" She turned to the governess. "He's made his point at eight years of age. Perhaps it is even a good point. I might have been a little severe. Xavier, we shall have a truce. Bring him a cake."

"I would like my toys back, please."

"What of the new toys?"

"A few of the old ones, then?"

"You are too old for stuffed toys."

"I'll have the bunny rabbit and the dog with sad eyes."

"Very well. I shall keep the adorable lion in my rooms should the bunny and dog wish to visit. I never told you, but that lion actually belonged to your father."

Xavier looked away for a moment to imply that he might counter. "When father and I make a deal, we pretend to spit on our palms, and then we slap them together in the air."

Lady Hollows removed her gloves. "I taught him that one. Why pretend to spit? Do we have a deal or not?"

In Xavier's day, a true gentleman was deathly skilled at blood sports. Xavier knew how to look dapper as he fished or fox hunted. He stalked stag and bagged pheasants at all the appointed times, but he was never in the least bit keen about it. He turned away when the fox met its end.

Classically educated, Xavier could quote Virgil and speak excellent French, passable German, and, of course, halting Latin. He knew his Chaucer and Shakespeare. He took heraldry quite seriously. As an engineer, he understood the universe through formulas and equations. He traveled to the Orient, the Middle East, and, of course, all over Europe. He never visited The United States, which he found culturally laughable. He considered the Americans he met to be excitable and prone to argument. If Xavier was a snob about anything, it was Americans—with the exception of the Wright Brothers, of course.

Popular at school and social functions, Xavier could dance and play the piano. He was assailed by young ladies who made vague promises of a sexual nature that somehow never came through. The sexual mores of that time prevented most people from talking about human reproduction. Children did not receive "the talk" as they do today. They were told about the Birds and the Bees. Kids had to extrapolate the sexual part themselves. This was true in Xavier's case as well. He was advised about his gentlemanly concerns by one of his mother's closest friends just after his first semester at college.

The House of Glass

Dianna Fisher was thirty-five and a mother of four boys. She was Catholic, half-Spanish, and far younger than her husband. She once caught young Xavier staring at her in that awakening way that teenage boys sometimes do. Xavier snapped out of it when she stared back and laughed.

Xavier rolled into the family drive behind the wheel of his 1912 Rover. He yielded way to the Fishers, who arrived in their chauffeur driven Rolls Royce Silver Ghost. Xavier barely acknowledged his guests as he walked around their car. Diana approached the young college man who suddenly remembered his manners well enough to offer a chipper Easter greeting. It took no arm twisting at all to arrange a quick test drive to the estate entrance and back in the fabulous luxury yacht. Xavier was surprised when Diana invited herself along. She was her usual chatty self, but she had to raise her voice to be heard.

"Xavier, you must listen. I have taken it upon myself to allay some of your mother's fears about certain obstacles of a feminine nature that might appear in your path now that you are out and about as a college man. She has reason to worry about your successful future. You are treading water with sharks, and you have no idea. Obviously, your mother would die if she knew we had this talk, but I see in you a certain liberality that must not go unaddressed. Slow down a bit, dear. I almost lost my hat!"

Xavier pulled to the roadside and cut the engine. "If my father is aware, he might send me a letter about it."

"That seems unlikely. Now, to the sensitive aspects. There are several things you need to know from a woman's perspective that, sadly, most men do not know. I wish someone told my husband what I am going to tell you now." Diana explained quite cooly that women should enjoy "the act itself" especially if they hope to conceive a child. "Do not be in a rush about it. The best ladies take some time to warm up to *the event*." She said nothing about technique, physiology, or anatomy. Memorably, she did offer that, "The French have an edge on the British in such things. Look there for answers. They seem to have the right proclivities for the task."

Then came the list of "do nots."

"You are not to deflower any of the young girls who, believe me, are ready and willing to marry you after the first date. They are your parents' friends' children, after all. The scandal would be unimaginable.

"Watch out for foreign girls, *especially* the French, but Germans too. The Scandinavians have a propensity toward nudity that is disquieting. They think it is quite natural. Italians call it artistic. Spanish girls are passionate and very faithful."

The lecture included a scenario on how he might be "caught" by an unplanned pregnancy.

"She will pretend that it is her first time, or very nearly so, but you will notice right away that she is comfortable with what is to happen. Nobody is comfortable the first time or even the tenth. Over time, one learns. It's really rather awful at first, actually. Ideally, it is the blind leading the blind, which is stupid on the face of it." Then, the conversation took an abrupt turn. Xavier was told where a gentleman of his station takes his urges.

"I can help you with the blind part by sending you to an expert. She will explain how to avoid disease and all of the distasteful details that I cannot bring myself to discuss. Here is the address. You may be shocked by who you see playing at sport, but I have researched this selection personally, and I am assured that no one in your father's circle frequents this establishment. Even still, go in and out with your hat on and collar up. Notice the name on the card. It is called The House of Glass. You shall see why. Ask for Geneva. She is the proprietor. I know her somewhat from many years ago before she went into business for herself. She will be expecting you, and she understands your special needs for privacy.

"Xavier, gentlemen, never, *ever*, discuss such things except in the confessional and when your doctor has to cure your venereal diseases. *Do not* discuss your visits to this gallery with your friends or, God help you, the servants. You are too chummy with them, dear. *Do not* take anyone with you. *Do not* meet the ladies outside of the establishment. If they are willing to do such a thing, something is wrong. So long as they are in-house, they are protected and so at this particular establishment are you. Let no photographs be taken, not so much as a sketch. Use an assumed name, of course, something forgettable. You are there for a service, not the sideboard. They will try to run up your bill. Do not eat, drink, sniff, or smoke anything they offer you. Bring your own flask. Tip heavily and promise a return engagement.

"I trust the proprietor, but all the same, do not dawdle. You cannot afford to be caught in just any…parlor. Stay with this one. The police have been bought off by people far above your lowly station and at great cost. The owners know that the only way to make money is to offer impeccable pleasures to highly discerning men. They are constantly on the watch for diseases amidst their…flock. If you ever do have a problem, you must come to me first. Do not involve your parents. People in their position lack the flexibility of mind.

"Now I believe I have done my duty. Keep your wits about you, young man. The world will throw itself at you. Do not underestimate the women who cross your path. Some of us are formidable, which is a hopeful thing, but most, I am afraid, are content to be fools. *They are the dangerous ones.*"

"So, which kind is my dear mother?"

"Your mother was a social assassin in her day."

"She was also hard on my rabbits."

"Your mother was not to be crossed or gossiped about. She was, and still is, quite stunning. That is where you get those handsome features of yours. Well, at least you have her nose. After your parents were wed, she became an extraordinary matchmaker, which is one of the reasons why so many fine people revere her.

"Go break a piggy bank. We shall explain our absence by saying our fancy automobile left us in the lurch until you used that mechanical genius of yours to set things right."

Despite the avoidance of any graphic content whatsoever, Xavier found the presentation on sex to be informative and, against the backdrop of the strict Victorian codes of behavior, quite liberating. He swore to keep mum about the talk and caught the first train for London the following morning.

Official Coin Mint, Wetterstein
Mountains, Germany 1671

Gunter Richter winced in pain as he pressed his fingers on the knife wound in his side. It was deep and blood oozed profusely from the gash. He looked about the room for something to staunch the flood and settled for a crusty neckerchief torn from the dead man at his feet.

The five men who so suddenly came for him, his compatriots, lay dead around the house. The total time elapsed between betrayal and their deaths spanned less than two minutes, but Gunter had one last man to go and that remaining obstacle was fond of firearms. He knew well that a wheel lock pistol was nearby, wound and ready to fire. The primitive handgun expelled a monstrous sixty caliber ball, and he expected to be shot at any moment.

Gunter announced loudly, "I knew you all would turn on me one day. We are partners in crime, which is to say that we owe each other nothing. But why turn on me now? Why today of all days?"

The last man pushed open a heavy door and entered the room with his gun leveled.

"Drop the sword, Gunter. You ask a fair question. I will answer, and then I have a question for you. Did you notice that my man, Klein, made the deliveries yesterday? Unusual for him to ride up here. He came all this way to warn me that Zimmerman has died rather suddenly. He also mentioned that they found an unexplainably large number of freshly minted coins in his possession. Apparently, that raised the alarm. Klein believes that a new inspector is coming up here, possibly tomorrow. I think we both know who that will be. No one else but that bastard Stoltz, and he won't come alone, either. He can likely count far better than our Zimmerman."

"I'm the one to worry over such things. You men have done very well by me these past two years. I may as well tell you now. I have a partner who shall we say sits at the head of the table. He will be crushed now that this is blown."

"Yes, yes, all your famous friends. We considered them. So, we thought Gunter won't run. He will lay off whatever they find on us. With all his secret allies, if we are caught, Gunter will go free and the rest of us will rot. So, we thought, it would be best to kill you. But then we also thought, why not take your share with us? After all, your pile is far more impressive than any of ours."

"But it wasn't where I left it."

"Noooo. We looked while you were taking your regular morning shit."

"You fools! This is…was, perfect. We are trusted by the people who matter because they are all fellow criminals, my investors. I paid them off. That came out of my share. Who is looking over our shoulders way up here? Nobody. We can see an army coming from miles away and can slip out over the mountain at this time of year without being captured if we must. So, Zimmerman is gone. What of it? Even if Stoltz wished to check every jot it would take considerable time. We could have studied the situation. We might buy him off like all the rest or get something on him and bend him to our will. At the very least we could have tried, and if we failed? He might fall off the cliff if nothing else."

"No. This is over. Your money, now!"

"You are twice the fool. I have hidden my coins so well that they won't be found for one hundred years."

"I will admit, we thought we had you when we discovered your little nook of a hiding place. Very clever indeed. To find it full of lead this morning was something of a shock. You have not dug any recent holes. We have been watching you closely since the last pay out. The coins must be in this building someplace, eh? So, you must tell me. Where?"

"I am spent. I will die, and you will choke on my secret. This is the best entertainment you are likely to get for my money. Otherwise take all these dead men's coins and be off. That's a princely sum."

Gunter was perhaps five yards away from the gunman, bent at the waist and weak in the knees. He kept his left hand on the stab wound as he breathed deeply. The last man thought his captive would surely fall and took a few steps closer.

"Oh, I will. And I will have yours too. Tell me or the pain I inflict will be worse than you can imagine. I'll cut your cock off."

"You know, the rest of them shouldn't have held back when they came at me. That's what cost them. Well, that and letting me reach my sword."

"I must admit that you did make impressively short work of the others, but none of us are warrior stock like you. If I knew you could fight like that, we would have grabbed you in your sleep. Thomas there was the only real challenge. Am I right? He got you, too I see. I wanted to kill him, myself. I might have. You ran him right through the heart, though. Very impressive."

The last man leaned in. "That's a great deal of blood on the floor. I always thought swords were foolish weapons until now. Coooo, that's a lot of blood. Some of it's yours, soon to be more. I am going to shoot you in your knee and stick my finger in the hole and you will scream for me to stop. Do you think you will answer me then?"

The last man's taunt was accompanied by an added bit of gesticulation that was meant to humiliate but only caused the muzzle of the pistol to dip. Gunter saw his chance and summoned all his remaining strength to spring on his former partner. He was marginally faster than the last man's reaction time. The massive pistol was swung, and the trigger was pulled, but the lock itself had to spin for a fraction of a second and the charge had to ignite which added another heartbeat to the process. The big ball flew less than a foot before it grazed Gunter's inner thigh decidedly close to what counts. It then ricochetted off the stone wall behind him. The ball lost most of its energy and was flattened against the rock, but its return flight hit Gunter in his left calf with considerable force.

The sudden pain added furry to Gunter's attack. He growled loudly as he grabbed the barrel and yanked the pistol from the last man's grasp. In an instant, he used its butt end like a hammer to savagely smack his opposite first in the mouth and then again on top of his head. The usurper wound up flat on his back choking on his own teeth.

Gunter dropped the pistol and flopped into a chair. "What's that you are saying?" Gunter leaned over painfully and picked up his sword. He used the point to turn the last man's head toward the wall. He jabbed, just once.

"That's all of you then. Jesus. Just me and the cat. That was an eventful breakfast. I did *not* anticipate that. Well. Lord knows what Stoltz will think of all this. Hmmm."

Gunther hobbled about the house removing heavy coin purses from his victims. He poured the contents into a large glass jug, corked it and made his way to the outhouse. The shithouse sump was good and deep. The residents and their visitors had been working on filling it in for six months. The bottle sank promptly. Gunter was satisfied to walk away but noticed the blood trail he left on the outhouse floor.

It took quite a while to set the hut ablaze. Gunter sat for close to an hour as he watched the remnants collapse into the hole. Finally, he slowly shoveled the dirt pile back into the smoking grotto. Each shovel full was delivered a little slower than the last. When he was done, the ground was flat and no more churned than anywhere else in the courtyard. The labor and loss of blood created fantastic thirst. The dying swordsman crawled back to the manor and sat in the scullery drinking wine.

The cat meowed as it entered the room. "Yes, I should be going. No sense lying about here. Nobody left to feed you, little one. I fear you are on your own." Gunter looked out the window and up the hill to the snowcapped mountain and smiled. He should have seen the outhouse, but it was erased. Gunter pushed open the window and looked down from his mountaintop perch. The sun was up, and the misty cloud cover over the vast valley burned away.

The pistol ball hit did not penetrate, but it caused a nasty bruise that throbbed painfully. The knife wound continued to trickle, and he felt a creeping chill in his bones. Gunter shuddered hard several times and then convulsed. When his head cleared, he slowly picked himself up from the floor. The best he could do was rise to his knees. He slapped the table smartly. "All is lost!" he cried. "All is lost."

Gunter limped to the edge of the cliff and squinted as he looked up to the sun. He listened for a voice, but he heard none. He held out his hand with his palm up as if to feel the touch of God, but he felt only the fading sting of his numbing fingers.

He looked up and shouted, "No? Well, I didn't think so. Is it just me, or do you do this to everybody? I'll just sit here on the edge."

Gunter reached for his purse and produced his cherished Roman coin. He rolled it in his fingers and pressed it to his palm and then his lips. He made a wish for his soul then threw it as if he were skipping a stone on water. He emptied the rest of the small sack into the thin air. A paroxysm of pain shot through his body. His heart burned like the sun. Falling several thousand feet solved the problem in this world, though not the next.

Stoltz believed that the mint house had been robbed by a particularly brutal force and Gunter was thrown over the edge before they made off with the loot. He had no idea that every cent's worth was still there, waiting to be found two hundred and fifteen years later in the spring of 1890.

The new owner of the old Mint House valued the property for its altitude as he was an astronomer and mathematician at the University of Heidelburg. Over the following decades this scientific retreat became a proper home.

Horace and Lydia Huckbolt were the proud parents of a newborn son named Heinrich who grew up exploring the ruins of the antient redoubt. He imagined the battles that might have raged outside the walls that stood above the clouds. Heinrich raised goats. He became an avid hunter of alpine game. He wandered the mountain trails and fished in the lakes and streams. At first, time spent on the site was more like camping than staying in a second home. There was no septic system. They had to dig a latrine and build an outhouse to cover it. Periodically, a new hole was dug, and the outhouse was shifted to a new locale. By the time Heinrich was ten years old, he had seen this process a half dozen times. Eventually, the new latrine perfectly aligned with the one that made Gunter smile.

Horace found the digging to be an excellent source of exercise and didn't mind the chore one little bit.

"You are sweating pretty badly. Let me back in there, father."

"No, no. I need to do this. The payoff is a healthy heart. There is a lot of ash and rotted timber in here. Strange. We might be digging through some sort of old burn pile. Who knows what relics are down here."

"Do you really think so, father?"

"No. But isn't it fun to suppose so?"

"It would make a fine story."

Horace was an exceptionally strong man with a mighty swing. He sank his pick and felt something give way. He thought it odd but took another swing and there, again, the impact felt odd. The third swing confirmed that something mysterious was under his feet. Horace assumed he was about to open an unmarked grave.

"Oh bother! Son, get your mother. But you stay at the house until I call for you. Go!"

Horace switched to a spade and carefully spooned up the soil. He noticed shards of colored glass and the mouth of a jug. Then he hit the coins. He knelt, quite stunned, and slowly reached out for one of the tiny shiny spots in front of him. He spat on the disk and held it up to the light. Horace ran his pocketknife around the edge of the glass and worked quickly to exhume the jug. He sat in the hole with five hundred and twenty-one coins of various types and descriptions, most being gold, and only a smattering of silver.

Lydia trotted across the lawn in her long apron. "What is it, husband?"

"Oh, so sorry to alarm you. It is nothing at all! No treasure here."

"No treasure?"

"Not much treasure."

"My God! What have you found?"

"What? This?"

Later that night, Horace and his wife shared a bottle of champagne and swore their silence about the find, especially around young Heinrich.

Horace knew that, "If word of this gets out, there will be treasure hunters poking around. The government here might well claim it for their own as this place was an official mint."

"Horace," Lydia said as she poured coins from one hand to the other, "this is our treasure, and I shall never say a word about it. Ever, to anyone, including our son."

"Very well, then. I swear the same."

"Husband?"

"Yes?"

"I married better than I thought."

The Huckbolt family made annual pilgrimages to Paris and London where they sold a few coins to various collectors who paid well and begged for more. In one extended trip from Spain to Sweden, Horace sold the equivalent of forty thousand dollars' worth of coins. So long as Horace used the treasure gradually, people just assumed that the Huckbolts had always been well-to-do.

Horace and Lydia fell asleep that first wealthy night with coins all over their bed.

"Horace, wake up!"

"What is it?"

"Husband, it occurs to me that this jug may not be the only one in that hole. We should check for more before the boy rises."

"My God! How did that not occur to me? You are quite right."

Horace dug by lamp light. As dawn broke, he excavated an additional three feet. In so doing, he tripled his fortune by unearthing four smaller jugs, each one deeper than the last. He dug another foot before he gave up the quest.

Dirt was piled high around the brim of the excavation as Horace handed bucketloads up to his wife who dumped their contents quite close to the deepening pit. The fortune hunter used a wooden crate as a step so that he might get a leg up and climb out of the hole, but between the digging and his wife's piling of the dirt, he found himself a little short. This caused a dirt cascade that pinned him against the wall. In a flash the alluvium was up to his waist. He called out one time before the dirt grip around his diaphragm was absolute and he could make no sound.

"Horace! I'm coming!" Lydia cried. She set the down the lantern, grabbed the shovel, and leapt into the hole. She could see very little but instinctively plunged the spade within a millimeter of her man's frozen diaphragm. She pulled the dirt back, and again, by pure desire to save her husband, the spade sank precisely where she needed it, though she sheared off his shirt buttons. Horace got a hand free and was able to breathe again.

When the two were finally clear, they laughed and hugged each other. Then Lydia slapped her husband.

"I thought you were smart. This gold has nearly cost me my husband, already."

"So, you want me to put it back?"

They didn't.

Life thereafter improved significantly for young Heinrich. He had his father's genes and grew rapidly. For most boys, this led to high-water pants and ill-fitting shirts, but Heinrich's mother bought him fine new clothes regularly so that he always looked proud and proper. The only child also benefitted from a healthy diet of the best fruits and vegetables that were carted up from town at great expense. His husky frame and huge hands belied a boy who still played with toy soldiers. As a small child he lived too far from town to attend local schools, so he was home-educated with a strong emphasis on sciences and his father's other passion, reading and writing poetry. Various tutors were brought in to come and stay for a few weeks of intensive instruction in English, French, and Latin. His mother encouraged her son to play the cello. This he did badly, and his musical education was allowed to dwindle. Once Heinrich turned fourteen, he was sent to boarding school in Switzerland where he learned how to end a hazing by punching out his hecklers.

Heinrich attended university where he excelled in academics but generally failed in the social graces. He was an imposing fellow, and girls somewhat feared him. He avoided sport and dances in favor of laboratories and workshops. In fact, he would never marry, though he did have a love affair or two with women who were impressed by his money.

Living so far from town, the Huckbolt family rarely attended church services, and they didn't fit well in the pews when they did. Horace was prone to arguing about religion, so their absence was appreciated. This did not stop Horace from giving generously to the community. People tipped their hats to the Huckbolts.

Heinrich's father had one of the best and most massive telescopes in Germany. It cost the equivalent of a small house, and astronomers travelled from all over Europe to be his guest. He was invited to lecture in England, Austria, France, and Italy. As a teen, Heinrich accompanied his father on several of these trips as his assistant, and when he was not needed, he was encouraged to wander about the greatest of cities on his own. When associates asked Horace if he worried about his son wandering about, he replied, "You obviously have not seen him. He looks like a Golem."

The sixteen-year-old Heinrich stood six feet, five inches tall and weighed in at one hundred ninety pounds. He was not handsome, but neither was he ugly. He had a broad nose and steel grey eyes that made everyone wonder, "Where is that odd man from? I'll bet there is something in their water." The traditional military cut of his jib suited his demeanor. The lack of socialization with other children his age robbed Heinrich of a child's innocent geniality. He liked to debate and lecture even his elders. Oddly enough, though, he had his share of useful insights. The lad read constantly and liked to quote his favorite authors. He learned his celestial facts at his father's knee and was a master at reading the night sky.

The pivotal event in Heinrich's early life occurred one morning in June of 1900. He was on a hike up to the lake when he saw a massive shape pull free of the clouds. It was the first zeppelin, a silver, grey banana of a gas bag with a black open gondola below. The ships stabilizers and the rudder were far too small to have a significant effect on direction. The angle of attack was set by a weight which ran on a long clothesline-like cable that stretched beneath the craft from nose to stern. Sliding the weight forward brought the nose down and obviously the reverse was used to bring the nose up to help with any climb.

From Heinrich's point of view, the aircraft was no more than a thousand yards away and headed directly for the mountaintop that crowned the Huckbolt estate. The boy waved and shouted with glee as he was unaware of the death-defying situation unfolding over his head.

As one might expect, three of the four zeppelin crew were new to the whole idea of flying and panicked oh-so-slightly when the engine quit, and they lost control. They saw the looming mountaintop sure as hell, and they attempted to turn and climb but the ballast cable jumped the wheel and was stuck fast in the nose down attitude. They attempted to add power which caused the engine to sputter and quit. As the hapless crew attempted to revive the powerplant, they sailed into a cloud bank and caught a tail wind which increased their speed considerably.

Heinrich used the zeppelin's disappearance to run back home. He could see his father standing on the telescope deck. It was obvious that he saw the airship too.

When it broke free of the clouds, the proto zeppelin found itself unable to turn fast enough to avoid a collision. The pilots jettisoned everything, but it was not enough. They covered the last thousand yards in only minutes.

Horace stood agog on the balcony. "My God! It's going to crash! No! Look! It is turning. It's going down on the boulder field."

The zeppelin gently lighted on the massive rocks and bobbed in the breeze. Though nearly a mile away it still looked otherworldly. Horace used his antique captain's telescope to assess the calamity.

The crew threw everything that wasn't bolted down overboard. Two men climbed down a rope ladder and worked underneath the gondola to get their adjustable weight back on its wheels. Meanwhile, the other two crewmen coaxed the thirteen-horsepower engine back to life. A gust of wind pushed the airship up the rock face, and for a moment it looked as if it might be dashed. The ship found its keel, and once it righted it began to climb.

"They are coming up again," Horace yelled. "Hey! Look out there! Two men did not get back aboard. Saddle the horses. We must be the ones to fly now."

The two remaining crewmen coaxed full power from the engine. Having lightened the load by two men, the pilot was just barely able to perform one of the first aerial emergency maneuvers. With only a few meters to spare, the ungainly ship slipped over the jagged crest not to return. It would eventually make a safe landing some miles away. The crew kissed the ground.

Horace and Heinrich rode up the mountain as fast as their sure-footed beasts could carry them. The day was fading fast, and even in early summer, freezing overnight temperatures on the windy mountain face could kill exposed men. The crewmen followed the sound of their rescuers' voices and escaped the boulder field before darkness fell. The aeronauts were beyond grateful for their salvation and were only too happy to discuss their airship and how it was designed over a massive dinner with many bottles of wine and schnapps. Heinrich was sore impressed and decided in that moment that he would somehow be an aeronaut himself.

To Heir on the Side of Safety

Xavier Hollows was primed for the aristocracy in every way. Wealth awaited him whether he earned it or not. His home was assured. His future was set if he could survive the war. It was thought that he might be an industry liaison—his father's private problem solver and go-between. As such, he could wear the uniform of an officer and putt about wherever he wanted, unburdened with responsibility or the need to get too close to the front lines. Many of his chums had similar arrangements. Some sharpened pencils while others made real contributions that gathered no glory. These men were not cowards, but they were resigned to a nonviolent reality, and that was a sensation Xavier could not tolerate.

Xavier was resolute about joining the actual fight, though he was also unsure how he would react to combat. He read the casualty reports and knew many of the boys who were killed or had gone missing. He fully realized that going to the front lines was very likely a death sentence. He thought about a death by poison gas, a death by machine gun, a smiting by artillery shells that took limbs, and a good old-fashioned bayonetting in the guts was in there too. One also had to factor in being burned alive, buried alive, eaten by rats, killed by disease, and strangled by some German's bare hands. There was death by naval action, too. This was mostly a matter of simply being blown to pieces, though a good drowning in freezing water was always in the offing. The sinking ship sucks the swimmers down.

Lord Hollows informed his son by mail that he was to consider which branch of the service he preferred. "Yours will be some form of administrative duty. You might find a way to do some good."

The industry liaison idea seemed a natural fit. Xavier knew a great deal about the engines of the time, which enticed him toward solving the trench-crossing problem in the newest of weapons, landships. The cover story was that the metal boxes were for watering the troops. Thus, these water "tanks" would be of little interest to the enemy. The idea was made possible by the success of the Holt caterpillar track. The tractor that used them could cover uneven ground and bear a great deal of weight.

This tank followed its king home from war in France.
Note the side sponson cannons and rhomboid shape
meant to get it through wire and over trenches.

The First Tank Men

The landship idea fired Xavier's imagination. He and his father were privileged to have a look at "Little Willie" in late summer 1915. It was an unarmed, lightly armored box that was too small to cross trenches, and it liked to shed its treads, but it was an impressive test bed all the same. Sadly, Xavier realized that, unlike armored cars, landships would be agonizingly slow. A few months later, he saw the new rhomboid-shaped vehicle, which made sense from a trench-crossing point of view.

The wide gun sponsons on either side of the tank impeded railway transit and had to be retracted into the vehicle or removed entirely for delivery. A special wagon was developed to move these sections around. Reinstalling the two-ton gun pods was a tedious process. It took quite some time to prep the vehicles for an attack, making their discovery by reconnaissance aircraft a distinct possibility. They certainly left an obvious footprint. The element of surprise, on which so much depended, would most assuredly be lost over the days it would take to assemble the force.

The original tank's weapons layout was a homage to a low center of gravity. A turret perched above the rhomboid tracks made the vehicle top heavy and prone to roll, so it was ruled out in favor of gun sponsons on each side. The only way to fire the tank's weapons accurately was to stop while the gunners physically manhandled the six-pounder cannons or machine guns to aim them. The side-mounted short-barreled guns could only fire in a 90-degree arch. What made tactical sense for one gun team might be a disaster for the gunners on the other side of the same tank. Stopping to fire was an open invitation to receive fire, so gunners blazed away while on the move with little real effect. The maximum useful range for any of the First World War's tank guns was about two hundred and fifty yards.

Xavier knew that once buttoned-up inside the machine, heat would be overwhelming, if not dangerous, within minutes. Visibility would be severely limited, and the air would be completely foul from a lethal combination of carbon monoxide, shell fumes, and even the enemy's poison gas. Operating inside a tank wearing a gas mask would likely render crewmen almost useless.

The worst issue did not show up until enemy infantry actually began to shoot at tanks with their rifles. Their desperate bullets mostly bounced off on the outside, but inside, each hit launched spall fragments that could blind a crewman and cut him in a dozen places all at once. Bullets wheedled their way in between imperfect riveting and open cracks in the armor. Most of these were not fatal wounds, but someone would have to dig the fragments out of the crewmen's flesh after the battle. A machine gun that futilely sprayed the oncoming monster might not stop the beast, but sure as hell, the gunner was cutting the crew inside with hundreds of shards. Tankmen were forced to wear defensive leather garb and fine chainmail masks that made conditions hotter and further decreased visibility. After 1916, the average armor thickness increased by a staggering two extra millimeters to prevent spall and fend off German heavy rifles that fired armor-piercing bullets. Two millimeters doesn't sound like much, but it added twenty percent to the armor weight and strained the overburdened engines even more.

The first dedicated anti-tank rifle was nothing more than an enormous single-shot Mauser action infantry rifle. The sights were crude but adequate for their task. The weapon's kick was stout but by no means unbearable. Under stress, I doubt the gunner would notice the punch at all. It would be fairly easy to shoot off a track or pump rounds into the driver's position. Certainly, the rifle was enormous, but it was easy to move, and unlike an artillery piece on wheels, it could pop up anywhere.

The landship's issues seemed insurmountable to Xavier, and nobody wished to discuss problems in front of Lord Hollows, who was also disappointed by the three-mile-per-hour top speed. Xavier kept his own council but told his father privately, "These things couldn't race mother, or grandmother for that matter. She could likely beat one to death with her cane, too. I can't imagine how dull a race between landships might be." The idea that such a ship might need to dash away from the Hun's artillery or rush ahead to secure an objective never occurred to the dozens of men involved in the design. Xavier decided to sound the alarm.

Of course, in 1915, even the most farsighted military technologists had no inkling of what the tank would become or what its influence on world events would be. The tank would see many uses aside from simply crushing an enemy beneath its hungry treads. When put on display, tanks inspired people to buy war bonds. When it comes to suppressing the populace, tanks rule. Want to stop a run on the bank? Park a tank out front. Reference British armored vehicles on the streets of Ulster Northern Ireland, Soviet tanks in Prague, or the Chinese tanks that crushed the freedom uprising in Tiananmen Square.

In December 1915, with his father's blessing, Xavier Hollows, engineer consultant wannabe, invited several dozen high-level engineers, industrialists, and military men to his family's estate to discuss trench-crossing landships. Colonel Ernest Swinton attended the conference. He was a celebrity within the group as it was he who first lobbied for some sort of weapon that could safely cross the machine gun-swept no man's land and deliver a blow right on top of the enemy trenches. He hoped to prevent another battle of Ypres. Swinton had his champions in the government who presented his ideas to cabinet-level ministers. He even received direct support from the Minister for War, Lord Kitchener himself, and the First Lord of the Admiralty, Winston Churchill.

Lord Hollows and son, not yet in uniform, greeted the mixed flock of soldiers and industrialists as they entered the main dining room, where the dinner tables were cleared to make room for schematics. It was all very hush-hush. The servants were shooed away before the blueprints and drawings came out. Soldiers stood at every doorway.

Lord Hollows made a speech about winning the war with brains instead of blood. He waxed poetic about Colonel Swinton's vision and the engineers at work on Little Willie and Mother. He praised his son for having an eye on the future, particularly when it had to do with all things mechanical. In a prepared address, Xavier asked the audience to pardon him for not yet wearing a uniform. "Have no fear," he joked, "I am not weak in the loins!"

Xavier promised that he fully expected the uniformed upgrade any moment and he was immensely proud to serve in His Majesty's forces. Boarding school speech classes and essay writing prepared him for the event. He eloquently expressed his faith in England and the average Englishman, especially when it came to designing weapons of war. He praised the Navy in particular, which was heavily involved in landship development. The audience was delighted and clapped politely. He quoted Kipling, and there followed more polite clapping. Then, his tone changed as he expressed concerns with the landship designs that were already well underway to realization.

"We have come far in the past year in landship development, but there are challenges to be met, and all of them are urgent before we throw this invention into the breach."

Xavier began with several paragraphs on the landship's engine and its placement. The room began to murmur. The English are polite, but they do heckle in their own way. Comments that began with, "Surely you are not suggesting…" or "You have forgotten about…" came fast and even a little hot. The consensus among the audience was that the Hun would run like a jackrabbit when these giant weapons made their assault. Whatever their faults, there would be hundreds of these landships in an attack. Most would get through, and when they did, they would putter on to Berlin, and the war would be over.

"Imagine it!" the crowd harrumphed.

Xavier never lost his composure. He painted his responses by describing what would happen on the battlefield if these vehicles were not *rethought*. "Imagine," he insisted, landships bogging down on soft earth. Operations would depend to a great degree on the weather. "Rain and landships do not go together. It is not a springtime weapon." He went on to the track shedding problems that were fresh in everyone's minds. Xavier believed that the new machines would suffer engine failure or become mired in ubiquitous shell holes, as well as easily prepared obstacles that the vehicle commander could barely see in front of him.

"We have determined the length of the vehicle by the average width of the Hun trenches which our ships must cross. Too short, and they nose in. How long will it be before the enemy realizes that he needs to widen his trench a few feet? We shall either have to lengthen the ship, build a bridge on the spot, or perhaps drop in some sort of block that we might drive over." Xavier's finale did no favors with the audience.

"Worst of all, these huge machines will draw fire from all over the battlefield. Once the artillery finds the range, these tanks will be destroyed because they cannot move fast enough to escape artillery attack. The armor is not sufficient to withstand any sort of heavy shell. They shall be knocked out by light cannons or even heavy rifles. If I were to hunt an elephant, I would use an elephant gun. Within a matter of weeks, anti-tank rifles will flood the front. Imagine a large machine gun that fires tank-killing bullets that are about six inches long at five hundred rounds per minute. One gunner so armed might take down a tank fleet just as a Maxim gun takes down a regiment of infantry at a time."

"Then we shall thicken the armor and increase the engine power."

"And the enemy will up-caliber their weapons. Which side do you think can implement changes or introduce new anti-tank weapons faster? What will these weapons look like in ten years? What if the war doesn't end? What will a landship, a tank, look like in 1926? We need to get this weapon right from the start so that it will end all wars. Otherwise, it's just another arms race that nobody wins. Let these be the only Landships we shall ever need."

The room was silent.

Xavier had already stepped in it when he changed his tone again to describe his idea of the perfect vehicle. It was more of a tracked Rolls Royce armored car than a battleship at sail on land. It had a turret and was manned by three or four men, not eight. Swinton quipped, "Sounds like he's been talking to the Froggies at Renault!" This inside joke, delivered by the crowd favorite, brought the house down. People had to wipe their eyes; they laughed so hard. This reference to the French industry deeply insulted Xavier's father and sealed Xavier's fate as a liaison.

Lord Hollow's son learned that change is hard. He listened to Swinton's presentation with a smile on his face, but it was his practiced grin. He entered one line in his diary that night. *Weapons designed by the committee are never as good as those designed by a single diabolical mind.*

There was some lasting indignation that evening from the designers who saw Xavier as something of an upstart. Walter Wilson, on loan to Foster Industries from the Royal Navy, pulled Xavier aside. He was largely responsible for the tank that first bore his name, then "Big Wille," and finally "Mother," the rhomboid tank. He designed the transmission, and he worked on the tracks as well.

"Give us a little time, sir. I have ideas for a new gearbox and steering. Best not to oppose this one. It's going to smash the Hun."

"I do beg your pardon. I regret being so blunt. I do not oppose it as such. I simply call attention to deficits where I see them."

"Yes, well… Best leave it to us then. You are quite right about the logistics. It will take a thousand men and a million pencils to compute all that lot. Perhaps you might lead such an effort once you are in uniform. That was a fine joke about Renault. The French will never make a usable landship. Look, I am still grinning at the thought. Excuse me, sir."

Other presentations were made. There were to be male and female tanks. The male had cannon armament, and the female was all machine gun armed. They would mix two females with every male. There was some conjecture about a troop-carrying version. Xavier pictured the troops spilling out of the vehicle after breathing carbon monoxide for an hour. Landship crews would be known for their vomiting after a fight. Any infantry they carried would be completely debilitated and helpless in the face of the enemy.

Tactics were not discussed. What was there to say? It was assumed that the machines would simply roll forward behind a creeping barrage until they met resistance. The mammoth ironclads would either smash the wire or drag it away with chained grappling hooks. Of course, they would put down any machine gun nests. The infantry that the tanks covered across open ground would then sweep forward with the tanks in support firing away with battleship-like multiple machineguns and cannons. It was going to be spectacular.

Xavier's took some pride in the fact that his logistical questions were never answered, though it was admitted that supporting a fleet of landships was a potential nightmare that could kill the whole force without the Germans firing a shot. Fuel, ammunition, spare parts for tracks and engines, oil, lubricants, and, above all, trained men were needed in vast quantities to keep the assault moving. So far, nobody had done that particular math. Just getting a working vehicle into production was a Herculean task. They had no idea what it would take to keep one going over hours or days, let alone weeks. Tanks that penetrated enemy lines had to be resupplied and likely repaired in their forward positions, but no plans had yet been made to bring fuel and the rest forward over a bomb-cratered landscape. This downtime could affect the tempo of the assault. The Hun would have time to regroup, dig up some elephant guns, and counterattack.

There was tremendous confidence in the final product, though nobody was one hundred percent sure what that would be. Many design flaws had yet to surface, though, thank the gods of war; nothing as bad as the French experience occurred with the early British rhomboid designs that for all their faults still stood a good chance of getting through the wire and over a trench. Early French tanks were remarkably bad. They would go on to produce the most innovative tank of the war but early on, their designs fell easy prey to deadly and insidious *uneven ground*. They produced an assault gun whose shape and forward overhang guaranteed that it would go nose-down into any shell hole or trench and never come back out. Like a turtle on its back, the French tank was helpless.

Where Do Pilots Come From?

As for Xavier and the tank men, the evening was almost a bust. After everyone calmed down and more drinks were served, the mood changed along with the closed subject of armored vehicle design. As it turned out, even the tank men were inspired by knights in the air, and, of course, they all hated the dreaded zeppelin. Aerial technology was meteoric in comparison to landships. The post-prandial liquor and cigars portion of the event covered little else. The engineers marveled. At the outset of the war, pilots were throwing bricks at each other. Then, they tried to shoot each other with pistols and rifles. It took no time to move up to forward firing guns and speeds that broke one hundred miles per hour in level flight.

New aircraft designs were tested almost on a daily basis that offered more speed, more maneuverability, greater structural strength and literally, above all, better climb. Xavier knew where the action was both in terms of velocity and technology. He threatened to learn to fly on several occasions during his teenage years when most people saw the airplane as something of a fad. Xavier was a good listener who asked the pilots he met smart questions. He read about aeronautics, but the published works were quite thin on the subject. He built balsawood gliders, flew kites, and dreamed of a day when he would own a kite that could carry him to the clouds.

Even after his landship speech was shot to pieces, Xavier dared to comment about aircraft. This time, his observations won him a little respect with the engineers. He approached the subject from the mathematical point of view, emphasizing "ratios" and "wing chord," the advantages of the biplane or even a triplane, and the laws of physics that rule the sky. He mentioned various engines by manufacturer and compared the power they provided. He offered a comparison of in-line and radial types. Best of all, he managed to lace in an almost artistic reverence for the adventure of flying. He did not shy away from how easy it was to be killed above the clouds, but to fly…that was…the bravest man's calling. Pilots were God-like, if not short-lived.

It took a few years to reliably get up and down, but by 1910, the Wright brothers, Glenn Curtiss, and many others demonstrated the airplane's relative safety and usefulness as a reconnaissance machine. As a teenager, Xavier flew on two occasions. The first was when one of his boarding schoolteachers arrived on campus in a Wright flier. Like the famous 1903 Wright Flyer of Kittyhawk fame, this plane had no real fuselage. The two riders had seats of sorts on the lower wing. The tail was a tall but simple rudder, and the stabilizer was actually out front of the aircraft. Xavier was the first to go up for a circuit of the campus at a heady thirty-five miles per hour. A flying club popped up two years later near the Hollows estate. Xavier toyed with the idea of learning to fly and took an extended joy ride that flew high enough to see the entire Hollows estate at once. A series of accidents and crashes soured the Hollows family on flying. Xavier was forbidden any more aerial adventuring, but he was given a motorbike as a consolation prize. He was asked to wear his riding helmet when he zoomed up and down the driveway.

It came as no surprise when Xavier announced after the tank conference debacle that he was off to be a flyer. The life expectancy of a pilot at the front in 1916 was only a few weeks. The "Fokker Scourge" of 1915–16 ate men and aircraft at an alarming rate. Pilots were said to be members of The Twenty Minute Club.

Xavier's parents experienced something close to panic when they learned of his plans to join the Royal Flying Corps. Phone calls were placed. Notes were written and sent by courier. Strings were pulled, yanked, and, in some cases, replaced by the promises of a noose for anyone who put Xavier in an airplane.

The family physician told Xavier that he had an inner ear issue that would keep him grounded. Xavier secretly reported for his own physical. The Royal Flying Corps physician who examined him found no such problem, and they shared a huge laugh about the inner ear ploy. His physical examination was perfect and a matter of military record. Then there were numerous paperwork problems. Basic training dates were changed repeatedly. Officer orientation took an unusually long time to arrange. Xavier hand-walked his applications through for a posting to flight school at Doncaster Airdrome.

At first, Xavier met little in the way of headwinds. He took his basic training very seriously, and nobody was allowed to make the least allowance for his position. Officers constantly yelled at him. He even got kicked a time or two. Very refreshing. His strict boarding school experience served him well.

Leftenant Hollows got his lowly rank, but his wings were another matter. His flight instructor in primary training politely failed him in every way he could despite Xavier's obvious feel for the air. The teacher made no pretense of fairness to his pupil and told him plainly that he was under immense pressure to keep Xavier on the ground no matter how well he might fly.

So, what to do? Luncheon invitations were sent, and protocols were twisted. Xavier used his clout, and Poof! The base commander and Xavier's flight instructor found themselves sitting at a small table set with white linen on the edge of the airfield. A cook tent was erected nearby where other officers and ground crews were served beer and sausages, all ostensibly provided by the Hollows family. A fair crowd gathered. Three gentlemen from the press had a table of their own and a motion picture camera on a tripod set up to catch the likely lad's landing.

The Spy

Leftenant Hollows was the only man in military history who qualified for a batman (orderly) ten minutes after signing in for flight training. He simply appeared and announced his assignment. Xavier knew that once he was in the field, a batman would be a great help. First and foremost, he assisted with communications either as a runner or acting as a message center. Other duties were menial. He dug the officer's foxhole. He moved the officer's kit and maintained its security. He made sure that his officer always looked the part. He maintained the officer's latrine. He carried the officer's weapons and cleaned them. He even acted as a bodyguard. The man selected for the job was raised near Hollow's territory and knew all of the landmarks and family names quite well.

At first, Private Linus Rigby was unsure what to do with himself. Xavier was busy learning to fly and had no need of a butler, but a sort of military buttle went on that produced spotless uniforms and shining shoes. He kept an eye on Xavier's growing stash of contra-band, but most of all, he spied for Lord and Lady Hollows. (He was granted a house on the Hollows estate where his mother could reside.) It took a few days for the two men to get to know each other, but the common background, at least geographically, helped the relationship along. Xavier took a shine to the strappy young man.

As it turned out, Rigby's extended family had connections with what he called "secondary markets" for everything from meat to petrol. "Shall I do some shopping for you, sir?" Soon, Rigby handled most of Xavier's financial affairs and carried his wad of cash when he was in the field.

Xavier marveled at Rigby's ability to change his demeanor and accent to match the moment. He spoke in perfect Received Pronunciation while in his professional capacity, but this dropped away and was replaced by an intimidating London parlance when he barked orders on Xavier's behalf. He was a lady's man one minute and an introverted reader the next. Xavier overheard his batman tell off-color jokes. He liked to laugh. But if the vicar were present, his manners were puritanically perfect. No matter what his role, Rigby loved his King and took every opportunity to raise a glass and ask God to save Him.

Most importantly of all, Linus was the kind of servant who knew the flaws of his betters, and in his way, he helped the misbegotten officers in his sphere to be better leaders. He had an excellent sense of timing. He might chime in once a week, but when he did, it was memorable and useful. He had a wry wit when the captains were callous and a soft come-hither for any child they encountered. Trips behind the lines brought Major Hollows and Rigby face-to-face with starving and sickened children. Xavier made sure that Rigby left a virtual trail of treats whenever they saw tiny desperate faces. The little ones loved him, as did any dog that happened along.

Those officers who knew Rigby well understood that this batman was unusually insightful, and they actually respected him for it. He could also lay his hands on just about anything one might…need. This changed the servant-to-officer relationship. Later in the war, after Xavier was given his own command, Major Hollows fully backed his man. There were times when Rigby invoked Xavier's name to give orders that his officer never uttered. Rigby sometimes failed to remember these little "directions" which could put the clueless Major in a bind.

Rigby asked a favor, "Sir, we are about to move the mess tents to the new location, but we could use a few more men. Could the pilots and officers turn out for a few moments?"

"Move the mess tents? What?"

Rigby cleared his throat and sent "the signal" which was his left hand in his pocket and his right hand over his heart.

"Oh yes, I remember now. I did give that order. I think it is a rather good idea. Why is it a good idea, Rigby?"

"The men do not need to eat on the edge of the airfield. An S.E. almost ran right through the tent, sir. It was a minor miracle that nobody was hurt. You literally could wind up with an aeroplane in your soup."

Linus was one part advisor, two parts assistant, and the remainder was all entrepreneur. At any given moment, he could have declared his equality based on his ability to get things done, but he was too smart for that. Linus Rigby was a batman fit for modern war. Xavier needed a guide for the military and the seamier world, and Rigby was happy to oblige. He soon fell under Xavier's spell and confessed his duplicity. Xavier, in turn, admitted that he suspected the same and couldn't care less.

"I can't have a private for a batman, Rigby. I have put in a call, and we will have you made corporal, at least. Good Lord. Let us hope that this war will be too short to see you make officer."

Corporal Rigby took his commissary function seriously. He stood by with iced tea in a pitcher, and as he served, he listened in on the commanding officer's party. Xavier took off in a brand new Sopwith Pup scout plane. He performed over the airfield what in those times passed for acrobatics. This included various loops and rolls. He deliberately stalled the plane and recovered beautifully. He did touch-and-go landings on the field and even briefly flew inverted.

Colonel Franklin rolled with the antics. He turned to his subordinate, Captain Knox, and said, "Dear God! He is a showman. The press over there will wonder why he has no wings on his uniform yet."

Knox snorted, "The sausages are first-rate."

"You wrote that he is a disaster in the air. The paperwork for his washout is on my desk. Oh yes, they are delicious. It suddenly occurs to me that you are in on this."

"Sir, I know what I was told to do, and I did it. I washed him out, but *you* have to sign the paperwork. *I* will not. Sadly, he is a fine pilot. Quite fine, as you see. His classmates see what is going on, and I will say that they are all on his side, as am I, I'm afraid. They call him Tex for some reason, and he puts up with it. He shines through. Quite annoying under the circumstances. Plus, he gave me an enormous supply of tobacco."

"Which you will share with the men. Starting with me. Well, his loss would be a disaster for the country. I am told he is a very eligible bachelor. For our nation's women's sake, we cannot lose him over some simple mistake. He flies well for a man with only fifteen hours of training."

Knox shook his head. "He acts like he has been flying for his entire life. He has had some prior experience with aircraft, and he studied aeronautics. Do not forget that he is a college man, an engineer. He races automobiles and motorbikes. Speed does not scare him at all, especially when landing. We should recruit other pilots with similar interests. Even with all the motoring, he's never had a wreck. Not one broken bone. He looks over the aeroplanes he flies himself because he doesn't trust the ground crews. He is always teaching them things when he isn't giving them cigarettes. *He* gave *me* a lecture yesterday about the fabric we use to skin the frames. He believes that it will go sour after so many hours, and he wants to develop a detector so that we might test for loss of strength."

"A fabric tester? You must be joking. Is it a bad idea?"

"Actually, no. He is quite right to wonder about the fabric. If the war didn't take them so fast, the fabric might go bad. We should be using lightweight metal or wood venire, not doped linen to cover the airframe. The disaster will be when he crashes because of some damnable, unseen, or unknowable mechanical failure. It will not be a lack of skill or caution on his part. The weather will get him, or he'll simply fly too close to the sun. His type always does. It would be nice to keep him on the ground, British soil preferably."

Franklin took a philosophical tone. "He's flying between two worlds. Nobody will want him in their squadron. The commoners will resent the special treatment. I don't care what the military says, his type plays by a different rule book. He might be a superb pilot, but he does as he likes. No military discipline at all. Look where we are. Look what he is doing. We are literally gobbling it up."

"But what would you expect of a man with his advantages?"

"You mean with a father like his. How well do you think his father knows the king? Quite well, I should think."

Knox lit one of Xavier's cigarettes. "I dare not ask such a thing, but I have wondered."

Franklin seemed exasperated. "I had hoped for a little insight, but he never says a word about his family or his relationships. He never drops a name."

"Yes, I know. He just acts like he is on holiday every day. He always smiles when he salutes like he is amazed his hand can make the gesture."

"I have noticed that. It's annoying and disarming at the same time."

Xavier climbed high over the field and into the sun. The spectators lost him for a moment, but his engine's rattle and whine grew louder as he headed for the deck. Knox looked worried. "Oh dear God, I wish he wouldn't dive like that! See how he pulls out? He began that right away. Very gradually. He has the measure of it, the angles. He just needs practice and a good dose of tactics. I will say that he has yet to show that keen hunter's spirit. Most of the men talk about the killing. They all want to get right to it. This one. He never mentions it. He's a fine pilot, but without that willingness to mix it up, he won't last any longer than anyone else at the front."

"Fine pilot and a fine table. Where *does* he find this fare? We can't just eat his vittles and then ground him. So, to sum up then, everyone knows that he is a superb pilot. He has the cameras here to prove his point. If I wash him out, he will just commandeer an aircraft and say send the bill to my father. Probably go off and fight the war by himself. Well, we shall have to slow him down some other way. Our young Hollows may be a better pilot than the two of us put together, but he is no match for military bureaucracy. I have conceived of a plan for just this contingency. I shall discuss it with Lord Hollows, but I am certain he will approve our next move. This is chess, and winning means keeping our Lord Hollows off our chicken necks."

Xavier ended his one-man air show with a very tight circle of the type he might have to pull in combat with a Fokker. The camera crew was up and running as he landed and taxied near the table. He dismounted his aircraft, removed his flight gear, and laid it neatly on the wing. He paused to run a comb through his hair and straighten his tunic before he marched over and came to attention at the very table he had set himself. The commanding officer traded salutes and then offered his outstretched hand.

"Yes, yes. Hollows. Damn you, I'll sign. You have your wings. You can call yourself a pilot in the Royal Flying Corps. Very amusing, all this. Wipe that smile off your face. You strain military courtesy with this sort of antics. Lucky for you that those sausages were so damn good. I'll hear about this too from your father and, worse still, from your dear mother. Pack your bags. It's off to advanced training for you with the rest of your class. That's another sixty hours in the air. Do be careful; I pray for you. These young pilots go down all the time. It was a roll of the dice to get you through this far. Once that lot is complete, I believe that you will be sent on a factory tour. It would seem you have some skills with these airframes and engines. Fly all the aircraft. Study them. Maybe you can help design the next models."

"Sir, as you well know, I wish to fly in combat. I have tried the industrial angle. No good at it, I'm afraid."

"See here, Hollows, all these antics of yours won't do at the front because there are no sausages, and soldiers up there already get all the cigarettes they want. Your father won't stop German bullets for you. You will distract the other pilots. You might get men killed. There, I have said it. But it needed to be said. The Flying Corps is not some posh club anymore. Surely, you have noticed your fellows here are common men. It's a physical issue, not one of character. Never was. Your squadron mates are shopkeeper's sons, not your chums from the polo team. This isn't some sort of ridiculous foxhunt. Leading them might not be so easy. As for the rest, rubbish. I am told you are an engineer. Your instructor here said that you wax on endlessly about these aeroplanes. You'll have a great deal to contribute. Think about it."

Franklin leaned in and put an arm around the young man's shoulder for a private comment.

"Well, Hollows, damn you, I see your consternation. I respect it too. You are obviously a fine lad for a lord-in-waiting. Consider this. You've got your wings, and you are on your way. You are doing very well against what I consider to be a serious headwind. Honestly, I am amazed you ever got off the ground. Try not to be a show-off in advanced training. That is what gets men killed. When you finish, you will be offered an opportunity to take the foreign aircraft factory tour. Keep an eye on what the French designers are up to. You speak perfect French, I am told, and you have an affinity for these kites. Think of what flying all their designs will do for your flying. They test new aircraft *near* the front, but I must stress that you should stay out of combat. Your family wishes this so, and command sees fit to comply with your father's desires. Bad enough that you have those wings. Do be careful up there, won't you?" He then muttered, "Still, being so close to the front... Perhaps you can taste it without being *formally involved.*"

2:14 a.m., 15,000 Feet,
Twenty-Eight Miles North of London

Captain Rahl Fausmann lacked Xavier's aristocratic swagger, but he more than made up for it with military vigor. His heart swelled with pride every time he flew a successful mission in a zeppelin. Most of these were reconnaissance missions and bomb runs over Paris, but as the war progressed and anti-zeppelin tactics developed, it was no longer practical to use zeppelins to attack such targets. That is, unless the weather conditions were perfect for an attack with low cloud cover. Zeppelins had to fly higher and higher to survive. The Germans literally rose to the challenge with zeppelins so large that they could lay claim to being both the largest and, for that size, the lightest weapons of all time.

"I hate this dead reconning! We'll get no help from the radio, either. They are working on it, but I am not hopeful." Leutnant Huckbolt snarled, "The damned British have blacked out the entire country. We *should* be over the Thames, but I can see nothing below us. The clouds that shield us tonight blind us as well. Kapitan, I recommend that we descend the ship to seven thousand feet, drop the spy car and attempt to get a fix on our location."

The captain pulled his navigator aside. "What are you saying? Are we approaching London or not?"

"We cannot know from this altitude. I need some reference. We have been drifting since we crossed the channel, but I cannot tell how badly. We are so high…the winds have us. We need to take the ship down."

"Drop any lower, and we will be subject to their aeroplanes and anti-aircraft fire. We must not unduly risk the ship."

"That is my point, sir. We can't see much down there, but sure as hell, there are no searchlights. Not below us or even in the distance. In truth, I suspect that we are over open country far to the north of London."

"One incendiary bullet is all it takes, Huckbolt. We bomb from up here."

"We don't know if we are killing cows or people. It is a waste of bombs! We must descend!"

Fausmann eventually relented, and the spy car was lowered with Huckbolt in it. The prone observer barely fit. He was tossed around inside by turbulence and quite unable to use his binoculars. Eventually this settled down to a dull thump or two every few seconds, distracting when one thinks of the fact that a slender cable is all that connects the observer to the mother ship. The world remained black and indefinite, though Huckbolt could make out some contours that did not remind him of tall buildings. His optics were excellent, some of the best in the world, but they showed him little he could use. There were a few dim lights. Here a house, there a cluster of houses. He spied for twenty minutes and found nothing useful. Then, a door opened someplace thousands of feet below and light-filled a driveway as a car with head-lights on pulled onto the road.

Dr. Oarsman was ten years past retirement and a little tipsy but still willing to take his black bag and make a house call. He knew everyone in the county and had seen most naked at birth, death, and various impositions in between. He was supposed to have one headlight blacked out and the other hooded, but the thought that he might attract enemy attention was so absurd that he never completed the work on his vehicle.

There were no other cars on the road for Huckbolt to track. Just one. That alone told him that they were nowhere near London, and the spy car ride was for naught. Huckbolt watched the vehicle and wondered what the driver would do if he realized that a monster was following him like a hungry prehistoric shark in the water. The car came to a stop. Oarsman's headlights reflected off train tracks. Huckbolt thought all roads (or, in this case, rails) lead to Rome. He consulted his compass and hit the retrieve button.

Fausmann followed the new heading at fifteen thousand feet for half an hour. Without using the spy car again, and over Huckbolt's strenuous objections, he salvoed his bombs and wrote in his logbook, "1:17 a.m. Struck London. Glory to the Fatherland!"

Huckbolt's diary read: 1:17 a.m. Bombed England, somewhere, from ten thousand feet.

The following morning, Huckbolt asked for a transfer. And as it happened, a group of officers were looking for just such a man…someone good but expendable to fly a one-way supply trip to East Africa.

By early 1916, the British produced effective countermeasures to the zeppelin problem. For London's defense, they placed anti-aircraft guns all along the likely avenues of approach. Zeppelins also had to overfly many airfields that bristled with defensive aircraft. For a while, the lighter-than-air ships were safe from these planes, but as aircraft ceilings improved, zeppelins had to soar even higher to be safe. Hypoxia became an issue for pilots and crew who carried no oxygen. Temperatures at such dizzying heights start off at Arctic winter frigid and drop from there. Zeppelin crews had their heated suits that lasted only so long as the generators worked. Once the engines quit, so did the suits. The Germans quickly developed oxygen tanks with long hoses so the airship crews could move around in the cabin. There were no masks at first. Oxygen hoses were fitted with a tobacco pipestem to grip with the teeth.

Fausmann had some influence with his superiors and advocated for high-altitude attacks. Even from twenty thousand feet, London itself was tough to miss. Fausmann boasted that he would find a way to make it memorably destructive, but it was his former navigator who made this a reality.

The British SE5a with Sopwith Camel in the background.

British Airfield, France, Spring 1918

In January of 1918, Major Xavier Hollows of the Royal Flying Corps was twenty-five years of age. He was by all accounts an excellent pilot pulled from research and development duties to run a frontline depot for aircraft and the warriors who would man them. In his two months at the front, he notched up three observation balloons and confirmed seven enemy aircraft. Three of these were two-seater types with deadly rear gunners. The other four were versions of the Albatross and a single Fokker triplane that wasn't painted red. It was so well camouflaged that Hollows thought his eyes were playing tricks on him when he first saw it. He had a superior altitude that he could trade for speed and the sun was conveniently behind him. Rather than aiming at the entire aircraft, he picked the pilot as his target. He fired a one-second burst from both of his guns at less than one hundred yards. The DR-1 flipped over and crashed. The entire engagement, from sight to fireball, took less than thirty seconds.

Hollows was a good officer who understood his purpose and tried to work with every pilot who passed through his command either to the front and combat or to the rear and home. The new men were over-eager and in need of a seasoned guide. The experienced pilots were often emotionally broken but had excellent insights about logistics, tactics, and training that command needed to hear if not for this war than for the next.

The single most important factor was to have superior altitude. Xavier practiced climbing into thin air above twelve thousand feet and even much higher until his engine sputtered, and he felt his extremities begin to tingle. Otherwise, when outnumbered, he harassed the enemy where he could. He hit and ran like hell and resisted the urge to hang about and confirm the planes he sent down. Even without kills to show for it, simply surviving these furious encounters was a hard-won thing. Twisting gunfights often started at ten thousand feet and ended at treetop level when both combatants ran out of bullets or their gas tanks were empty.

Hollows survived a ramming attack that narrowly missed taking a wing. The German's guns had jammed, or he was out of ammunition. Either way, he wasn't giving up. He could see the grimace on the German pilot's face as he rolled over the enemy plane and wound up less than ten yards behind it. His Vickers gun killed the pilot and his engine with the same twenty-seven bullets.

Major Hollows used his broad experience with aircraft to test tactics. He was vitally concerned with just how much stress an airframe could take in a dive without shedding a wing or two. During a dogfight, part of his analytical mind remained detached, and he observed what the German planes could and did not want to do, especially how tightly they could turn and how quickly they could roll. He saw an Albatross fighter shed its wings during violent maneuvers as it tried to evade Hollow's approach. He questioned other pilots about their encounters with the German type and summarized his findings in a letter which Rigby distributed to British and French designers he met along his rise to command. These epistles were enthusiastically received, and invitations followed that command would only be too happy to grant. Hollows passed on the opportunity so that he might remain in action.

Most pilots were taught how to fly a specific aircraft. While they might be able to generalize their knowledge and fly anything in existence at that early point, few pilots lived to get the chance. Xavier flew several types of planes prior to and in combat, including the Sopwith Pup, the Sopwith Camel, the S.E.5, and the new S.E.5 "a" version of biplane fighter that was the pride of British aviation. He flew the Bristol F.2 two-seat fighter and practiced dropping bombs on the factory range, though accuracy was universally poor, not just for him, but for everyone.

Prior to his frontline posting, a fresh-faced and eager Captain Hollows flew the Royal Naval Air Service (British) Triplane and a float-equipped Sopwith seaplane. He thought the triplane with its narrow chord wings was remarkable but under-gunned. The experience helped him months later when he first encountered the German Fokker DR-1 triplane in action. He avoided the turning fight and instead chose to use his superior speed to dive away and gain a little separation. He used his momentum wisely and pounced on the triplane twice without giving the maneuvering enemy dancer a chance to fire back. The fight was a draw but formulaic for what was to come.

As for seaplanes, Xavier thought them romantic but admitted that he did not relish navigating over open water or landing on a moving surface. He did it once and pronounced himself over-practiced. He flew a Handley Page bomber which needed every inch of airfield to get airborne even when unladen. God help the pilot who lost an engine not just on takeoff but at any point in the flight. Other than just prior to combat, this was the only time Xavier actually felt fear in the air.

Captain Hollows accepted an assignment to tour a French aviation factory where he examined their production techniques in detail. Xavier was something of a celebrity in the press. Cameras followed him through several test-flights in the latest Newport and Spad scout planes. Xavier was impressed with their performance. The French offerings became a secret benchmark that Xavier held for all his mounts. In a press interview, he pronounced French aviation to be a good match for the Americans. The French press and military in attendance looked stunned to receive such praise, but after a heartbeat, they applauded enthusiastically. Hollows admitted to being extremely impressed with French aviation and the amazing products of their war industry.

Xavier also fired a French automatic rifle called the Chauchat, which rattled away reliably despite looking cobbled together on a plumber's bench. It was hoped that one man in ten might be armed with such a weapon. His report on French weapons also included considerable detail on the French two-man tankette made by Renault. He concluded with:

> *While there were those in British Industry who laughed at French tank designs, there is no denying that their two man tank is revolutionary. The Germans will not find them amusing at all.*

Great Mistakes: The One-Man Turret

The French Renault Model FT was a modern tank executed by a seasoned but well-beaten military-industrial complex. It was the first to have the now familiar modern layout with the driver up front, a turret in the middle, and the engine in its own compartment behind. It weighed seven tons and had armor thick enough to defeat small arms, some anti-tank rifle fire, and most artillery fragments. The frontal armor was quite thick for its day and double that of the Mark 1 tank fielded by the British only a year or so prior. The FT had sprung suspension, though it could only do about five miles per hour across rough country. It was an odd-looking contraption with massive front wheels that were actually made of laminated plywood and a trench-crossing extension referred to as a tail. With the exception of the British Mark A Whippet, no other tank could match it for maneuverability. Yes, the French made the best tank of the war, at least from a World War One perspective. It was the right starting point for every tank that clanked along thereafter.

The FT would be known postwar as the FT-17. American forces operated the type and were commanded by none other than George Patton. He left the comforts of the command post to personally direct and lead his tankers on the battlefield under fire. He did this at Saint-

This is a postwar FT-17 tank with some sort of mockup for the main gun. It shows the now standard layout of driver in the front, the flawed one-man turret amidship, and engine at the rear. A German anti-tank rifle (A 59) would be hard-pressed to stop this vehicle firing from head on. AAF museum, Danville, VA.

Mihiel and again at Meuse-Argonne. He knew what he could ask of the new tankette type because he had been to the factory where they were produced. He studied them in fine detail and was deeply steeped in fledgling tank terminology. He even authored influential papers on the subject. Patton managed to get himself shot in the leg or ass—depending on who one reads—while leading tanks in action. Reports make him sound almost delighted to have been winged. One would think that he was in a tank, but it is my understanding that he was exposed on foot.

Patton commanded tanks with full traverse turrets that mounted either a small cannon or a machine gun. It was, however, a one-man turret, so the tank commander had to detect the enemy, load the cannon, aim the gun, and then observe the fall of the shot. This is disorienting in the supreme and leads to low situational awareness that will positively get you fragged on the battlefield. So long as the tankettes operated like a swarm of insects, they provided each other mutual support as they advanced. Dividing them up among infantry units breaks this strategy. The one-man turret is largely responsible for the pitiful performance mounted by French armored forces in World War Two. It was a war-losing mistake that the French did not make alone. Many nations fielded tanks with one-man turrets, particularly in the light or tankette class such as the Japanese Type 95. Patton's exposure to fire was essentially caused by his attempt to be the second man in every one-man turret. He was doing the reconnaissance and target spotting for the entire fleet coming along behind him.

French tank designers never realized the one-man turret deficit, and so, between the wars, they made a plethora of two-man tankettes. They were relatively speedy and small targets that might have done well in the infantry support role against Panzer I and Panzer II tanks of the same class. Their SOMUA tank was splendidly armored and mobile. It was in many ways the best in its class, but that one-man turret slowed everything it might do. An infantryman knew that if the French tank was firing, its commander was not watching his ass. As it was, the French fought badly against Czech-made Model 38(t) tanks with two-man turrets and some Panzer III and IV tanks with modern three-man turrets, which were still in short supply. Yes, in the most common tank, the 38(t), the German commander had to load the gun, but the rest of the time, he was looking around the battle space while his gunner was doing the deed. So remember, armor thickness and firepower are good, but that second, or even better, third man in the turret is everything. I'll take a third brain and set of eyes over an extra armor plate any day.

The tank commander should have a good cupola with 360 degrees of view. He should also have a radio tuned to the platoon net. Heinze Guderian, Panzer Leader and victor in Battle of France, well understood these basic needs and equipped all his tanks with radios and a fifth crewman to man the complex set. The French had very few radios and relied on dispatch riders and telephone lines for communications. These methods often broke down, leading to battlefield paralysis at worst and slow reaction times at best.

During the First World War, tank commanders viewed the world through vision slits and gunsight apertures. They had a few periscopes with armored glass. German infantrymen were drilled to aim for the vision ports, and every once in a while, they got bullets right through. Down goes the commander or driver. A rifle bullet could stop a tank, and with a couple hundred soldiers firing, someone was bound to get lucky.

Tankers signaled other tanks with flags that must have been impossible to see through smoke and the ejecta of a battle. Messages to the rear echelon were sent by carrier pigeons. Long-distance communications were obviously one-way and super iffy. Inside the tank, communications were little better. There was no interphone. The eight crewmen shouted and used hand signals to be understood over the engine noise, creaking tracks, and gunfire. Do not forget that all eight men in that small space were reacting to things that no other man could see. The four gunners and the commander were all yelling about separate targets, threats, obstacles, friendly troops, braking, and calls for ammunition. Each side of the tank was in its own fight. The brakemen had it the worst as they stood at the back of the vehicle listening for orders yelled from the commander and driver, who did not face them, and they might not have been able to see.

The first tanks were hideous for their crews and not much more than a nuisance to the enemy. They pushed the Germans back at Cambrai, and at times they achieved some local successes, but as Lord Hollows predicted, the Tank's shock value was quickly lost, and their potential was often squandered due to lack of vision and the limits of their technology. The lessons taught in World War One were only half-learned by the weapons designers who toiled mightily between the conflicts.

British Aircraft Development Late in World War One

Major Hollow's "S.E." (Scout Experimental 5a) wood and fabric biplane scout was more heavily armed than the machine gun-carrying FT tankette. Its *two* machine guns were both .303 caliber and were easier to load than the French Hotchkiss machine gun used in the FT, which fed from stripper clips of thirty rounds. He could also carry a light load of bombs. The belt-fed Vickers gun fired through the propeller disk and used an improved interrupter mechanism. The gun itself was semi-recessed, which offered better streamlining. The weapon's muzzle seems to point a few degrees high as if someone made an installation mistake, but this is intentional. The extra elevation allows the pilot to get a few extra degrees of lead when he is pulling a tight circle behind a defending aircraft.

A secondary Lewis gun was mounted above the top wing on a Foster-railed mount that allowed the pilot to change the pitifully small forty-seven-round pan magazine without standing in the cockpit. He could draw the weapon with its pie pan magazine down on a track to windshield level right in front of his face. The muzzle in this position pointed more or less straight up, and the weapon could be fired from this setting quite effectively. This tactic was deadly against early German bombers, which had little in the way of protection from directly below.

This reloading system was nearly suicidal to use in combat as the pilot had to cease maneuvering and looking about for danger to focus on the gun. Changing magazines while wearing heavy gloves required practice. A fumbled magazine on the cockpit floor could interfere with peddles and cables. Toward the end of 1916, a larger magazine that held ninety-seven rounds was developed for aircraft use. Hollows had two spares, both forty-seven round pans. The easy grab was over the instrument panel. The other was under his seat and a measure of last resort. It is up to the reader to decide if having the ability to fly under a target and shoot upward is worth the trade of a second Vickers gun.

Early German scout planes had an initial advantage over their British and French adversaries when they fielded the Fokker Ein Decker, a single-seat monoplane with forward-firing single or paired Spandau machine guns. These weapons only fired when the propeller was clear of the muzzles, a miracle made possible by what was called an inter-rupter mechanism tied to the engine itself. Fokker gets all the credit for this invention, but several inventive engineers from Russia, France, and elsewhere were all working on the problem. The British were inex-plicably late to the interrupter party with such a system of their own and resorted to pusher prop aircraft with the engine behind the pilot so that they might fire straight ahead.

Just a brief aside to mention that last bit again. Would you pilot an aircraft that has a whirling Cuisinart food processor right behind you? Lost your hat? Don't reach back for it. It just got shredded anyway.

A Lewis gun could be mounted in the nose of the pusher engine airplane or even set on a pedestal so that a resolute gunner could fire in just about any direction so long as he didn't mind standing up while in flight. While the Lewis was in widespread use as an observer's weapon, or a secondary gun mounted above the wing, the mechanism prevented use with interrupter gear.

Aiming the machine guns was still a primitive matter with open sights consisting of a large ring sight and post that had to be aligned while the pilot's eye was perfectly square behind the gun. The British produced an excellent scope like the ALDIS gunsight, which was fitted in the center of the windscreen. Using this apparatus, the pilot could aim with both eyes open and with his head at any angle behind the unit. He had only to put the enemy in a large circle to see if it was in range, lead the target, and fire.

Pursuit planes of that time were made basically of spit and tissue paper with no armor to protect the pilot or other vital areas of the airframe. Thus, most hits passed right through the target without doing much damage. A hit to the engine or the bracing and struts that held the wings in place was another matter.

Early machine guns were often less than reliable. The Maxim and Vickers mechanisms were essentially identical, heavy, and sound. They were among the most successful small arms ever designed. From a statistical standpoint, when we consider how many rounds these weapons successfully fired during the war, they rarely ever jammed.

Machine guns of this era used cloth belts that swelled when exposed to moisture. This could jam the mechanism. Another culprit behind so many malfunctions was poor quality control of the ammunition itself. Underpowered rounds, dented cases, and faulty primers ended many a dogfight. Pilots could do little to clear a malfunction other than recock the guns and hope for the best. If a case was stuck in the chamber, the pilot was out of the fight. Some popular films about World War One fighting planes show pilots hammering the weapons in an attempt to beat them back to life. Much like whacking your old-timey TV to get better reception, I cannot see how this might help.

The worst thing that could happen in the swirl of a dogfight was to shoot off one's own propeller due to interrupter gear failure. This is thought to have killed the very man who is wrongly credited with the first use of the mechanism in combat, Max Immelmann. In fact, the first German pilot to shoot down a British aircraft by firing a machine gun through the prop blades was Leutnant Kurt Wintgens on July 15, 1915.

Immelmann and Boelcke are the most famous of the early fighter pilots. Their intense competition to be the best of the new breed captivated the German public. Immelmann eventually shot down fifteen enemy planes. He was clipped by a French pilot on June 3, 1915, but he skillfully made a dead stick landing behind his own lines to walk away without a scratch. Later, he managed to shoot off his own propeller when his interrupter mechanism failed. He deftly handled the emergency by shutting down his engine before the vibration could shake his delicate kite apart, and again, he made a dead stick landing.

Immelmann participated in extensive testing of the interrupter mechanism. Attempts were made to put up to three Spandau guns on an Eindecker monoplane. Testing this array led to two more dead stick landings when, yet again, the propeller was shot away and the engine lost its balance.

The Germans cite either interrupter mechanism failure or ground fire for Immelmann's death on the 18th of June 1916. The British, on the other hand, credit George Reynolds McCubbin with Immelmann's loss. The lethal attack was a classic pounce from above as Immelmann was in a turn that would become synonymous with his name. McCubbin would later state that it was his burst that took off the German's propeller blade. The wreckage was so bad that Immelmann could only be identified by the initials on a handkerchief found in his pocket.

Two-seat observation planes and bombing aircraft often mounted a rear-firing defensive machine gun or even a mated pair of guns operated by the observer. Scoring hits during violent, swirling aerial skirmishes must have been exceedingly difficult for the rear gunner. Larger bombers such as the Gotha and British Handley Page bombers had to fly straight on and take it as they were hugely underpowered and aerodynamically clumsy. They did have two or even three dedicated gunners, and when they flew in tight formation, the concentrated defensive fire was dangerous from any angle except below. Late in the war, German designers solved the underside blind spot problem on their Gotha bombers by creating a conelike tunnel under the rear fuselage and mounting another machine gun to cover whatever field it could manage. The crew remained a nose gunner, a pilot, and a rear gunner who had to jump back and forth between an upper and lower gun.

British observation balloon crew wearing an early parachute harness. Note how they designed the leg braces. This man holds his parachute tether as there was no rip cord until the mid-1920s.

Early Parachutes

All aircrews were in an equally dangerous situation as virtually none of them had parachutes. The technology did exist, and as mentioned, parachutes were in use by observers floating helplessly beneath observation balloons. They were more difficult to deploy for scout plane pilots. Early parachutes were very bulky and did not mate up with a pilot's seat. Picture wearing a small square suitcase on your back that fits into a recess where the back of your seat should be. In an emergency, one had to fight inertia and lean forward enough to clear the back of the cockpit with the parachute box just begging to hang up the pilot. This seems like a simple fix. The incentive was there, but development was slow. A few successful parachute exits were made, but pilots faced being burned to death, eating a pistol bullet, or leaping to their fate right through the end of the war.

The real hindrance in issuing these life-saving devices was a matter of esprit de corps. It was thought that pilots might well choose to use the parachute rather than fight to the last bullet. The Germans issued a parachute system on a limited basis in 1917. Ernst Udet used one to save his skin so he could thoroughly foul up the Nazi Luftwaffe in the next war. His incompetence was so bad that he committed suicide. Whoever folded and packed his parachute did the whole world a favor.

Udet was a Nazi Party national treasure, but completely out of his depth as an organizer and industry leader. That being said, he understood the reality of the strategic situation and gave his boss, Herman Göring, strong warnings about the rapidly growing power of the Soviet Air Force. In fact, Udet realized that Germany was falling behind in aircraft production. Göring gambled that the war would be over so quickly that any Soviet advantages would not materialize in time to save them. He did *not* pass Udet's sage observations along to Hitler, and when things went badly for the Luftwaffe, Göring actually blamed Udet.

Whenever Hitler wanted to string Göring up, Udet took the hit, but the old ace was so publicly loved that he never quite lost his job. The stress that caused must have been unimaginable. Göring always tried to make up with his old friend with lavish parties and hunting trips, but Udet visibly withered. Eventually, he shot himself while on the phone with his girlfriend. That's the act of a man who wants someone he trusts to hear his final truth. I am certain it began with, "You can tell that fat fuck, Göring to..."

Of course, this was hidden from the German public. It was put out that Udet died at the controls of an experimental aircraft. In reality, at least before he joined the Nazi Party, he was a respectable and fearsome combat pilot who survived one of the earliest parachute escapes in combat. Even better, the story goes that his parachute became entangled on the tail of his stricken plane. One wonders how he escaped that one. Observers said that the silk didn't properly bloom until he was less than three hundred feet from the ground. It was a narrow escape, but it saved a veteran pilot who would claim a total of 62 kills.[21]

Early parachutes were heavy and thought to reduce aircraft performance. Sure, in experiments, they worked most of the time if you had the altitude and the harness held together, but a full third of jumps from aircraft were unsuccessful. There must have been fifty reasons why, beginning with the complete absence of parachute training. Pilots were not briefed on how to roll on landing. One learned it on the job, or one didn't.

The pilot was more tethered to the aircraft than the parachute, which was either in a tube behind the pilot or later in a pack that he sat on. There was no ripcord until the mid-1920s. Some of the earliest parachutes were packed into what would appear to be a garbage can lid which was suspended under the aircraft where it created a lot of drag. This was fine for an observation plane but a nonstarter for combat aircraft.

It was hoped that the lack of a parachute would *incentivize pilots* to get every plane home that they could. Max Immelmann won an Iron Cross for nursing a badly shot up plane back to German hands. The British and Americans resisted the parachute until September 1918. The reluctance on the part of Britain can be traced to a report of the Air Board: "It is the opinion of the Board that the presence of such an apparatus might impair the fighting spirit of pilots and cause them to abandon machines which might otherwise be capable of returning to base for repair."[22]

Rather than jumping, the best fighter pilots sought every advantage they could find and thought nothing of fine-tuning their aircraft

---

21. The highest scoring ace to survive the war was Rene Fonck who downed 73 planes.
22. Ralph Barker, *The Royal Flying Corps in World War I* (2002).

themselves. This usually took the form of improving speed by lightening their mounts. This suited Hollows. Before the war, he fancied automobiles and motorbikes. While the rest of his family was at the stable with the new roan or chestnut racehorses, he was in the carriage house disassembling a motor car or tractor engine. He was entirely self-taught and known to take a motor down to the bits and get it back together without schematics or professional assistance.

How Xavier Became a Texan

Back in those days in the Hollows household, like aristocrats sometimes do, nicknames were lovingly bestowed or approved by the patriarch and matriarch. Major Xavier Hollow's family nickname began with "Tinker" because, as a toddler, he was constantly drumming on anything he could find, particularly steel pots in the kitchens. It was his father who first called him "X" for short. As he grew, X began to race on motorbikes and, later, actual automobiles. He developed a racer persona around his boarding school friends, who called him Tinker X.

Xavier's beloved younger sister, Beatrice, had a serious speech impediment and rarely spoke. She had no difficulty whatsoever in saying her version of this alias: *Tex*. This name, ultimately, was the one that stuck, yet virtually nobody understood the true origin of the playful monicker. This annoyed Xavier, which delighted his friends who chided him endlessly. It even resulted in a Stetson hat that still resides under glass in the Hollow's estate library. The exhibit is accompanied by a twisted wreck of a Lewis machine gun and a battered black-and-white photograph that Xavier carried in his wallet throughout the war. It is a picture of Beatrice taken in his workshop when she was perhaps ten years old. She beams in her assistant role with goggles on her head and a grease gun held between two man-sized work gloves.

Hollows was a fair artist and painted a large B with goggles and pigtails behind the cockpit of his personal aircraft.

Like most British aviators of that time, a newly promoted Leftenant Hollows honed his aerial maneuvering skills during advanced training in the Sopwith Camel, which, compared to the S.E., was highly unstable. This fighter used a rotary engine and had some torque that the pilot had to counter when he banked the airplane. The Camel could snap out a right turn that was tough to follow, though the pilot had to be ready for the nose to fall. Turning left caused the nose to rise and might stall the plane if the attentive pilot did not compensate. The Camel also employed a "blip switch" which the pilot used to momentarily cut engine power rather than adjusting the throttle. This is what gives the aircraft that engine-on-and-off sputtering sound. It was not a beginner's aircraft, but neither was it untamable if the pilot had some proper British grit.

The Sopwith Pup was more forgiving, but hands down, the Royal Navy's Triplane was the most maneuverable airplane in British service. In experienced hands, the Camel's unpredictable tendencies made its pursuit more difficult. Even when expertly flown, however, it was a tricky gun platform and tended to swim about in a diving attack, which could waste precious ammunition. Hollows preferred the Camel's two Vickers machine guns to the single gun in use on the Pup or the mixed armament on his S.E. While Camel pilots had to hone their skills and instincts to keep from crashing, the Sopwith itself needed little adjustment. The designers did a splendid job. In a little less than a year, the Camel flamed thirteen hundred enemy planes.

The S.E.5a was an equally British bird but with an entirely different soul. First, the in-line engine largely solved the torque issue. No matter how a pilot turned, he never had to fight the gyroscopic qualities of a radial engine. This steadied the S.E.5a when its guns chattered, making accurate shooting a real possibility. The guns and sights had to be harmonized, and there was some debate as to what range to set the guns. A distance of fifty to seventy-five yards was optimal. Some pilots were better shots than others. The bird hunters, who were accustomed to shotguns, likely downed the most planes as they understood how to aim in front of a target when shooting from any sort of angle.

The pilot sat fairly far back in the S.E. Visibility was good, with a minimum of struts and wires and a fair view both above the top wing and downward over the sides. The long nose and positioning of the landing gear demanded a pilot's full attention when setting down. Unlike the Camel, however, the S.E.5a just begged for a good tweaking. The British made a practice of issuing each squadron an extra aircraft of their type so that the pilots might experiment and discover improvements that the designers missed. They compiled their findings into monthly reports that were studied back at the aircraft factories. Hollows flew the experimental plane as his personal aircraft.

The first things he adjusted were the needlessly long exhausts that ran outside along the fuselage to a point just past his shoulders as he sat in the cockpit. These were shortened for considerable savings in weight, and the exhaust stubs were put back on. With his engine at maximum power, flames flickered from these shortened spouts. They were harmless but a little distracting. He debated removing the elaborate and somewhat heavy semi-enclosed glass canopy, which could easily be replaced with a simple glass windscreen. Most of the pilots who issued this plane thought the new canopy quite ridiculous and stripped it immediately, but Hollows did see one advantage in the heavier glass. He was always cold in the cockpit, no matter how many scarves and sweaters he stuffed beneath his flying coat. In addition to the flight helmet, Hollows wore a leather mask that completely covered his nose and cheeks. Even still, his face was usually numb on landing and stung as it thawed. The new canopy vastly improved the airflow and promised a more comfortable mission.

The S.E.5a's seat was quite high in the cockpit, which gave the pilot an excellent view all around, but it also exposed him to the slipstream and required the pilot to lean forward to use his sight. Though reworking the seat put Xavier low in the cockpit, he felt less exposed and he was perfectly aligned behind his gunsight. He even removed the hump behind the cockpit in an attempt to improve rearward visibility. By the time he was finished, the major picked up another five miles per hour in top speed. This sounds like nothing, but added to the S.E.'s stunning basic performance, Tex could call on perhaps twenty miles per hour over his most feared opponent, the Fokker DR-7. He could climb just a smidge faster, too.

Raise your glass to Captain Overstreet and his Sopwith Camel.

Hollows in Command, Western Front 1918

The moon crested the airfield. A newly promoted Major Hollows walked out onto the flight line, unbuttoned his trousers, and took a long piss. It was a remarkably clear night. He looked up at the stars and thought for a moment about the existence of God, or more specifically, where He'd gotten off to lately. This relief took some time, and as the process continued, Xavier noticed that the dogs had stopped barking, and the guns were all silent. The repair crews were not hammering. No orders were shouted by angry sergeants. No engines sputtered. He could hear leaves rustle. So long as his urine lasted, there was peace on earth. He had been drinking tea and sherry off and on for most of the night as he paced from hangar tent to hangar tent, but not enough to win the war. Sure enough, as he did up his last button, the distant sounds of war crept back in.

Xavier personally oversaw the maintenance of his squadron's planes and often found fault with the ground crews who were still learning their craft. There were some talented men behind the wrench, and Hollows made it a policy that despite rank, these men had the last word on what was cleared for action.

Two mechanics exposed Hollow's in-line Wolseley Viper Hispano Suiza V-8 engine. It was lightweight compared to other powerplants as it was made with cast aluminum lined by steel where needed. While the initial batch of S.E.5 aircraft suffered from unreliable power, the "a" model had these kinks mostly ironed out and added another fifty horsepower to the problem. The technicians stopped what they were doing, stood up straight, and saluted smartly but differently. Hollows offered a cursory return as he tossed them a pack of cigarettes.

"You salute like an American."

"Yes, sir, from Wyoming. Half of the new ground crew coming in are from the States and Canada. Some Irish, too. We're not really soldiers, so I apologize for my salute, sir."

"You must learn a proper salute. This is England, not…where was it?"

"Laramie, Wyoming."

"Cowboys?"

"Indians and tumbleweed, too."

"I have the right hat for that someplace, and as you can see, I wear my revolver American style, right hip."

"You'll still need a horse if you want to fit in. Actually, sir, that might not even be enough."

"Hmmm. Quite. Know this engine well, do you?"

"She's just right, Major. All two hundred horsepower purring and no leaks. Smooth as silk."

"Let's see, shall we?" Hollows made his own inspection. He reached in to swipe a finger on some suspicious part and was pleased with the result. He sat in the cockpit to check the function of the louvers on the tombstone radiators that flanked the propeller. He pulled the stick and worked the rugger pedals. Satisfied, he climbed down to do a walk around. He ran his hand over the skin where a few ground fire hits were patched. He tugged on cables and struts. He had only one very minor, "Let me show you something" to offer.

"Very well, men. Very well. Just make sure the rest of them are up to it."

The mechanics smiled and offered casual salutes as they cracked the pack of smokes and hustled off to the next plane.

The various Allied squadrons required thousands of mechanics. The British alone had to staff enough fitters and mechanics to keep two hundred squadrons in the air. Early in the war, the RFC recruited the trained people they needed on their own quite easily. But as casualties rose and other war industries sucked up labor, it became increasingly difficult to keep pace with the demand for skilled aviation workers. Sixteen thousand mechanically minded men were brought in from the USA and another six thousand from Ireland. Boys as young as fifteen were apprenticed, and approximately twenty-five thousand women were used as drivers and stores handlers. The oldest hire was Thomas Cox aged sixty-two. A technical school was established at Reading that could graduate one thousand trained technicians every eight weeks.

Just after midnight, Hollows walked into the armaments tent to find twenty machine guns lined up on tables awaiting routine maintenance. The ammunition used corrosive primers and dirty cordite. Left unattended post-heavy use, the grime and worse that caked the moving parts could slow the cyclic rate and eventually cause the weapon to seize. The interrupter gear might fail, which was never helpful. Nothing short of bathing the mechanism in solvents followed by a scrubbing with a wire brush could bring a filthy weapon back to useful status. Proper lubrication was also essential. Too little and the weapon fails; too much, and the lubricant becomes a sludge when it comes in contact with carbon. Some lubricants did not do well in the cold at higher altitudes. A steady supply of the factory-recommended oil was required. Prepping the guns was an art and a time-consuming science. Soldiers didn't do this sort of maintenance under fire. It was essential that machine guns be serviced whenever there was a lull in the fighting. This went double for airplanes that often carried two or more guns.

The squadron armorer was a manic young man who muttered as he worked. He scurried about checking tolerances and looking for cracks in receivers or bulges in barrels. Over the hour Hollows spent working on the guns, he saw springs swapped out, extractors and ejectors replaced or adjusted, barrels were deemed dead and swapped out, and interrupter housings were repaired and readied to reattach to the engine. A pile of discarded parts littered the tent floor.

The enlisted men doing the gun work were known to cut corners to be ready on time. Hollows good-naturedly shooed away the private who was cleaning his two machine guns so that he could do the job himself. He took off his jacket and rolled up his sleeves. Xavier had *his* Lewis apart in seconds. He had done this process after each of his kills. This particular Lewis gun was in on all of them. The Vickers was one of many, but the Lewis was special to Major Hollows. He cracked the corrosive residue that encrusted the bolt and other moving parts. The barrel took considerable effort, and he accepted a little help from the men who felt at ease with their new major. Tex paid particular attention to his weapons' chambers. Both gleamed reassuring once he was done.

Hollow's hands were black with carbon as he rinsed and lathered and scraped under his nails. Back in the dispersal hut, he had a shave as he chatted with new pilots. He combed his hair carefully and adjusted his collar and cuffs. His squadron mates snickered. Tex was famously fastidious, even a bit of a dandy in his impeccably clean uniform.

The fatalists and religious pilots slept like babies before a mission. The rest of the pilots, particularly the newest arrivals, did not slumber so well.

Several of Hollow's men shared his anxiety-based insomnia and milled around reading, smoking, or playing cards to pass the time. Some were veterans and morose about it. They were sent down because of exhaustion, stomach issues, alcoholism, and various assaults from slaps right on up to attempted murder of a superior officer. These were mostly decorated soldiers with many kills, not men a King would just throw away. All the same, their low morale was not needed back home, either. For these pilots, a modern description of Hollow's unit might be a halfway house for pilots who were too good to quit but absolutely needed to.

On operational days, when they had to complete a morning patrol, Hollows slept a few hours in the afternoon and sometimes a few more after dinner. When grounded by weather, he and his men slept all day. They read German newspapers to learn all they could about the famous aces who opposed them. Very few pilots were captured. There were no heroic dinners where enemies sat together to talk shop. Some pilots scoffed and called the news stories propaganda, but they all secretly feared the next Boelcke, Udet, and Richthofen. They shared an utter respect for Fokker's designs, particularly the triplane and the recently introduced DR-7 biplane fighter that was as fast, sturdy, and maneuverable as anything in the Royal Flying Corps inventory.

Hollows quizzed the newer men on hand and maneuvering signals as well as the best strategies for staying alive. Breakfast came before the first light. Hollows forced down some oatmeal and toast. With the pilots assembled and all of the planes inspected and ready, the Major reviewed the plan over maps and chalkboard. Their target was a group of observation balloons that could spot the big Krupp-made guns hidden far behind the front. Another worry was that the Germans might see troop movements or even supplies coming forward that might presage a coming attack.

The Dawn Attack

Hollows lit a rare cigarette as he considered the map on the table. He passed the pack as he counted noses. With his pilots gathered around, he used a MK VI bullet as a pointer. "I will lead the formation with the three S.E.'s at five thousand feet. We have finally received a few cases of explosive rounds, and I am told that these may be the last we shall get. It will be our task to bust the observation balloons first and then the barrage balloons as this ammunition allows. You, new men, expect the barrage balloons to have cable aprons spread between them. I would be remiss if I did not remind you strongly that these will hang a considerable distance, and they are next to impossible to see, so don't get caught in the spider web. You either have to get beneath them, and that just pushes you into their anti-aircraft system, or stay above them, which serves you up for their patrols. So pick your poison.

"Captain Overstreet, you shall lead the Camels and fly high cover for the rest of us. It won't take long for the opposition to come to the rescue, so be ready to pounce on the Fokkers when they show up. The four Bristol fighters have the most dangerous assignment. You men will take off first to strafe and drop bombs on the anti-aircraft positions. For God's sake, you too must watch the cables, but if you can strafe the winches. That would be ideal. Again, ideally, we will make one pass and be on our way, so keep a keen eye and shoot well."

Overstreet caught Hollow's arm as the men dispersed. "Major Hollows, sir, I am going to talk to you as a friend."

"Nothing less. Please do."

"You know, Tex, I would remind you that as our commanding officer, you should not be on this mission or any other for that matter. I can lead this flight. You needn't expose your family to ruin. Let me take this."

"Have you pissed yet? Come on. It's my new tradition. I had Rigby set it up. Good for morale I should think."

An early war German spiked helmet sat atop a short stake in the middle of what the men called Le Pissarrie. Hollows fired first. "I shall soak this helmet down every time before I go up. Join me."

Overstreet needed no encouragement. "If this is my last piss, it's a good one."

"I shall never miss the opportunity. My friend…despite your offer to spare me, I must ask you not to risk yourself unduly over me. Up there, I am just another Englishman. For those few minutes, I am my own man. It feels…even if I die, as if I am liberated. Please understand. We have pissed on the helmet. We have to go now. Logic, you see. I studied it in school."

As the planes rolled out in pairs, Hollows felt his flying coat's breast pocket. He had his lucky bullet. He said the Lord's Prayer as he opened up the throttle.

Other than reconnaissance flights, the Germans rarely ventured over British or French territory. They were badly outnumbered and sought to keep every pilot they could from being captured due to all too frequent engine problems. Even operating behind the lines, friendly fire was a constant danger as the men on the ground assumed every aircraft was coming for them. Anti-aircraft machine guns and light artillery were very effective. In fact, it is likely that the Red Baron himself, Manfred Von Richthofen, was brought down by ground fire and not Captain Roy Brown of the Canadian Air Corp with whom he was dogfighting.

When Hallow's group arrived on target, there were far more balloons than expected, yet only two or three were manned by observers. They were set farther back from the front than expected, which gave the Germans more time and space to shoot at British planes as they penetrated German lines. The Hun used the ground well. Rolling hills concealed balloon landing areas from direct fire. Manned by highly trained and specialized troops, barrage and observation balloons were grounded by massive but mobile diesel-powered winches that could rapidly bring thousands of feet of tether to heel. Though they were attached to only one cable, it was woven steel and had a phone line running through it. The observers had powerful optics and good maps to work with. They could see troops massing and the fall of shot.

Hollows flew high enough to make out the explosions caused by the four Bristols as they made their runs, but he had no way of knowing if they did any real damage. He banked his plane and strained his eyes to see which balloons had baskets beneath them. It took several long moments to find them and another few to plot an attack through the barrage balloons arrayed at staggered altitudes. Hollows climbed until he was perched above it all. The manned balloons beneath him showed their awareness with blooming parachutes and rapid retraction. The barrage balloons remained and were separated by perhaps two hundred fifty feet on each side. Hollows planned to dive steeply, make his attack, and then run out under the barrage balloon net. This would put a great deal of stress on the airframe, more than Hollows had ever asked of it before. All the stick and rudder time in different aircraft translated into harmony with any aircraft he flew. He felt confident that his plane was up to the attack.

All three S.E.5a fighters assigned to downing observation balloons used standard bullets in their Vickers and incendiary/explosive rounds in the Lewis guns. This was a useful countermeasure to zeppelin attacks which were common over northern France and southern England earlier in the war. While a standard machine gun might put dozens of holes in a zeppelin's gas bags, the slow leaks were not often fatal as the crews scurried inside with patches and glue to save precious hydrogen. An incendiary round, however, could ignite a hydrogen-filled gas bag with instantaneous and oh-so-satisfying results…at least for the British pilot. The trick, however, was to create a large enough gas leak to mix with the oxygen around it. Once these conditions reached critical mass, a single .303 "Buckingham Bullet" could fell a giant.

First introduced in 1915, the MK VI incendiary round was resisted by the British high command as, technically, it was a violation of the rules of war, which forbade such rounds on humanitarian grounds. They were the perfect response to zeppelin raids, which were in themselves seen as terroristic and likely a violation of the rules as well. The British justified the bullet's use against the zeppelin itself and somehow not by extension on the helpless crews. For a time, Royal Flying Corps pilots who used such rounds on observation balloons feared being forced down and captured with these bullets in their machine gun belts. They were issued written orders signed by high-ranking officers that explained the situation and hopefully absolved the pilots. The absurdity of this solution led pilots who used the Lewis gun to load their magazines with the offending rounds. At least, these might be tossed prior to capture.

Hollows' attack was recklessly steep, and the huge grey target quickly filled his gunsight. He opened fire with his Vickers gun at a considerable distance. His weapon rattled away without jamming. Hollows saved his magic rounds until he was within three hundred yards of the target as he suspected that they quickly burned out and, over longer distances, were no more lethal than any other cartridge. His incendiaries passed through the balloon and a fireball erupted that quickly fell to earth. Hollows scared himself as he pulled out of the dive. The S.E.5a was less than one hundred feet up as it passed over the German gunner positions. He banked hard to spoil the enemy's aim and clawed for altitude amidst the field of barrage balloons. He saw cables that missed his plane by scant yards. He passed a very angry German observer descending by parachute. Flaming debris lighted on his canopy, and it quickly caught fire. The Hun fell several hundred feet onto one of the winches.

The Major looked back over his shoulder and expected to see other balloons burning. No hits were scored on any of the other targets by the other S.E. pilots. He rolled his plane to look for wrecks and saw an S.E.5a down between barrage balloons. The pilot was out of the plane and in a shell crater with a thousand yards of no man's land to cross before reaching his own lines. The third S.E. was nowhere to be seen. Hollows continued his climb. The powerful Hispano engine obliged him. He winged over and dove, hell-bent on destroying the remaining observation balloon just as he had the first in a single pass that ended low enough to get under the cables. Again, he held his fire, knowing that the Lewis was good for perhaps one more good hosing.

Fighter pilots talk about the problem of target fixation, where the engagement focuses on the enemy before them, and they lose greater situational awareness. This leaves them open to an unseen interloper who might get a free shot from dead astern. Hopefully, a wingman would protect his leader's tail, but such tactics were in their infancy in World War One. Hollows knew nothing of the greater battles going on both above and below him. He did not see two Fokker pursuit planes drop down from top cover to attack the Bristols. Captain Overstreet, climbing steeply, traded shots as he passed between them.

The DR-7 and Sopwith Camel had very similar strengths and weaknesses. Overstreet could turn just a little tighter than the Germans, but they had a speed advantage, and there were two of them. Their firing pass hit him everyplace, including his right leg. He could barely keep pressure on the rudder. The Germans smelled blood in the water and came around for a final bite.

The captain strained to look over his shoulder for the planes he knew were about to rake him. His aircraft was tattered. The engine was still running strong but there was no escape. No matter which way he turned, either the Germans would get him or his aircraft would fail. His Camel lost energy as he climbed too steeply. If he stalled, he was done for and the engine told him that a stall was in the offing. Overstreet's final hope was that Hollows saw him and was on the way, again, as he was that time before.

The Germans could not believe their luck.

Tex just wanted to kill another balloon. He bore in and took his shot while kicking the rudder to spray as wide an area as possible with the last of his incendiaries. The balloon exploded, and the avenging S.E. flew right through the debris field. The cloud of flaming fabric and sooty smoke had no effect other than to distract the pilot from other dangers. He pulled out somewhat higher this time and again braved the ground fire. He circled steeply and found himself perfectly aligned to fire on a barrage balloon.

Hollows fired his Vickers gun, seemingly to no effect. He passed over the balloon so closely that he thought his wheels might well brush the top. This was just the moment a German officer on the ground had been hoping for. He threw a switch that detonated the barrage balloon as if it were a flying landmine. Hollows was almost one hundred yards away when it actually exploded. The overpressure of the blast caught his S.E. and tossed it like a child might throw a paper airplane. The sturdy British fighter shook off the bout of heat and flame but went into a spin. Harrows had precious little altitude to give as he applied power, rudder, and roll, which saved him, but again, he found himself flying dangerously low and headed in the wrong direction. He came about as every German beneath him opened fire.

Holes appeared in his wings and clipped one of the two outer struts that connected the portside upper and lower foils. While the hits were not immediately fatal, he felt wing flutter and knew that jinking too forcefully or diving his plane might well result in the wing coming off, which would most assuredly kill him. With his throttle wide open and his upgrades assisting, the young Major thought that he would be clear of danger in moments. There were plenty of other targets in the swarm, and he trusted his luck.

This turned out to be a very bad idea. The German DR-7 pilots were ecstatic as they added Captain Overstreet's aircraft to their list of victims. Their combined fire killed the British pilot, tore off the top wing, and set his plane on fire. They winged over having used up most of their ammunition, but the leader saw Hollows far below and calculated that his dive speed would quickly bring him into range. The German pilots did violate the rule about flying beyond their lines, but the leader was sure of a kill before overflying Tommy territory. Even with their added speed, Hollows almost slipped their noose.

The DR-7s bounced the Major on his starboard side at a near ninety-degree angle, one stacked above the other. Shooting with such a degree of deflection was unusual for that era as most pilots tried to approach the enemy from astern. Hollows was stunned to see the gayly painted Germans just as they began to fire. Their winking Spandau 7.9 m/m guns were expertly aimed, and the British fighter flew through their hale with disastrous results for his engine, tail, landing gear, and, worst of all, his fuel tank. He did not notice the petrol leaking under his feet.

Hollow's superior speed carried him past the German fighters and over his own lines. The now withdrawing Sopwith Camels drove off the DR-7s. One of the Bristol fighters formed up with the crippled S.E.5a to inspect the damage. The engine was still running roughly, but Hollows was losing speed and altitude rapidly. The S.E. had suffered mortal wounds. The rear gunner in the Bristol wildly waved his arms and pointed at something behind Hollow's field of view. None of his engine gauges were working, but he knew at once that his craft was leaking everything needed to stay in the air. This would almost certainly lead to engine seizure and, worse still, a fire, if not an outright explosion. He needed to land immediately.

The battlefield below Hollows was impossibly shell cratered with barely any roads or pastures to give a safe haven. Every open space was littered with the flotsam of battle, including numerous immobilized tanks that broke down before even reaching their departure points. There was, however, a rather large pond directly in front of him. As predicted, his engine quit, and the S.E.5a began to drop. Fire licked over the nose, but he was protected by his lowered seat and the much-despised canopy. Unable to see forward through the smoke and flames, for a moment, Hollows thought he would not make the pond. He barely cleared a barbed wire fence, which ripped what was left of his wheels from the lower fuselage and pulled the husk downwards. This aided in the ditching as the S.E. obligingly skipped on the surface twice before sticking.

The bottom wings held, but the top wing broke loose and flipped back over the fuselage. Water filled the cockpit and promptly put out the engine fire. Hollows had the wherewithal to tighten his seat belt prior to ditching but was knocked unconscious when the departing Foster mount hit him square in the face. When he came to, his vision was blurred, but he made out a considerable number of green-clad soldiers standing on the bank looking at him. They presumed he was dead and made no attempt at rescue. Hollows waved weakly, but no one waded in, and there were no boats on the way. He did notice that most of the soldiers either wore gas masks or held handkerchiefs to their faces. Blood streamed from Hollow's nose, and for several moments, he was unaware of the fact that he successfully landed in a massive cesspool. He was saved by the scat of ten thousand men.

Major Hollows spent several hours in a frontline medical station. Medics at the crash site stripped off his offensive coat, mufflers, shit-filled gauntlets, and uniform. He was doused with what passed on the front lines for clean water, wrapped in a blanket, and put on an ambulance truck. He was badly concussed and unable to explain who he was or what happened to the young frontline doctor who examined him. Only his identity disk offered proof that he was an officer. It took a fellow flier with a bullet through his shoulder to sort out Hollow's family status. Everyone in earshot stopped for a moment with an I'll be damned look on their faces. This promoted Major Hollows to priority transport and a hospital bed behind the lines where a comprehensive exam was conducted.

Doctor Ernest Hood was an older gentleman not known for sudden moves. He shot bolt upright, and some would say that he veritably dashed straight to Hollows's ward when he read the Major's name on his ever-lengthening patient roster. Before he entered the private room, the doctor composed himself. A nurse handed him the chart and filled him in on the details of the crash, the subsequent disinfecting, and the rumor that he was being considered for some sort of medal. The doctor knocked, and unlike every other patient in the hospital, he waited for someone to say, "Do come in."

"Good God, Major. And here I thought I would find you full of holes. I am Doctor Ernest Hood. I am the chief surgeon here. It looks as though someone hit you in the face with something solid."

"I think it was the war. I don't recall *exactly*. I have a splitting head-ache. I am a little nauseous. My ears are ringing. Am I speaking loudly?"

"Think nothing of it. Can you sit up? Let's have a look at your eyes, shall we? Hmmm. Well. Yes. You are quite concussed." The doctor main-tained his banter while asking his clinical questions. Hollows found him reassuring. His smock was slightly blood-stained, evidence of a difficult calling in times of war. Hollows liked the doctor's grey hair, spectacles, and neat uniform. He was pleasingly British as he poked and prodded the young officer. He spent considerable time checking reflexes.

"So, landed in the proverbial vat, did you? I hope you killed some Huns for your trouble. What do you remember?"

"I downed two observation balloons." He tried to snap his fingers and failed. "I am certain of that. A third exploded right underneath me. I was pretty badly hit by two nasty German Fokkers. I thought I was done for. Less than two minutes later, I was down. That's just about all I can remember. Just a great whoosh of hydrogen followed by a tremendous splash of shit. And then the rest is…mysterious."

"That's a concussion for you. Yes, very brave and a good show, to be sure. The best tradition of your family too. I recall your father served with distinction in South Africa."

"He was a staff officer. Never fired a shot in anger."

"Oh. Is *that* what he told you? His expertise was cartography and land navigation. He was always in the field and, as I recall, regularly taken for a target. Well, it is none of my business. It was another good show. I treated men who were there the day he…did what he did. We were school chums of a sort, you know. You must remember to give him my best when you see him. Well then. My diagnosis. I shall be blunt. The war is over for you, I'm afraid. I'm sending you to London for further treatment and observation. We might use the Roentgen process to look at your skull and spine. Have you had an X-ray? What do you think of that?"

"No, never. Doctor, I am sure you understand that I would prefer to return to my squadron."

"My Lord…"

"Wait, none of that. My father is Lord Hollows. Please, Dr. Hood, just call me Major, Xavier, Tinker, X, or Tex if you must. People like to call me that when they think I am not listening."

"Very well, Tex… Oh my, that felt self-indulgent. I shall say, Major. As I said, Major, you have suffered a nasty concussion, and it is a miracle your neck was not broken. You can barely turn your head. It will take some time to recover from that. Weeks, very likely more, and only then if you allow yourself the time and space to get well. So, then. No. You cannot fly airplanes with a neck like that. To the good, however, I do not believe your skull is fractured. There isn't anything we can do about your nose. Someone was a little sloppy with the set. We will never know who. You shall still be a handsome fellow. Maybe a little bump there. Better than losing a limb. As for your command, well, in my medical opinion, that, too, would be too much of a strain. It is quite out of the question."

Xavier winced in pain. The doctor put a reassuring hand on his shoulder. "My God, man, you look like a raccoon. Here, stand up. Let me help. Straight. Stand at attention. No! Not really. That was my attempt at humor. Not so easy, is it, laddy? Sit. Admit the vertigo and take a vacation. You have earned it, have you not?"

"No more than any of my men. Please, doctor, I have my reputation to consider. That landing was…messy. I have to go back to the front. My reputation, you see, is…"

Hood raised his hand and shook his head. "Besmirched is the word you are looking for. Literally, too. Come, come. Stories like yours are the bright point of this damnable war. Think of the headlines back home. A heroic Lord's son miraculously lands in the muck pond after taking down two observation balloons at once."

"I don't know how heroic it was."

"Well. Maybe it was symbolic. Whatever the metaphor, it is priceless for my morale. The people back home will love you for it. The House of Lords will be all atwitter. You are a brave lad, and that is sure. Two balloons at once, you say? As for the rest…as I understand it, and I know nothing of these airships you fly, but I should think that even a messy landing like yours is a good one if you can walk or, in your case, be dragged away alive."

"You should add that I was covered in other men's dirt."

Hollow's last action left him somewhat spooked. He had never been shot down before. There were close calls and bullet holes in the wings, but he had never faced an engine fire. He always landed gracefully, well, almost always, and the indignity of putting down in a cesspool gnawed at him. Thanks to the general horror of events, the ignominy of the cesspool landing soon wore off. When your fellows are being gassed, machinegunned, and buried alive, a little trip and fall in the outhouse was no big deal.

Xavier was desperate for news of the day's action and could get no reports until Rigby finally made it to the evacuation hospital two days after the balloon attack. He learned, to his horror, that one of his best pilots was lost that day. Five airplanes went down, including two S.E.5a's, two Bristols, and a Camel. Two other Sopwiths were borderline write-offs. The squadron was essentially out of action. Morale was bad. The pilots and ground crews missed their leader and, to a man, swore that the cesspool landing should be taught in flight schools.

Rigby set out on his rescue mission two minutes after the survivors made their report. He knew that Hollow's S.E. was on fire as it went down, but it did land basically intact on a pond. Finding one man amidst the torrent of torn bodies coming your way at that time in history was nearly impossible. One had to fish for a person by watching the right spots. Rigby put out the word by telephone and wireless that Lord Hollow's son was missing and assumed to be among the wounded.

So, it was a considerable relief when Linus found his mate. He gave a smart salute when he entered the room, but Xavier extended his hand in return. For the batman, this reunion was an answer to a thousand prayers. He shook his fellow's hand but noted that his friend's grip was unusually weak. Linus pulled up a chair. He composed himself and said at last, "Fucking hell, Xavier, you look like shit."

"Thank you, Linus, my friend. I am so very glad to see you too."

"Sir, I didn't mean to be too familiar. We all heard how you cheated a fire. But, sir, I must make a report about the mission. Brace yourself, sir."

Linus kept it simple as he watched his officer's head drop and shoulders stoop with every lamentable detail. The British strike force was decimated at the cost of a few ballons. The strike force lost one quarter of their aircraft. Seven men were killed including Hollow's executive officer. Two other pilots were missing and assumed dead or captured.

"Not Overstreet. Dear God. Bad luck. Bad luck. Pissing on that German helmet doesn't help I suppose." Hollows wiped an eye. Rigby had seen this before and almost came to attention as he looked away.

He offered, "I'll help you pen Captain Overstreet's letter if you can't focus on the page. My penmanship will…"

"Yes. Poor, dear Overstreet. Now, *he* was a man. I thought he would make it. Oh my. I'm a little overcome. Excuse me." Xavier was struck by a visual memory of Overstreet's plane clawing for altitude, and all at once he realized that had he been thinking, he would have seen this as the last act of a desperate comrade. He should have seen the closing DR-7s. As he thought about the dogfight, he flashed on moments from the fight, some without color or sound, while others were too clear and begged to be believed. Xavier did not know what was real and what was created by his guilty mind, the concussion, or both.

"Oh my God, I could have saved him. I remember, but I was dedicated in my own attack. I would have had to break away, and I chose not to."

"The mission was to shoot down observers. It was a sky battle, and you were fighting it as best you knew how. You can't start second-guessing yourself, sir. Not over flying machines."

"I want to sob. Dear God. The despair feels limitless tonight."

"Must be the hit on the head, sir. Pay it no mind. That letter will wait a few hours, sir. I will stand outside. I will see that you are not disturbed."

Hollows took a deep breath, turned away, and wiped his eyes. When he next met Rigby's gaze that durable English emotional venire was back in place. "Not necessary, Rigby. But I thank you. You know me well. It was an ambush. That last. An ambush. The balloons, all of it irresistible for us. For me. The way they set it all up, the DR-7s waiting to pounce like cats on a mouse, the extra gunners on the ground and maybe even, now that I think of it, the barrage balloons were rigged to explode. We had to do it, but it was an ambush all the same. I should have realized. I don't know what I might have done differently, but I should have seen it right off."

"Blame it on the Hun, sir. Here's an amazing thing. The men at the aid station sent your flight suit back to the squadron. Imagine that."

"I remember something, most dimly. I asked for my coat and my Lewis gun."

"Yes sir, they sent both."

"Impossible! Really?"

"I checked the serial number, sir. It is your old gun back from the depths. Somebody had to fish it out. It had muck in every cranny. There must have been ten men who volunteered to clean it for you."

"Good Lord! They should have left the damned thing in the shitter."

"As for the coat, sir, I burned it. Stank to high heaven. No saving it. We'll soon have you another, but I did find your wallet and your bullet in the vest pocket. I saved them for you. They stayed clean. Here you are, sir. See, it has that little nick you put in it. I brought you a fresh uniform, too, your Webley and Colt revolvers, and your best footwear. When they let you back in uniform, which revolver will you wear, sir? I'll even load one up if you like."

"We don't need to go that far. This might be my last opportunity to wear my revolver. Will I be seeing any Americans? I'm not prepared for a showdown, but I will wear my Colt revolver American style."

"You know this is one of the reasons why junior officers and senior officers, for that matter, call you Tex."

"You do know that the name has nothing to do with a dreadful place like Texas."

"What about the hat you so famously joke about? I can't promise who you might cross paths with this far behind the lines. Americans are everywhere. Not one of them knows a thing about you. I should think you would like that. We will have you looking smart, if not nationally confused, in no time. Your belongings are all packed and in your staff cars. Your drivers are guarding them with that Lewis gun. Yes, I bought it. You won it fair and square. How many balloons with that gun and planes, too? It's difficult *not* to be sentimental about it. If they knew how many cigarettes and bottles were in that car, we would need the gun to hold the bastards off, sir."

"I am very touched, Corporal Rigby. Very touched. See that the lucky bullet makes it into my next flight suit, will you? And I think we have actually just stolen the Lewis gun. I know I said I would, but it really belongs to the King."

"No sir, it belongs to the bottom of a cesspool. We wrote it off the books, sir. We are at war, and you have to fight with something. Am I right, sir?"

"I will only keep it until the war is over. Then right back it goes."

"If anyone asks, I will tell them the same. You really don't look like you see the world in focus, sir. Shall I read you this telegram from his

Lordship? I have already read it. It's quite nice. To paraphrase, your parents send their regards. They are both very glad you are not dead, and now that you are ostensibly out of the fight for a while, they wish to see you as immediately as medically and militarily possible. They have spoken with Command, and you are released from duty for medical reasons until your doctors determine that you are fit to return to combat duty. They are anxious for your return as there is someone that they would very much like you to meet. They wish to know where you would like a boat sent for your Channel crossing."

"They love to make the Navy do tricks."

There was a long silence. Rigby stood in a state of limbo. Hollows rubbed his knees and twisted his torso. He tried to stand but could only lean against the wall. He looked in the mirror and touched his new nose. He flashed on a party scene where scantily clad young ladies would laugh and try to touch it as they flirted so well. That sealed the deal. A trip to The House of Glass would go a long way toward his recovery, not so much for the physical release but the chance to just sit and talk with beautiful and charming Geneva.

"So, home then? Maybe I will take a vacation. Would you like to go on a vacation, Rigby?"

"Duty calls, sir. Where it takes me is up to you."

"We should take the boat. You are a lucky Sargeant."

"Sargeant? How grand. Thank you, sir. Sargeant Rigby. I quite like the sound of that, sir."

"You'll be an officer by the time we cross the Channel. Where we are going, a little brass goes a long way. No more batman for you. I shall no doubt soon be promoted to colonel, which will assuredly end most of my flying. Perhaps we can explain you away as my aide."

"Many thanks for your continued benevolence. So, who is the mysterious person your parents are so keen on? A lady, perhaps?"

"No doubt. I predict she will be well-bred and possibly wealthy in her own right. Remember, it goes title, money, then beauty is often a distant third."

"For me it is the exact other way around."

"You are far smarter than I am. I shall do my best to fall in love with her, but I am reliably advised by a woman who knows a great deal about such matters that this is an unlikely outcome."

"It's a different kind of battle then?"

"Quite. And a fight I am delighted to lose in comparison to recent events. But, truth be told, this is something I have dreaded for most of my life. It has kept me from chasing love except in the most fleeting sense, and any woman of means knows that, for me, an arranged marriage could come along at any moment."

Military Convalescence Hospital Burn Ward, Bulgaria, Late Fall 1917

Kapitänleutnant Huckbolt sat up in bed and contemplated his painful wounds. The burn ward in which he languished was sixty miles from where he crashed at the zeppelin field in Jamboli, Bulgaria. He was badly burned over forty percent of his body and initially not expected to survive after the crash of L-58, the world's largest zeppelin, on September 26, 1917. The hospital ward was full of hopelessly disfigured aircrew.

It was the fourth test flight, and as the acting kapitan, Huckbolt was desperate to please his superiors with a quick shakedown cruise in the face of imminent but not immediately inclement weather. He made a bad call and strayed too far from the field. He did not outpace the incoming cold front, and the ship was swept by sudden high winds. He attempted to land, but he couldn't control the descent. The ship smashed down on the landing field which broke her enormously long keel. At that moment, everyone but Huckbolt jumped ship. Not that he didn't try. He simply forgot to bend at the waist when he reached the hatch. He smacked his forehead soundly, which knocked him backward and off his feet. It took only a moment to recover, but it was time that Huckbolt did not have to waste.

The flames likely began when an engine struck the ground. Huckbolt made his jump just as the flash overtook him. The fire licked him hard even as he ran away from the exploding hulk that chased him like a flaming rolling pin. Many of his crew were killed in the conflagration, while others with whom he shared his current space were horribly disfigured.

Huckbolt endured the endless wrappings and unwrapping of treated gauze that clung to what was left of his back, arms, calves, and hands. He longed for morphia and laudanum to dull the pain. He was able to stand and use the toilet normally, which helped his outlook, but the opiates he took played havoc with his colon. He understood the problem, and without complaint, he freed himself from the opioid addiction and began to eat again. He also developed a fixation that consumed all his attention, but it was accepted as beneficial to his recovery, and he was humored when he asked for maps, charts, a slide rule, and a desk by his bed. Draftsmen came and went from the zeppelin sheds to show him their work. One brought a cutaway model airship that broke into three sections with all sorts of details inside.

Huckbolt was delighted. "It's like a doll's house of death. I can move the bombs and machine gun emplacements around like furniture."

Huckbolt's plan was inspired by a picture in a local paper of a near disaster involving an airship undergoing experimental docking with a mast that would be useful on ocean liners and navy ships at sea. Unfortunately, the winds came along and snapped the other ground lines, causing the zeppelin to stand on its nose at the top of that mast. Everyone inside was thrown about rather badly. If it had lost any buoyancy at that moment, the mast would have perfectly skewered the ship, and there would have been sparks. Fortunately, it remained afloat and was quickly recovered. That ship was saved, but Huckbolt seized on an idea that would skewer another zeppelin in spectacular fashion.

Huckbolt was due for release from the hospital in December 1917. A bout of pneumonia set this back considerably. He defied death a second time, and by the beginning of March, he was fully recovered, and his discharge was set. Huckbolt had no idea that his medical progress was of interest in Berlin.

There was a hint of springtime just outside the burn ward window when an Imperial Navy officer came to see Huckbolt. He stood at attention at the foot of his hospital bed and saluted. Nurses scurried and brought curtained dividers to give the two men some privacy. Huckbolt tried not to look surprised. He knew what this all had to be about. The officer opened his tunic and removed a small envelope.

"Sir, I am Leutnant Albert Brock. I am sent here today to speak with you about a certain letter you sent to my superior, Grand Admiral Von Holtzendorph."

Huckbolt looked sour. He expected to be arrested. "Not very official stationery for a court martial inquiry."

"Oh, this is…no, read it," the officer insisted with a smile. Huckbolt opened the envelope. "You did all that planning, all that design work from this bed? I must tell you that there was considerable debate about your ideas at the very highest level. Some said the plot was mad, others inspired. A weapon capable of truly massive destruction…that was the term they used."

Huckbolt read the message to himself several times before he said, "My God. My plan… *Your designs have been reviewed and approved. Construction will begin with your acceptance of this mission. Report to Friedrichshafen with the volunteers. You will be met by our representative*—I assume that is you, Leutnant—*Top secret. Strictest security. Von Holtzendorph, Chief Naval Staff.* My God. I must find a crew."

"Congratulations. You have been promoted to the rank of Oberstleutnat. Your new uniform must bear no reference to the zeppelin service, and we shall move you to a private room. You shall have any assistance you require. To preserve security, you will continue to work on the mission from here where you will, at least on paper, continue to be a patient until you are discharged to undertake this mission. Do not leave this area. I need to be able to reach you at all times. I will provide you with anything you need and handle all your communications. Send no letters or telegrams or make any phone communications without my direct presence. May I have that letter back? Finally, I am to escort you and your men when all is ready. What shall you say to these men? After all, it is a suicide mission."

"Look around you. I shall say we are in luck! Our days are numbered."

The Zeppelin's Longest Mission

After Huckbolt accidentally killed the first mega zeppelin ever made, it took sixteen days with crews working around the clock to produce another just like it. This ship would quite famously carry only military cargo on an epic run into East Africa, where German colonial troops were in a lopsided fight with lavishly supplied British forces supported by troops from India. The Zeppelin was designed for a one-way trip. It was to land and be dismantled by the Germans, who would find that every last bit of it had a secondary use. The internal walkway leather was to make boots, and the ship's enormous aluminum frame and empty gas bladders could make impressive shelters. The cargo carried included a dozen machine guns and hundreds of Mauser rifles. These would fire the countless cases of ammunition stacked up in the ship's hold. There were medical supplies aplenty, a radio station, and hundreds of pounds of other essential stores for a guerilla army on the move. In all, the care package from home contained thirteen and a half tons of war material.

Nobody had ever attempted a zeppelin flight over a desert where temperatures fluctuated wildly by day and night. Zeppelins do not deal well with such change, not that anybody knew that. The L-58 was testing all the aeronautical theories ever postulated on a mission with no prior knowledge of the weather ahead or, for that matter, an exact place to land. That would be sorted out when they somehow located the German forces that were technically on the run. The plan was to fly over the battlefield, looking for German troops from two thousand feet. Once spotted, a junior officer would parachute jump into the area, make contact with troops on the ground, and signal by flare or morse code what to do next. As it happened, the Germans in Africa were routed before their skyborne supplies could save them. I'll bet that junior officer was one relieved jumper when the mission was called off, and the world's largest zeppelin came about for home.

The L-58 had a few harrowing moments staying aloft. The crew experienced both superheating of the hydrogen gas and super cooling while flying over the desert. At one point, the nose dropped, and the ship fell at one hundred fifty feet per minute. They had to jettison quite a bit of their stores to stay aloft, but by that point, they had been recalled anyway. German ambitions in the region were deemed unachievable. There were other near catastrophes on the return flight, but they did make it back to Jamboli, Bulgaria, having completed the longest zeppelin flight to date. It was the rough equivalent of flying from London to Miami.

Meanwhile construction crews were busy in the massive zeppelin construction sheds at Friedrichshafen with a plan to convert any existing zeppelin to L-58 scale. An experienced team of one hundred craftsmen began construction of something that was entirely new to them. It wasn't a complete airship, just two new ingenious parts that changed its character utterly.

They began a new series of fuselage rings with a triple keel that gave the giant barrel great strength for its short length. This structure held two additional standard hydrogen gas bladders up top with a bomb bay and redesigned ballast system in the space below. Fuel was held in four bladders sandwiched between the two. Fully loaded, the ship carried forty thousand gallons of aviation gas.

The bomb bay was somewhat different than normal as it held a unique munition. Each device was actually four fifty-kilogram tanks of pressurized mustard gas. They hung bat-like in the bay, each on its own little trapeze. This ensured that no matter what attitude the zeppelin took in its attack, the bombs pointed straight down so that their parachutes might deploy cleanly. Two of the four tanks were set to disperse deadly gas as the platform fell. This allowed the wind to take the contaminating droplets everywhere, rendering real estate dangerous to touch for several days. Traces of mustard gas would be found in every puddle, on doorknobs and railings, streetcar seats, and windowsills. The other tanks did not expel their fifty kilograms of gas until the bomb hit something solid. This second cloud of mustard gas might roll down the narrow streets to kill a great many people who did not expect such an attack and would have few protective masks. The gas would creep into cellars and basements to take even the sheltered. Huckbolt could call on twenty gas bombs plus a full rack of normal high-explosive and incendiary bombs for use in the airship's final strike.

The new section's ultimate destructive power was housed in a ring of forty-eight aluminum boxes that spanned the circumference of the ship. These were accessed from the outside of the superstructure. Each static-proof, cardboard-lined box held two hundred fifty pounds of explosives and was covered by a fabric flap that prevented moisture and natural electricity from coming in contact with the structure of the ship. It also matched the external flat grey finish.

The new ballast tank connected by fire hoses to a large ballast tank in the new nose, which was under construction in a separate shed. Water could be pumped forward to influence the zeppelin's angle of attack. This was not new, but the size was unusual. The builders realized that the nose tank was far larger than it needed to be. If it were overfilled, the zeppelin would nosedive with catastrophic results for the crew and anyone at ground zero.

The trip from Jamboli to Friedrichshafen took Huckbolt and his crew more than a day. They traveled with a nurse who administered pain medicines and worked on bandages more or less constantly. None of the men could sit comfortably, and most resorted to lying on the floor in the aisle.

One of Huckbolt's crew was undone by the constant click and clack of the train ride. Every tiny jostle caused him a paroxysm of pain. Medicine was administered, but upon arrival, he had to be carried out and brought to the base hospital by ambulance.

"Damn! We are down a man already," Huckbolt complained. "He was the best of us, too."

"Who will work up in the superstructure now?" the flight engineer asked. "More importantly, who will man the spy car?"

"Either we shall have to do without, or I shall find us a new volunteer."

The ride to the airfield included schnapps and ham sandwiches. Huckbolt got a little tipsy and almost spilled out of the car. A beautiful young girl helped to steady him. It took him a few moments to remember that he was on a mission.

"Huckbolt? Is that you, old friend?"

"Oh, Jesus Christ."

"No, it is Fausmann! Do you not remember? We bombed London together and got out to tell about it. You have met my daughter, Gretta."

"Nice to meet you, Gretta. You are a vision, so tall, even next to your father, who is an idiot. We bombed British cows together or maybe it was pigs that we killed. What are you doing here, Fausmann? You have nothing to do with this mission. This is *my* mission. I was giddy there for a moment. Have I been burned again?"

Fausmann turned to his daughter and sighed. "Excuse us, my dear. Uncle Huckbolt has forgotten his manners." They stepped aside. Fausmann's tone was ominous. "Well, you see how this mission might be something sensitive. Yes? The High Command needed a go-between with the authority to give you anything you needed and…no questions asked. I volunteered when I found out who authored this plan, and quite a plan it is. I have studied every detail. It is a brilliant ploy, and it will work. There, are we now friends again?"

"We were never friends, Fausmann, but perhaps comrades. There, that is the best I can do, comrade. I thought the young Leutnant there was the man among men. Now I see it is you. No time to be appalled. I would see to the ship if you do not mind. You see that my crew gets the best of everything, including any women you might have hanging around. They shouldn't be too squeamish."

"Of course. We have anticipated your wishes. I see that they have taken your zeppelin badges."

"They have been especially strict about security."

"Here then." Fausmann removed a decoration from his tunic. "I have a zeppelin pin for you. Put it in your pocket to remind you that we are on the same side."

Huckbolt took the pin, and for just a moment, he softened. Then he took a step back, clicked his heels together and shot back a smart salute that made Fausmann's eyes widen. The salute was returned, and the men shook hands.

Huckbolt turned to his crew who looked desperate to find a bed. "Men, be comfortable. I am going to see our little bird with the kapitan. Weather, it is always the weather with us. I need to see the predictions. I trust we still have sources for such things."

"Fewer and fewer. We may not be able to predict the weather accurately, but then, we never could. The reports look promising for the next four to five days."

Fausmann extended an invitation. "Come, let us walk to the sheds. We have many details to discuss."

"Let us drive. I'm counting every step anymore."

"Are you still keen?"

"I have pain. And I am stiff, but I am still keen. If we make this work, we change the war. That is what I tell myself."

"The British will know fear again and respect us on the battlefield, which is now everywhere. The psychological blow will break their spirit. This will be devastating."

"Have the special weapons arrived?"

"Four trucks are under double guard as we speak."

"The perfect weapon for a man on his way to hell, don't you think?"

"What did the American General Sheman say about war? The more cruel it is, the sooner it ends."

"Don't quote Americans. It has to be bad luck."

Huckbolt's airship had no service number. It was assembled from an existing zeppelin that was split in half and expanded with the new center section. The new nosecone looked more or less identical to the original, but the changes added considerable length and weight. Nobody was too sure that the joining was going to work, but when it was briefly flight-tested with Fausmann in command, it handled well enough. The ballast system functioned, and the nose rose or fell a few degrees quite reliably with the water transfer system, though the new tank was only partially filled. Any time the nose rose or fell, it created a tremendous amount of drag and rapidly slowed the ship. When an airship stalled, it did not fall; it rose. Huckbolt sold the innovation as a way to stop the ship in flight so that he might more accurately bomb his targets. Absurd, but at that time in history, who knew otherwise?

The second flight tested the new zeppelin's rate of climb and maximum altitude. The ship climbed to fifteen thousand feet and did enormous figure eights for two hours before ascending to twenty-one thousand feet. The oxygen system was tested and found to be satisfactory. Huckbolt struggled with the ship's ladder, but he made the climb into the upper structure to inspect the hydrogen bags and emergency venting systems for the ship's 3.8 million cubic feet of hydrogen gas. He did have some trouble getting aboard. The hand-up he received from one of Fausmann's young crewmen felt like he was losing an arm. Fausmann's crew was efficient and wore the heated suits quite comfortably. The new zeppelin food, which required no external heating, was foul beyond all belief.

On landing, Huckbolt made a full and positive report to Fausmann who quietly relayed the news up the chain of command by telephone. His superiors were impressed and congratulated him for his efficiency. Fausmann was given full latitude to launch the attack at his discretion once he received the code word. The authorization to continue came by telegram three days later. Fausmann read the two words. His heart pounded, and he had to sit.

It read: *Brimstone, confirmed.*

The ship performed as expected in all tests. Huckbolt only asked that stools be put in for his crew's comfort and the light on his map table be changed to a red bulb. The work order was turned in, but in Fausmann's hurry, he wrote, "Change map table bulb." He never wrote the words "to red."

Huckbolt worried that several of his men were not up to the flight, and with no crewmen to work inside the fuselage or to man the upper defense positions, if anything went wrong deep inside the ship or up top, the mission would come to a sudden end. The most important crewman was the flight engineer. He kept the engines running, monitored fuel and oil states, and controlled the ballast tanks. One engine in five was "rested" on a rotating basis as they flew along. It took the engineer's touch to get them restarted from his station inside the gondola. While there was little repair work to be done aloft, the engineer's preventative measures and nose for impending problems prevented calamity. This engineer, Leutnant Michael Berg, was missing two fingers on his left hand and half of his left foot. Burns melted his face. People looked away. Berg said that he would have shot himself if not for this mission. The rest of Huckbolt's men felt exactly the same. Their suicides were expected in the burn ward, even encouraged by physicians who could do little more than control the pain with large amounts of morphine administered wherever the remaining skin would allow. To a man, they all wanted a spectacular exit, and Huckbolt had little trouble selling the mission.

The crew kept to themselves in a local hotel. They were a pitiful picture, so none were taken.

The mission preparation went on apace. A scaffold was erected with a winch for dragging loads up from more than seventy feet below. The ground crews slowly loaded the box ring with bags that looked remarkably like artillery charges. Incendiary and high explosive bombs were loaded, though not yet fused. The "special" munitions were taken aboard by a designated team and only then, in seclusion. Each parachute tube and weapon took considerable time and attention to install. Their bay doors were sealed, and guards were posted prior to launch. The forward hold was stacked with boxed explosives. The hydrogen gas bladders were filled to ninety-five percent capacity. Each huge bag had two valves at the top that could be used to release gas rapidly. One of these was a safety valve designed to open at twenty-two thousand feet. The second opened electrically on command from the flight deck.

The final tests revealed no issues, and the landing went smoothly. The unmarked zeppelin was taken back to her shed to await a weather report and priming of all munitions.

Huckbolt visited the base armory to draw weapons for the strike. This included a hodgepodge of handguns for his crew, mostly .32 caliber pocket pistols. Ammunition was in short supply, but his men only needed one round per pistol. Huckbolt had the only proper Luger. Machine guns were added to the forward gondola but not the center gun pit on the top of the fuselage as there were no men available to man the weapon. This was not a fun place to do one's service. The oncoming air was already subzero and going sixty miles per hour. Turning the gun against the wind was a jerky process when smoothness was required. Imagine your hand sticking out the car window on the highway; only your hand, in this instance, is a Spandau machine gun.

The engines were tested and retested daily. All the components were brand new, and confidence in their performance was high. The sponson engines could not be reached in flight, but the main engine behind the forward command cab was. There were actually two engines clutched together to drive a single propeller. They performed flawlessly in-flight tests. The radio was also used and pronounced perfect. All was in readiness.

Huckbolt grew increasingly morose as he waited on weather reports in Fausmann's office, where at least there was hot water for a proper shave. The crew knew that they might be called to action at any moment, so they couldn't get completely obliterated. None of the men wanted female companionship. Several wrote letters that were taken from the post and never delivered. Indeed, there are no records of who they were or who paid their tab, for that matter. For all we know, this was the Kaiser's idea. He was in a weak position at the end of the war, and a single hyper-destructive act correctly timed might win him some respect at the negotiating table—if there was to be one at all. The Gotha bombing raids were thought to give him this kind of credibility, but the damage they caused was a pinprick if anything at all.

Gothas might drop five 150-pound bombs in an average sortie. They could carry a heavier load, but range, speed, and even the weight of oxygen canisters had to be factored in. Huckbolt's zeppelin would carry seven tons of explosives in the outer ring alone. A further five tons would be carried in the forward hold. The full bomb racks carried the fragmentation aspect of the blast. These were the largest bombs of their type.

The Hydrogen Kamikaze

The plan was to dive the zeppelin into the target area at as steep an angle as the engines would allow. The angle would depend on enough air passing over the tail fins to give the pilot control of the ship as it fell. In theory, running the engines at emergency power would drive the ship into the ground. Huckbolt could choose two methods of attack. First, and this was his preference, he would apply full power to the engines, move ballast forward to the nose, and assume a more or less forty-five-degree angle. This would give him time to spot a target and make for it. He would spread the destruction by dropping mustard gas cylinders and incendiary bombs on the run-in. Half of London might be affected in one hyper-destructive dive from high altitude.

The second method of attack allowed for no real adjustments, but the rate of fall would be spectacular, and anti-aircraft guns would find it impossible to hit the dropping target. Any zeppelin falling horizontally is so wide that it acts as its own parachute, and the whole fall from grace thing happens very slowly at about 150 feet per minute. Once the ship was fully on its nose, Huckbolt had to hit but one switch to vent enough hydrogen to turn his zeppelin into a nearly eight-hundred-foot-long gravity bomb. Once in this posture, it would be impossible to drop the mustard gas or bombs, and the gas would be consumed in the massive fireball, so a trigger was designed that opened the valves in the event of freefall. With the bomb bay doors open, the gas could still take to the wind and cause panic on the ground.

The real damage would be caused by the gun cotton ring, which was sympathetically detonated by the immolation of the hydrogen gas and remaining aviation fuel. This blast would likely occur one hundred feet in the air causing considerable damage several city blocks in diameter. The zeppelin's frame, lightweight though it was, would be transformed into seventy tons of shrapnel. Even those buildings left standing within the extreme blast radius would be roofless and shaken so badly that they would be unsafe to reenter. The final explosion would also include the five tons of explosives in the hold, which would pop at ground level along with any bombs in the forward bay. The fragmentation effects were predicted to be especially horrific.

Think of the concentration of explosive force. This was to be no pathetic pattern of hits, each its own little ditch waiting to be shoveled in. The entirety of explosives was going to land in one specific place. This hit alone would topple Windsor Castle or even the Tower of London. Other than massive tunnel mines, this blast would be one of the largest of the war, certainly the largest ever delivered by aircraft.

This air attack would change everything. Zeppelins could be retrofitted, and if flown correctly at the highest of altitudes, they might make a one-way trip to carry a whole squadron's worth of bombs and enough hydrogen or poison gas to obliterate a city center. The crew needn't perish. They might parachute away at the last moment. Better still, what if a "zeppelin bomb" could be fitted with an aircraft that might fly the crew home? One has to admit, it sounds so doable. Soon after the war, the Americans launched the dirigible, the USS *Macon*, which carried five small Curtiss F9C biplane fighters that were launched and recovered by a trapeze bar.

On this trip, there was only one parachute. It was a standard issue on the L-58, so the designers included one on the new ship as well. It was the observer type and meant for use below a few thousand feet. It consisted of a hefty canvas drum with a stuffed parachute, a tether, and a harness that did not easily fit over an electric suit. The user had to hang the drum on a special hook outside the gondola entry hatch prior to the hop.

On the last morning, after a night of waiting for a weather report confirmation, the new and still unmarked ship sat in its hanger with the massive doors open. A car arrived, and a young feldwebel trotted into the shed office.

"I have an urgent delivery for Kapitan Fausmann. Where can I find him?"

The short-statured sentry pointed down the corridor. "First office. He's the tall one. Can't miss him."

The feldwebel found Huckbolt hatless, tunic off, and shaving in Fausmann's office. Fausmann's Kapitan's hat sat on the counter next to the sink.

"I have a letter and package for Kapitan Fausmann. It is marked urgent, Fausmann only, sir."

Huckbolt said without a moment's hesitation, "I am Fausmann. Leave them there. Dismissed."

"I am to wait for your reply, sir."

"Yes, well, the water is hot, and my lather is perfect. You have had a long drive. Go to the mess. I shall find you with the necessary."

The feldwebel needed no encouragement.

Huckbolt looked at the tiny envelope with a deathly sinking sensation. He had seen this stationery before in the hospital. His hands shook as he opened the communication whose contents he correctly guessed. He pocketed the note, toweled his face, and hurried over to the zeppelin gondola. He found the largest flight suit and put the letter in the internal pocket. He took the package from Fausmann's office to his own. There, he carefully opened the lid to find a simple time bomb with a twelve-hour clock. He estimated how long it would take for the return drive and added an hour for good measure. He wound the mechanism and connected the wires that set it to explode. He then repackaged the box and marked it "delicate." He put on his flight helmet and leather flying coat to cover his rank insignia. He trotted over to the camp mess with the box held casually under his arm. He found his man looking fat and happy as he smoked his pipe in the morning sun.

"Fuel up your car on my authority. Take this back to Von Holtzendorph. He asked for the original note. I have included it with my own note inside. So, here you are, with my compliments. This is what the general so desperately needs. Leave immediately. This is most time sensitive. Take it directly to his office. You do not need to wait for a reply."

Huckbolt made his way to the meteorologist office and was waiting impatiently for the lead officer to appear with the morning reports. He practically ripped them from their envelope when they arrived. He looked at the weather map and summoned the totality of his education and experience to make one of his last decisions.

Huckbolt picked up the phone and asked the switchboard to connect him to the flight shed.

"This is Oberstleutnat Huckbolt. We will launch the mission within the next two hours. Stand by for confirmation from Fausmann."

Shortly after breakfast, the ground crew rolled the tethered and tested super zeppelin out onto the airfield using large tractors. Fausmann showed up with a weather report in his hands. Huckbolt gambled that the intercepted letter was the only communication with the High Command's cutoff man. Fausmann showed no sign of apprehension. Rather, he was flamboyant, like the director of a play on opening night.

"Huckbolt, I have confirmed your order to launch the mission. The conditions are right. Perfect, if true. You must launch immediately if we hope them to hold."

"When I woke up this morning, I felt it in my bones. If we launch soon, we can do the eight hundred eighty miles and strike London shortly after midnight, hopefully before two if we meet headwinds."

"Yes! Huckbolt. Look what Germany can build, and even with your broken German heroes at the helm, this ship can still win the war for us! We shall show the King of England what destruction really means. Assemble your crew immediately. Let us go aboard to make all final preparations."

It took less than an hour to get the crew situated for the flight. They ran through their checklists quickly, and the engines were warmed up without incident. Huckbolt wore his cold weather suit and tested its function. Other than Gretta, no spectators assembled.

"Well, Huckbolt, this is your moment. Perhaps you will change history today."

"Your daughter came to see us off."

"She has no idea that you won't be back."

Huckbolt tried to smile. "Stand in the door with me, Fausmann. Let us wave to your little Gretta."

"The mission is upon us, Huckbolt. This is goodbye. Navigate her well. Good Luck in the world to come."

"Fausmann, do you know what would make this trip even better?"

"A direct hit on London Bridge?"

Fausmann felt the barrel of a gun pressed against his back.

"No. Keep smiling. You should come along. Come back in now. Watch your head. Close the hatch. Take the helm. Let Gretta see you fly her out, or I will shoot you and toss you out for spite alone."

"Huckbolt! You're mad!"

"I need one fit man for this mission, and you are the perfect choice. Let us see if we can hit something important this time."

The flight from Friedrichshafen to London proceeded at an average speed of forty-five to just under sixty miles per hour. Huckbolt was pleased that his predicted arrival over London would be close to midnight. They climbed to fifteen thousand feet. The heated suits worked well. The engines behaved. The command was given to take the ship to twenty thousand feet.

As for Fausmann, he melted down. He complained bitterly as he put on his flight suit. He begged Huckbolt to land the ship and put him off anyplace that wasn't an Alp top or the English Channel. It didn't take long to tire of the whining, so with some effort, the men bound the officer and sat him by the radio.

Huckbolt asked, "Tell me truly, is there another bomb, Fausmann?"

"Another bomb? Is there *a* bomb? Whose bomb are we talking about? I promise you I have no idea."

"A remarkably bad mailman brought you one yesterday, but I happened to pass for you. I was shaving and out of uniform and what with both of us being so tall, it was a fortuitous mistake. You were supposed to sabotage the mission. They lost their nerve in Berlin. Personally, I think it is the poison gas that disturbs them so much. We could have gone without. If you had no hot water in your office, I would have shaved someplace else. No doubt you would have planted the bomb. Instead, I marked it for return. You can think about that. Gag him. You and your Shakespeare. You fit the mark perfectly. A romantic warrior threw in his lot with a crew of dead men on a suicide mission. The obituary writes itself, don't you think?"

Return Mail

The return post upon which Huckbolt's sentiments were so set detonated in a traffic jam. The driver and postman were both out of the cab when it went off. The feldwebel surmised that the package he carried was responsible for the blast, and had it not been for a log jam of epic proportions at a damaged bridge, a high-ranking officer and his staff would all be dead.

The Feldwebel kicked what was left of the front left wheel. "I need to inform my superiors of this bomb. Obviously, their plans have been thwarted. This Fausmann is clearly off his rocker."

The driver shrugged. "We are miles from any telegraph line. It may be hours before we are over the bridge. We are on foot now until we flag someone down. Your warning will come too late, my friend, and you will be blamed. Are they expecting you?"

"Yes."

"Too bad. Otherwise, I must point out that the whole army is confused, and you have open travel orders. Even if questioned, we are safe. We are less than two miles from where I grew up. I say, let's go home."

"Well, I suppose we do have some latitude. I mean, who is to say what happened here? How long were we knocked unconscious by the blast?"

"Quite a while, I should think. No need for us to hurry. I have not seen my parents for years."

"Start walking."

And with that, the German leadership believed that the hideous mission was scrubbed utterly, while, in fact, Huckbolt was in his glory.

20,000 Feet Somewhere over the Western Front

Four hours into the mission, the sky began to change. A blanket of white clouds at eight thousand feet covered the world below.

"Huckbolt turned to his charts. He consulted his instruments and used his rulers. The pilot reported, "Kapitan, as you can see, we are now above the clouds."

"I am taking no chances. We are flying right over the trenches now. Is everyone getting oxygen? Take us higher."

Hours passed with nothing but a clear sky around them and a blanket of white below. There was no turbulence, but the cold on their exposed faces was bitter, and the oxygen stems kept freezing up. Huckbolt spent all his time at the navigation table as the engineer started and stopped the engines every few hours. Radio messages were coming in hot and heavy, asking for progress reports. These, of course, went unanswered. The radio operator was amused.

Huckbolt kicked the prostrate Fausmann. "Let them think we have gone down. I would love to see their faces in the morning."

Huckbolt flew his zeppelin over the English Channel well south of the British mainland. He tracked a westward course that took the ship past Brighton, Worthing, and Portsmouth. He was still thirty miles or more from the coast and unsure of his exact location. The direct route to London was a lot easier to follow. Ideally, one would fly right up the Thames. By late in the war, this route was lined by the largest concentration of searchlights and anti-aircraft guns ever assembled. There were airbases aplenty and scout planes galore flying standing patrols at altitudes up to fifteen thousand feet. Huckbolt's flight plan called for a ninety-degree turn over Portsmouth, then on to Reading, where he would turn one final time to begin the final dive on London. The penetration would take the ship over relatively open country with few defenses. German aircraft did not have the range to fly this route. Zeppelins could make the distance, but they had proven to be so vulnerable that their use was completely discounted. Never dismiss a giant, no matter how ungainly he might seem.

Huckbolt stood over Fausmann with Luger in hand. "By my calculations we should be over England in two hours and ten minutes time. London in another hour and twenty minutes at this speed. I must decide what to do with you, Fausmann. History will record that this was all your idea. You went rogue male and took a bunch of suicidal men on your mission. Even you must have figured this out by now, correct? The High Command will be happy to say so. If this works, and we so stun the British that they negotiate, you will be a hero in Germany. Well, maybe I will throw you out of the zeppelin with the parachute. Maybe you will actually get away with this. I will never know because I will be dead. I will be the happy one. Imagine that. Serendipity for me, a noose for you. Now let me ask you, should I take the ship down and use the spy car to make sure of where I am before I toss my dear comrade overboard?"

Fausmann nodded.

"Not afraid of enemy planes? Not atremble over their anti-aircraft lights and guns?"

Fausmann tried to sit up straight. He shook his head.

"Then get ready. You are the only one fit enough to be our spy. I don't recall you ever having done this duty, have you? It is quite a thrill. That slender line is all you have keeping you alive. One nick is all it takes, and you are the bomb."

As the mission ran on, crew fatigue became an issue. The man operating the tail surfaces had to make constant small adjustments to keep the ship level. At one point, the ship had a series of rises and falls, like a dolphin leaping from the sea as it swims alongside a boat. Huckbolt took over the position himself. The crewman slumped to the floor, curled up in a little ball, and died.

Huckbolt whispered something to himself but ordered, "Leave him how he is. We will not throw him overboard. I can step over him. He is going all the way with us."

The Hollows Estate, Late Summer 1918

Beatrice was overcome when she and Xavier were reunited. Neither could believe how the other had changed. Xavier was a trifle gaunt.

His warm smile was all but gone. Beatrice had crossed the threshold of adulthood. Though she hugged and kissed her brother, she said nothing. Her speech problems were not improved. She pulled Xavier close and hummed in his ear, "My Tex." Everybody who saw them embrace wiped an eye, even Lord Hollows himself.

Life for Xavier Hollows, military hero and super-wealthy bachelor, was pleasantly dull. His return was triumphal in the tradition of his social class. The young lady was as predicted, though her pedigree showed her mother to be…American. Olivia Armstrong preferred New York to London, and she made no bones about it. "The fashion, the shows, the cuisine, and not one bomb crater to slow you down."

Olivia spent part of her childhood in the Texas oil fields where her mother's people were heavily invested and wildly successful. Back in those days, she wore pants and cowboy boots. No petticoats were found in her Texas armoire. She rode horses Western-style and wrestled haybales. She slopped pigs and tended the chickens. She helped cook for the cowboys, who loved her like a little sister. Olivia cried for an hour when she found out it was time to head back East. She did another Texas tour in her late teens, where she learned how to square dance, drive a brand-new Ford Model T, and shoot guns.

Olivia attended school in New England, where she excelled in languages and music. She played the piano like a virtuoso and the flute more than moderately well. Olivia was well-read and philosophical by nature. She was of Presbyterian stock, and her mother could be a little severe about it, but Xavier found that his would-be girlfriend cared nothing for the faith. Many young men made a play for Olivia's hand, and she had once been engaged, but her betrothed died of yellow fever contracted while touring Panama. She did not take the loss well and swore off love for several years.

As an adult, Olivia Armstrong was a woman of leisure and had many friends in far-flung places. She traveled extensively before the war. The Armstrong and the Hollows families met at Ascot Racecourse and took to each other immediately. Xavier was away at school and did not have the occasion to meet Olivia. Mrs. Hollows, however, was a keen observer. She pulled Olivia's mother aside, and a plot was hatched. A little bird sang in Olivia's ear about the son of a certain Lord Hollows. Not only was he handsome, but he was also reputed to be as rich as she. A rare equal, but better because this one was British. Once Mr. Mystery returned from the front, the two would meet.

Like Rigby, Olivia could turn her cultured British accent on and off. She fell back on a New York or Western American drawl. She artfully used the skill to amuse her friends and would-be relations. Xavier found himself laughing for the first time in a long, weary year. Olivia played the piano and drew the partiers together for a sing-along. She played a medley of recognizable classical bits and bid the crowd guess the composer. Finally, she asked Xavier to sit beside her on the piano bench and let their four hands tickle out an original tune. This delighted the entire room. Xavier's mother almost fainted.

Olivia might have been put on display, but in her mind, Xavier was trying out for the part. At first, the two tried not to pay too much attention to the other. There was a bit of side-eye going on as Olivia chatted with Lord and Lady Hollows. It was late afternoon before Xavier asked if Olivia would like to see the family horses.

"I'll drive us down to the stables. My automobile awaits."

"That would be marvelous. As it happens, Xavier, I learned to drive a motorcar in Texas when I was seventeen years old. May I? How much trouble could we get into on your own estate?"

"I have only recently taken greater chances with my life." Xavier smiled broadly as he watched Olivia climb behind the wheel. She wore a long gown and had to hike up her dress just a bit. Xavier took in the eyeful and said nothing as he signaled the valet to crank the engine. It was Olivia's turn to smile.

"I don't believe I have ever sat in this seat," Xavier said.

Olivia settled behind the wheel. She reached about for a moment as if to refresh herself with the controls. "I think you shall enjoy the ride. The trick," she said confidently, "is not to stall as you get started. I took some time on that. But look, I still have it! Off we go!"

The couple hustled right along the local road. Xavier was a completely smitten passenger. Olivia's hair was coming down, and she cleared it from her eyes. "I can drive a motorboat, too. I jump horses, I like to swim, and I bait my own hooks." She bumped shoulders with Xavier, "Never been to war, but I killed a rattlesnake with a shotgun in Texas. I didn't ask; I just got the gun and did it. My father, as you no doubt noticed, is proud to be Scottish, but he calls me his Texas Tomboy."

"Would you like to learn to fly? You are literally halfway there now."

"Well, I like the idea of a lady pilot, but I also prefer my nose the way it is." Olivia pulled over in front of the horse barns and stopped the motor. She hiked up her skirts considerably and waited for Xavier to come around and help her step down. "What do you think of these? You don't have to answer now."

"I will not comment until we have run a race."

"I am quite fast. You would be lucky to catch me."

Olivia walked from paddock to paddock, looking over the Hollows' breeding stock and riding horses with a studied eye. She turned to face Xavier, who said, "I am told they are magnificent specimens, but in truth, I don't know enough to form an opinion. You should talk with my sister about that sort of thing."

"I am ready to render *my* judgment." She reached out and traced the bump on Xavier's nose. She touched his cheek and turned his face to take a closer look.

She leaned in. "Ouch. That must have hurt."

Other than a handshake, this touch was the first moment of tenderness between them. Xavier thought he might melt. His heart pounded in his chest as he looked into her green eyes. Medical science in those times had no idea about cascading brain chemicals and synapses firing, but Xavier would have said that all of his went off at once, and they all screamed the same message. All that worry about his parents making the choice of wives was for naught.

"I do like this little bump. Makes you look like a pugilist. Everybody has a war wound these days. You need to make the most of it, especially around strangers. Maybe you earned this nose in a bar fight in Galveston defending my honor."

"I got it killing Germans, but I like your tale far better."

"You crashed your airplane into a giant toilet to make the world a better place, and that nose is what you got for it?"

"Did I mention that the airplane was on fire? They may award me a medal, too. Not so much for the landing but the balloon-busting part." Xavier came to attention, saluted, and said solemnly, "I did it for my sister and the King."

"She is adorable and becoming a beautiful young lady, I see. Did you notice the way she looked at your aid, Sargeant Rigby is it? So sad about her speech, but she does have a way of talking all her own."

"Oh yes. I hear her quite clearly. She has a million little gestures that we have all come to know. She says a great deal with her eyes as well. She is terribly sweet, very loving, but not particularly gentle, and the scamp never asks permission for anything. She just does what she likes."

"Yes? Well, her eyes were on your aide, and I know that look."

"Well then, I shall have to promote him again or send him to India."

"She would run after him, I think."

"Linus is an awfully good man. He looks after me. Beatrice and a beau? My God. He lacks social standing, but he seems to have my parents under a spell. If they were to be married, that might be tricky. Military rank might be enough under the circumstances. Yes, I should promote him again. I shall make him a field marshal if I have to."

"So where will you be when this stupid war ends?"

"Right here, I suppose."

"But alive and well? No more soldiering from here on?"

"No. I will be but a simple engineer designing airplanes."

"Before you get to all that, would you like to take the boat with me to New York? You could use a little tiny taste of America. Desperately, actually."

"Well, I said I never would, but suddenly I long to go."

They kissed. Xavier came away from round one short of breath, and Olivia, too, was a little dazed. She had to kiss him again to be sure it was all real, but that choice only ratcheted up the heat. The first kiss was honest. The second was earnest, and the third, for just a moment, went a little primal before it lingered gently and became feint. The horses snorted as if on cue. The couple held hands and actually giggled.

Xavier managed to say, "I…huh." But he was thinking, *Goodbye Geneva.*

Olivia replied, "How eloquent. Ooo, lipstick. Let me take care of the evidence. You must think me awfully forward."

"No, no. Not at all. Somebody important said that in war, one has to kiss where one can."

"It's not the war, Xavier. It's the damned American in me."

"Well, now we shall have to go to New York. Just as soon as we sink all the Hun submarines and not a second later."

"Wouldn't it be grand if we could just fly over them?"

When the couple returned to the party, Olivia's lipstick was perfect. More perfect than when she left the group for her private outing. Every woman in the room read the touch up instantly for what it was. They entered arm in arm and all ablush. Beatrice made her *I'm wise to you* gesture, and Xavier returned the look with a nod toward Rigby. Beatrice wrinkled her nose and made a finger gun. Champagne was served, and the families were toasted.

"Did you see the horses, my dear?" Lord Hollows enquired.

Olivia chimed right back, "Yes, we did, and they saw us."

Major Hollows, with Olivia by his side, told his war stories, even the shit ditching with an actor's panache. He quoted Olivia's observation about making the world a better place, one splashdown at a time. The assembled friends and family laughed heartily and clapped. They all stood and toasted the King, England, and Captain Overstreet.

Toasts and prayers or no, Overstreet's death still bothered Xavier, and though he was medically excused, he felt remiss for not being at the Front. His vision improved, and the effects of the concussion passed, but beneath it all, Xavier's confidence was shaken. He longed to fly again. Getting clearance was the problem. This time, the wrap against his physical ability was legitimate. It took several weeks of doctor visits and vision tests before he was approved to fly, but he lacked a highly placed mentor to give him a squadron, and his father be damned. Instead, Xavier returned to his industrial duties and authored a report about the S.E.5a that was well received.

Back in the Saddle

The Royal Flying Corps medical report on a recovering Major Xavier Hollows recommended a period of rest and recovery followed by a few quick flights to test the waters, but there was no hurry about the process. With America in the war, the tide was changing in the Allies' favor. It was thought by most that the conflict would soon end, and there was no need to send recovering pilots back to the front when the pipeline of new talent was wide open. Besides, even a partially recovered Major Hollows was certain to be useful at Sopwith.

The doctor looked at Hollows's x-ray. "This all looks very well, actually. My concern is with your reflexes, reaction times, that sort of thing. Any headaches after a flight?"

Xavier reacted defensively. "Back to those tactics, are we? No need to hold me back from combat now. I have fought my parents for this entire war to be my own man. You have no idea how they meddled in my military career."

"Sir? I do not understand your reaction. I am on your side, Major Hollows. My diagnosis has nothing to do with any outside influences. Be assured. I will say that you have done your bit and then some. How did you get off your parents' leash?"

"As it turned out, all I really had to do was promise to follow orders and quit any antics. I insisted that status was not to be considered, only my merits as a flier and leader. I had no idea what a fool I had been until I reached the front lines. All those stunts. Childish. After I snuck out and downed my first Albatross, I changed my ways. I was supposed to be on leave, and I switched places with a pilot who was to ferry an aircraft to the front. I sent my motorbike ahead for the return trip from that field. As you no doubt guessed, I flew right past the airfield. I didn't have to find the Germans; they found me, and quickly, too.

"I was so close to the man I killed. I saw his face. He was wearing what looked like a white fur coat. We were very low, sometimes less than twenty feet up, jumping trees and houses, going round and round. He got off plenty of shots at me. I thought I was all for it several times. Then, I would pull around on him, but it was impossible to get enough lead to fire. Finally, I shot, and I saw his wings come off, and he slammed the earth. Hard. Pieces of the airplane went everywhere. I circled and watched for the pilot to get clear, but the whole thing burned and exploded.

"I am ashamed to say that it felt good to kill the enemy. Ashamed. I feel the same way when they kill the poor fox, but right then, at that moment, I wanted to be cruel about it. That feeling didn't last long; by the time I landed, I decided not to claim the kill. It would only get me in trouble anyway, so I said a prayer for my enemy, reclaimed by bike and set off for the rear. That unknown German taught me what I needed to know. Of all my victories, by far, the first taught me the most. I felt terribly low, but he was trying to kill me, so I got past it.

"I had a favor coming from highly placed friends at Sopwith, and they helped me plead my case up the chain of command. I was promised that eventually I would receive a fair hearing, but I never had to appear and make my case. They made me Major and put me in charge of a pilot dispersal depot. I informed my parents that I wasn't expected to fly, but of course, I did. I redirected the wayward survivors and green newcomers to their new postings, but we fought as a squadron as well from time to time when a push was on and every last man was needed.

"The idea was to improve new pilot survival by gradually getting the inexperienced men into action. We had some seasoned pilots come through, and it was hoped that some of their knowledge would brush off on the greener pilots. This was seldom the case, as morale was very bad. Some men were returning from hospital or were awaiting reassignment after their squadrons were decimated. Some units lasted only days before they were at half-strength. Within two weeks, they ceased to function. The stunned remaining pilots cycled through depots for the lost souls of the Royal Flying Corps, waiting for reassignment. While in that Limbo, they belonged to me.

"Our aircraft ran the gamut. Unlike frontline squadrons where equipment was uniform, we had too many types to keep up with. They came and went with the pilots. Some were spanking new, but most should have been put down like a lame horse. I pulled people from my factory tour to come up and train the ground crews. I worked with pilots who lacked practical knowledge that could keep them alive. That started on the ground. They had very little idea how to inspect an airplane prior to a mission. I caught countless things that would certainly have killed a pilot. Pointing them out was the best part of my curriculum. Pretty soon, we reliably had twelve to as many as fifteen planes that could fight, but pilots were often reassigned just as we were coming together as a team.

"There were always a few completely bewildered new arrivals to worry about. We were stationed in a fairly quiet sector, I will say that, but trouble found us, or we went looking for it. I couldn't tolerate balloons for some reason. We lost quite a few pilots. I wrote too many letters. It saddens me, but I am a better man for it... Band of Brothers and all that. It's all true. Very true."

Though technically still in recovery and with no expectation of flying in combat, Xavier accepted a position with Sopwith as their lead flight instructor and test pilot. He was overjoyed to be in the air again, but every time he landed, his head throbbed sometimes so badly that he took aspirin and had to lay down with a compress over his eyes. He kept the symptoms to himself as he analyzed the cause. He deduced, quite correctly, that altitude was the issue. Where possible, he flew below eight thousand feet. So long as he didn't fly above ten thousand feet, he was relatively symptom-free—most flights. He also found that when he used experimental oxygen tanks, he could fly quite high with no symptoms at all.

Major Hollows, the flight instructor, lost his S.E.5a but took to a new plane that he enjoyed greatly, even if it did resist tweaking.

Enter the Sopwith Dolphin

In the late summer of 1918, the ultimate British scout plane to serve in the war had already entered service. Its progenitor was virtually identical and was ordered into production in mid-1917. The appearance was somewhat unique as the lower wing stood slightly farther forward than the top wing. For some reason, British troops thought that such a design just had to be German, and it is said that many Dolphins were fired on by skittish British gunners. This aircraft had the distinction of having four firing machine guns if the pilot didn't mind having two guns positioned to take off his head in the event of a crash landing. The left upper gun spit empty brass right across the pilot's face and into the slip stream. They must have come up with some sort of deflector or passed on mounting the port side gun. Hollows did not expect to fire his weapons and flew with only his Lewis and no ammunition to lighten the plane. The top guns could be pointed upwards for underside attacks, but they were difficult to aim. Though early French-made engines for the plane were unreliable, production flaws were ironed out, and eventually, the Dolphin was known as a highflyer capable of taking down airplanes at twenty thousand feet.

In point of fact, Major Hollow's Dolphin was nothing special, but it was equipped with the afore mentioned oxygen bottle that clipped on the outside of the fuselage next to the cockpit. This added some weight and drag and would be quite deadly if struck by a bullet. A short hose connected to a mask made of a rubberized canvas that fit over the pilot's nose and mouth. The mask was slightly oversized on Hollow's face and uncomfortable. One didn't wear it until it was thought needed. It hung loosely about the neck on a single lanyard. A second strap was supposed to run over his ears and be pulled tight for use. Without gloves, this was just barely possible one-handed.

Hollow's plane was also equipped with a new parachute system that was stored in a canister that opened about a foot behind the cockpit. The pilot was connected to it by a twelve-foot lanyard that was tied to a single point on a harness that ran over his shoulders, around his waist, and somewhat uncomfortably between his legs. The tube was covered with wax paper but essentially it was open on top, and the pilot's falling weight deployed the parachute. The chances of a hangup on the tail or wing tip were excellent.

Hollow's orders sent him to Andover Aerodrome, about seventy miles south of London. This was the first stop on what was to be a tour of units equipped with the Sopwith Dolphin. Specifically, Major Hollows was to train the squadron in high-altitude bomber interception. Largely built by German POWs, Andover was the home of several squadrons, including Handly Page bombers, which were being fitted with radio directional devices that could guide them to Berlin and back. Hollows arrived by air while the rest of his crew, commanded by Lieutenant Rigby, arrived in convoy with engine parts, oxygen equipment, and a few parachute kits.

High-altitude tactics were not taught in initial flight training. It was generally understood that most pilots began to make poor decisions due to oxygen deprivation at twelve thousand feet. By fifteen thousand feet, this could be a serious problem, but pilots climbed on without knowing the physiology behind what was happening to their brains. Some men handled it better than others. Before his shoot down, Major Hollows made a practice of climbing to high altitudes before it was fashionable or necessary, but his abilities in thin air were rare.

Bottled oxygen was helpful, but the supply per canister was short-lived. A pilot might have enough of the precious gas to get to altitude and not enough to get him back down again. It was also a good idea to come down somewhat slowly to let the body reacclimate to the rising air pressure. Pilots complained of extreme cramps on fast descents.

German bombers were the desired prey of scout interceptor squadrons stationed in Southern England. Two types were used. The Gotha was smaller than the Zeppelin Staaken R.VI bomber which had a wingspan damn near that of a World War Two B-29 Super Fortress bomber. The Gothas were common, but the larger ships were more destructive with much heavier payloads than the Gotha. The massive Zepplin Staaken had an enclosed cockpit, which was unique at that time, and carried four defensive guns. It was powered by four engines and crewed by eight men, two of whom were mechanics along to service the engines. They walked from the flight cabin across the lower wing to access the engine's compartments *in flight.* The two tandem pusher/tractor units had a combined one thousand horsepower and drove two fourteen-foot pusher propellers. This giant traveled at about eighty miles per hour and carried somewhere in the neighborhood of one thousand pounds of explosives. It could fly as high as fifteen thousand feet. These aircraft were seldom used over England, and none were lost in attacks on London, though two failed to return to base from missions. By contrast, twenty-eight Gotha bombers were shot down by all means over England.

When the phone rang at the Andover airfield dispersal hut, Xavier was the only man wearing a flight suit as the entire squadron's planes were taken off flight status by faulty pinion gears in the French-made Hispano-Suiza 8B engines. He landed just as the sun was about to set and went straight to the officer's mess for some long-expected dinner. He relaxed and sipped brandy with fellow officers who were fascinated by his stories of life at the front, shooting down Germans and landing in a cesspool. A few men at the table were back from the front lines. Like Xavier, they were the lucky survivors, the statistical outliers who ought not be. These pilots shared their moments of survival more than memories of their kills. They passed on their techniques with little brutal quips and sarcasm that began with a gasped, "Oh!" As in, "Oh Lord, whatever you do, don't do that!" Or, "Oh good! You have found yet another way to kill yourself." They were sometimes physically scared, even burned, and tight lipped about how they got that way. Xavier was a member of that society, and their impromptu decompression went on for some time.

The squadron's CO entered the mess and called for Xavier. "Hollows! Get over to the dispersal hut. A picket boat more than fifty miles out saw a zeppelin at low altitude cross the full moon with a bearing they estimate is right our way. The report said that it was unusually large and climbed away rapidly. We're instructed to put everything we've got up. That is you, if you want to go."

"A zeppelin? You must be joking. Of course, I am going up. Rigby! Fuel and arm my Dolphin and bring up two oxygen bottles from the trucks." He turned to the CO. "Let's go look at that map. Where was that boat? Did they estimate altitude? When will the zeppelin make landfall, and where do I have to be to kill it? It might make, at best, sixty miles per hour. Balls! I don't have time for this. Get your best navigators on this. Bring me the information on the flight line. I must prepare the airplane."

"Major Hollows, this is an interception, not Christmas. Do be careful. I don't much like the weather tonight. I fear turbulence at altitude, and we have no MK VI rounds in the ammunition dump. We didn't expect to see a zeppelin over London again. Shoot up his engines if you can and the gondola. Maybe the wind will blow him out to sea or better still, Ireland."

"Huh. That's funny. I have one MK VI bullet right here. It's my lucky one. I've had it for a few years now. My little war crime. What the hell? I'll put it my Lewis gun."

"Get moving. Good hunting."

Leftenant Murphy and sergeant Burrows were the best navigators on the base. They were fiendishly good at their job and thought of the situation like a chess game with a healthy dollop of physics thrown in to give it modern flavor. They discussed the weather and wind direction. Maps were laid out, and lines were drawn. At first they disagreed. The experts challenged each other but quickly reached a consensus. Numbers were rechecked. The CO made a final measurement for himself.

The squadron leader challenged his experts. "If we have guessed his speed correctly, he has already crossed the coast. His plan is obvious, if not a little insane. London is heavily defended in the southeast. He thinks he will get behind the anti-aircraft guns, but first, he has to sneak by a few airfields on the coast."

"Yes, sir. If he had not dropped low enough to get some sort of bearing when he was out over the Channel, that picket boat never would have seen him."

"The cloud cover is clearing. That's what will do him in, I hope. Perhaps it's down already."

"Possibly. The other squadrons received the same report that we did, so they are up there. Still, it has been some time, and we have heard nothing from them. If they had insufficient warning, they would never have time to climb high enough to reach the intruder before he slips past. He must be carrying a staggering amount of fuel."

"Sir?" the navigator asked. "I have a question. How will he run out after the attack? Surely not back the way he came, and heading out over the Channel through alerted air defense is suicide unless it can climb so high that it cannot be reached by our aircraft. In which case, why come around the back way? Maybe his target isn't London."

"Well, we have no way of knowing, no idea at all. But London is the best bet. An attack on any other city isn't worth the effort. We need to get cracking. Hollows is in for a long climb to the southeast. Run these instructions to him. He'll be ready to go any moment now."

Rigby helped Hollows situate himself in the Dolphin's cramped cockpit as the engine warmed up. Even without the extra Lewis gun, it was rather like putting on a glove. Adding to the sense of confinement were the two oxygen bottle brackets. The hose was fairly long and clipped to the pilot's chest to keep it from flapping around. Oxygen flow was controlled by an on/off valve on the hose itself. Hollows chose to fly with a second oxygen canister and hose but not a second mask. Though it was not designed to do so, he found that he could pull the hose from the on/off valve and reinstall the hose from the other tank. This left him with two valves to open, but it worked all the same. The issue was finding the second hose when he needed it. He was already covered in seat belts and the new parachute harness, which he wore somewhat haphazardly more as a promise to Olivia than any belief in the system. He rolled up the second hose and tucked what he could into a nook meant for a flare gun. He tucked the pistol under his seat where the other Lewis gun magazine was supposed to be.

Hollows tended to his engine warm-up and did not notice when Rigby opened the as-yet-unused parachute canister behind the cockpit. The ever-faithful aid withdrew the chord and wove it over the wing spars, which ran behind and above the pilot's seat. Hollows smiled when he heard the huge hook click.

Rigby patted Xavier on the head and shouted, "I promised your sister."

South of England over the English Channel

Fausmann was prone to making motivational speeches in the *Henry the Fifth* tradition. Every mission was decisive or pivotal. Names would be remembered and a new weapon immortalized. He liked to swear that he would never stoop to using a parachute. He would face his fate. But, after being hogtied for several hours, he wanted that parachute option more than anything in his entire life. "I'll cooperate if you let me jump for it."

Huckbolt nodded and turned to his pilot. "Take us down to a few hundred feet over the cloud layer. Damn, they are starting to clear out here over the water. If they catch us, now will be the time, but we have no choice. Come on, Fausmann, it is time to earn your silk."

The climb up the ladder from the control gondola into the underside of the zeppelin was nothing for Fausmann but agony for Huckbolt, who went first so that he might turn and cover the only able-bodied man on the mission as he came up. His hands did not like the grasping, and his knees were barely up to the lifting. The rest of the crew had their pistols out as Fausmann followed his captor.

Huckbolt had the spy car hatch open and beckoned Fausmann to reach inside for the phone. Huckbolt listened on his set and nodded in readiness. Fausmann was broad-shouldered and had to squeeze himself into the bulletlike housing. Of course, this meant that he had to unplug his suit. It would be a cold ride.

Huckbolt toggled the control button and watched the parasite disappear into the gloom below. Inside the spy car, there was a distracting whistle from the hatch. Then, the buffeting began as the clouds closed around him. He could see nothing for more than a minute. Just when he thought the car would come unglued, it broke through the overcast. The full moon was largely blocked by the cloud layer, but there were breaks enough to see a reflection of the ocean and the fall of land.

Fausmann used the phone, but the whistle was so loud that he could not make himself heard.

"Huckbolt! Huckbolt! I see the coast. Repeat, I see the Isle of Wight! We are slightly west of Portsmouth!" he screamed. The car began to rise, and the turbulence began again. The hatch gave way and flew off into the slipstream with a thousand feet to go before reaching Mother Zeppelin. Fausmann buried his face in his gloved hands as he felt the cold find his spine. His exposed neck burned with frosty vengeance, and he cried out in frustration and fear.

The spy car lost its aerodynamics when the hatch blew off. It whipped and bucked against the current like a foul-hooked trout on a fishing line. Huckbolt was unsure if the car would line up with its opening in the zeppelin's substructure. The cable snapped and slipped in the massive reel. In the final yards, the car hit the underside of the ship where it was pinned by the winds. The cable kept pulling and Huckbolt thought for sure it would snap. The car was slightly askew and did not align with its portal. It could not be fully retracted to its starting position. Huckbolt saw Fausmann climb from the car onto solid footing, where he clung without moving for about thirty seconds. He snapped out of his shock and waved a fist at Huckbolt who was calling for him to get moving.

"Fausmann, you pathetic bastard, climb! What did you see? Are we over the coast?"

"You did not hear? It is blacked out, but I clearly saw that we are slightly east of Portsmouth. We are over the Isle of Wight. Let's get down to your table. I can plot a course for London. If memory serves me, we are maybe seventy to maybe ninety miles from our last turn at Reading."

The Kapitan nodded enthusiastically. "My plan is going to work, Fausmann. If we can slip through at altitude, there will be nothing to oppose us, especially from this direction."

"Be careful on the ladder, Huckbolt. I would hate to lose you in your last hour of life."

The zeppelin rose back into the darkness as it neared its final destination.

Far below, telephones began to ring, and searchlights switched on.

"Look, Fausmann, in the extreme distance. Searchlights. There is London, and they are looking the wrong way."

"Yes, but they are looking. They may know we are here."

Hollows is Airborne

Hollows cleared the runway and pulled back on the stick as he spiraled upward. He knew his prey would be above the cloud layer, but flying through it was thought to be unadvisable, especially at night, as rough air could potentially rip a wing from the frame quite easily. Here and there, the moonlight lit the cotton above him, and he thought the clouds thinner and perhaps penetrable. He circled looking for a hole and was rewarded at eleven thousand feet. It wasn't particularly large, but the Dolphin slipped through with only moderate buffeting. Above the clouds, the moon was full, and the stars shone brightly. He made a circle towards London as he passed fourteen thousand feet.

After liftoff, it took Hollows a little over twenty minutes to reach sixteen thousand feet. He attempted to don the oxygen mask, but the lanyard that was to go over his ears was stuck on his collar. He had to remove his left glove for a moment, but he couldn't figure out how to both fly the plane and remove a glove. It was baffling. The plane continued to climb past seventeen thousand feet. Hollows added a tingling sensation in his fingertips to his list of odd sensations. He focused on the mission and looked about for the zeppelin he hoped to flame. But then there was something else… He knew he was supposed to do something, but he could not for the life of him remember what it was. He climbed still higher.

It took thirty-five minutes to reach twenty-thousand feet. He felt swimmy and started to sing, but he couldn't remember the words. Then, he decided to stretch his legs. He pushed the rudder pedals back and forth. The plane violently flipped over. Hollows felt his full weight pull against his safety belt. He took both hands off the stick and stared at it as if it had a mind of its own. The Dolphin stalled, and the engine sputtered as the aircraft lost altitude. The oxygen mask hit him in the chin. He focused on it, and from some dimly lit cave in the nether reaches of his brain, a command was passed to his tingling hands. With the mask on it took only a moment to realize that the situation was dire. He pushed the stick forward and added power. The Dolphin took a moment to decide what it was going to do. It shuddered as Hollows pulled out just above the cloud layer. He took a moment to count his blessings and test the airframe. He felt no shudders or flutter. The roll rate felt right. Engine temperature was within limits. He still had half a tank of fuel. The mission could continue. He marveled at the blanket of meteorology beneath him. He began his climb again but rolled to take a last look at the wispy white heavens lit by the moon.

At first, Xavier thought a little raincloud was mixed in the white. It was a strange shape, like a dart, and it was moving. Hollows made sure the oxygen bottle was flowing as he traced a line with his eyes from the odd shadow cast by the full moon and a monster streaming along at eighteen thousand feet. It was barely perceptible to the eye, and the rushing wind rendered its noisy engines silent. Hollows crossed seventeen thousand feet, and his engine purred lovingly for him. For a few minutes, both the shadow and the zeppelin disappeared, and Hollows thought it had gone even higher.

He crossed eighteen thousand feet forty miles southeast of London, but the target was gone. Then, ahead of him at about a mile he saw a light. It was Huckbolt's map table lamp showing Hollows the way. The new clear bulb shone brightly. It was only lit for a few moments, but it was enough to set a course.

For its day, the Dolphin was a near-perfect high-altitude interceptor if the pilot had enough oxygen to pull off a battle. Hollows sensed that his first bottle was about to run dry, so he took a mighty lungful and closed the valve. He decided to press his attack but ran out of air before he could close to fire. He took another shot of oxygen, but it wasn't much, and again, he felt swimmy. The zeppelin loomed, and he ducked beneath it without firing a shot. He found himself directly behind the port side rear engine that hung below and slightly outboard of the ship on a long sponson. A quick burst of the Vickers guns stopped it for good. It burned for a moment and then blew out. Hollows slew over to the other side and repeated the shot. He then circled up above the ship and looked at the stars.

This crucial move in the battle had nothing to do with triggers or bombs. Just rubber hoses. Hollows decided to put the other bottle on his oxygen line. How or why this one rational idea took hold was a testament to his experience. His head began to clear. He had one urge: *land the plane immediately.* This he did, making a perfect three-point touchdown on top of the zeppelin. He sat in the cockpit with the engine at bare idle, breathing deeply from the mask and slowly coming to the realization that he wasn't on the ground.

Huckbolt's Play

Huckbolt saw the Dolphin just before it opened fire and destroyed two of his engines. He leaned out into the slipstream to look back at his assailant as it rolled and climbed away. He called out to the remainder of his crew. "Do you see it? Where did it go? Fausmann! Put on the parachute harness! Quickly, we do not have much time. I cannot fathom why he didn't just shoot us with those damned explosive bullets."

Fausmann pulled the chute from its locker and stepped into the harness.

Huckbolt ordered, "Take us down. Transfer ballast to the nose tank. I will vent the forward bags at ten thousand feet. We'll just have to hope that we are over something worth blowing up below us. Once we are through the clouds, I will hit the button. Say your prayers! Fausmann, you better jump before I hit the switch, or you'll land right in the middle of it!"

Fausmann kept up his preparations. "What is it you said to me on that last mission together? A killer of cows, you said. Not so easy, is it, Huckbolt?"

"Fuck you, Fausmann. There is a letter in your flight suit. It is my confession. I want the British to know who was up above the clouds tonight. Stand in the door. Prepare to jump. This will be a record fall for both of us."

As the airship sank, the oxygen level came up. This, combined with the leaky mask's supply, brought Hollow's world back into focus. He was aware of the airframe vibrating. It made tiny hops as if it wanted to leap free, but its master wouldn't let it run off a leash. With the throttle back and the zeppelin moving at barely forty miles per hour, the Dolphin wanted to stay where it was with not one gun pointing at a target six feet beneath three muzzles. Hollows dreamed of using his flare gun to blow up the zeppelin. He reached for the pistol but found it gone; its recess used to house the second oxygen line. It took a few seconds to remember where the gun was. He produced it, checked to see if it was cocked and loaded, then held it over his head and fired it straight up into the air. He watched the flare arch and thought it pretty. He then dropped the pistol over the side.

Hollows airborne airfield began to tip and fall. The Sopwith rolled forward toward the unmanned central gun pit. If its wheels fell into that position, the likelihood of pulling out was not promising. Xavier opened the throttle and raised the nose. The Dolphin rolled over the pit. The landing carriage struck an edge, but the Dolphin vaulted into the night sky.

Xavier banked his airplane hard and lined up for a firing pass. He remembered that his Lewis gun on the upper gun rack had a Buckingham bullet in the pan. The gunsight was useless in the darkness, and Hollows had to break away before he rammed the giant. His burst was aimed by his usually trusty instinct, but this time, he missed the gas bags by a mile. He did hit Fausmann who had just hung the parachute tube in the gondola doorway. The explosive bullet holed his chest. The damage was massive, but he still managed to bend over and step out of the hatch. The tether raced behind and pulled the chute from the tube.

The other crew was riddled by the burst as well, except for Huckbolt, who scrambled as best he could to find something solid to stand upon now that the zeppelin was nosing over. The double engines in the back of the gondola did not like the angle and began to smoke. The dead engineer was not there to cut the fuel. The remaining two outboard engines choked as well.

Hollows sprayed the gas bags with his remaining ammunition. He watched with glee as the zeppelin stood on its nose and began to fall away rapidly. Inside the Gondola, Huckbolt braced himself with a foot on the aluminum window frame. He reached for the gas release valve that would send his ship to Earth like a meteorite. He stepped onto the glass. The pane cracked. His reflexes were slowed by mental resignation, but he managed to flip the switch.

Xavier saw Huckbolt fall as he circled the zeppelin. By jousting standards, he had unhorsed his man, and yet his opponent's massive airship still had a plan of its own. He counted down to an expected explosion, but instead, the massive airship gathered speed as it fell. The last effects of oxygen deprivation had yet to subside, and Xavier seized on the thought, *I have to ram*. His duty was clear. England Herself was under direct attack below him. Without hesitation, Major Hollows of the newly named Royal Air Force banked his Dolphin and aimed the nose at the center of the falling giant.

He closed the distance in a few seconds.

There was no time for Xavier's life to flash before his eyes. He didn't consider what his parents would say or how they would feel when he was gone. He only heard one voice. It was his little sister, and she said quite clearly, "Tex, don't be a damned fool." Beatrice reached out through the cosmos to touch her brother's heart. She moved his hands on the stick and caused his feet to press the rudder. The suicidal dive crossed the zeppelin upside down and so close that Xavier could lift his hand above his head to touch his enemy and count coup like a Plains Indian warrior.

Huckbolt's switch vented the center gas bladders, ejecting thousands of square feet of hydrogen gas in seconds. Hollows flew right through the flammable cloud. The sparks from the Dolphin's exhaust did the trick.

The Freefall

The explosion that followed began as a fire in the zeppelin's forward compartment. Hollows saw the nose glow for several seconds. This shot up the internal walkway that spanned the full length of the ship. The incendiaries in the forward bomb bay were the first to explode.

Everything else went off within milliseconds, just as planned. It all happened above the clouds at thirteen thousand feet. The mustard gas was vaporized in the flame, and the debris that fell over farmland was so small that nobody ever put it together with a zeppelin attack.

Hollow's Dolphin was caught squarely in the blast. The pressure buckled his portside wings and blew off his propeller. The plane began to spin like a bullet in the barrel of a gun. The shattered Dolphin nosed over and fell into the clouds. Xavier pulled his head and shoulders down into the cockpit as the rest of the top wing departed. For a moment, the spinning stopped with the cockpit facing up.

The upper wing had two spars, front and back, with no fabric over the cockpit, so the pilot's visibility was excellent. The rear spar ran immediately behind and just above the pilot's head, and the parachute tube was right behind that. Rigby attached the parachute tether over the rear wing spar so that if the Major did bail out, the chute would not have to be dragged under the spar before it could deploy. He did not consider what would happen if the top wing were lost. It pulled the parachute tether so forcefully that it yanked the parachute from its tube. It was perfectly folded and threaded its way to a clean opening. Unfortunately, on the other end of the tether, Major Hollows was still belted into the falling fighter.

The parachute was well stitched, but the forces put on it were far beyond anything its designers ever anticipated. A truly savage snap pulled at Xavier's abdomen and crushed his testicles. The loosely fitted harness rode up on him and began to rip. He pulled the seat belt buckle release and rocketed from the cockpit. It took only a moment for that speed to turn to free fall. He always wondered what these last moments would feel like, and he had plenty of altitude to think about the terminus. He watched his Dolphin disappear into the blackness below.

The falling slowed considerably. The parachute was attached to a single riser behind his head, so the passenger had no control over where he landed or what direction he was facing. The silk was torn from overstress, leaving a hole that accelerated the fall. Hollows spun completely around twenty times a minute. He found the spin combined with the nether-crushing quite nauseating. This process went on for some time, several minutes, in fact. He landed like a sack of hammers in the middle of a pig farm wallow. For a moment he couldn't catch his breath. The pigs panicked and shot around the enclosure protesting loudly. The parachute was still abloom and pulled on the prostrate flier. A farmer with a shotgun took for him for an enemy pilot until he heard Hollow's accent.

"Dear God, man! The harness is trying to kill me. Grab the parachute. Quickly, or I may never have children."

The farmer leaned his shotgun against a fence and began to gather the billowing parachute.

"You'll have to pardon the gun-pointing, sir. A dead German pilot landed on my barn. I thought it might be raining Germans tonight. I saw an airplane crash."

"Yes, on both counts. I believe that German is one for my game bag, and that crashed airplane would be my Dolphin. My aid will no doubt pop by to clean this all up."

Hollows returned to earth with one hell of a story, but he and the farmer were forbidden to tell it. He expected a medal, but none was forthcoming. Secret negotiations were ongoing. A massive bomb aimed at England's heart might be off-putting to the peace process. The zeppelin's high-altitude detonation was heard as far away as London, but the mystery of the explosion went unfathomed.

The loss of Hollow's Dolphin was written off as a structural failure at altitude. It happens all the time. So what if a dead German pilot was found hanging from a parachute? Yes, as was said, it happens all the time. The theory was that he fell from a Gotha that was badly off course, but his identity was never tracked down. He had a letter in an envelope in his flight suit vest pocket, but the combination of the explosive bullet and the subsequent torrent of blood ruined it. It was a little weird, but hey, this sort of thing happened all the time.

Huckbolt's body was not found until 1921. He landed in a swampy area smack in the middle of a vast cow pasture. A farmhand saw a boot rising from the muck. Between the burns, cuts from the glass, high velocity impact with the earth, and a few years soaking in the bog, Huckbolt's bloated body was among the most hideous ever seen. His uniform was still somewhat recognizable, but no identity tag was found. A zeppelin corps badge was found in his pocket. Whoever he was, his twisted remains were too long for the stretcher. Lord knows how they got him in the standard-sized coffin, but it had to involve a crosscut saw. A news story wondered who the unrecognizable German was, but nobody took up his cause. He was buried in a pauper's graveyard without a headstone.

"Sorry about the mud, sir." The farmer was embarrassed as he brushed Hollow's flight jacket.

"What? This?" Xavier sniffed his sleeve. "This is just mud. I hadn't even noticed. Not a bit of it, my good man. This is a serious step up for me. Let me sit here a moment. I am still spinning. The ride down was a trifle alarming. My doctor would say this was a good landing, and I trust him completely. Any landing one can walk away from, you see? I will be walking here momentarily. Oh my Lord. I am very happy to be on the ground. I might not leave it again. Actually, this is one of my most memorable impromptu landings."

"It would have to be. I suppose you know all about the horrendous explosion up there. What the hell was that?"

"I was compelled to kill a giant. Just that simple."

"I guess that makes you Jack then, doesn't it, sir? Had your fill of magic beans?"

"Jack? Hell. My name is Tex, and, as I like to say, I have a hat to prove it."

"What? Buffalo Bill's Stetson? I very much doubt that, sir. Clearly, you are an Englishman. There is no way a hat such as that would ever fit on your head."

"Well said. I am an Englishman. Truth be known, I do hate that hat."

Acknowledgments

The author would like to acknowledge the following soldiers, teachers, historians, curators, and family for their help with this book. While this is not a scholarly offering as such, it has been extensively researched. These acknowledgements and the bibliography are meant to reassure the reader that my creative tether is tied to an understanding of history that goes beyond the armchair. I was an educator on the college level and a grad student for many years before that. Be assured, I have grown to despise the scholarly tone and stringent documentation of higher education pulp. This will be a different kind of history lesson.

I wish to praise four specific soldiers. All should salute Audie Murphy, whose story is told here. Second, Chuck Yeager's interviews about air combat and tactics were word-for-word some of the most useful observations ever posted. I am truly appreciative of my former (step-) "Uncle Cliff," whose Vietnam story is recounted in Chapter Two. Finally, I save my greatest appreciation for mortar platoon leader Lieutenant Eugene Folks of the United States Marine Corps, who served with distinction at Guadalcanal and Okinawa. He was a family friend and business partner for many years. I grew up on his war stories. We have made his 1911 .45 something of a shrine. Gene was the finest, most decent man I ever knew and an exact representation of a noble citizen soldier. This book is for him.

As a teacher, I know how hard it can be to kindle a love for any subject in a student's heart. I had an amazing history instructor in high school by the name of Mark Olcott, who wrote *The Civil War letters of Lewis Bissell* (1981). He taught a reverence for world events. His creativity and enthusiasm for the past was truly infectious. My junior year English teacher, Micheal Kennedy, gave me confidence both as a writer and a critical thinker, even if I couldn't spell my way out of a wet paper sack. I give credit to The Field School and The Pomfret School for having the highest academic expectations. I had but one college professor at the University of Richmond who helped me to be a better writer. Dr. Todras, wherever you are, thank you for teaching me the value of the well-chosen word.

Next, I must *begrudgingly* admit that YouTube videos by various personas have motivated me all along the path to publication. Yes. I know. New media is often the *Monarch Notes* of understanding. Longer format presentations, however, often offer new details and perspectives that prompt me to further investigation. I must give thanks to "The Chieftain" Nicholas Moran for his videos on all things tank related. I would also like to thank Ian McCollum for his work with small arms history on his channel, *Forgotten Weapons*. Similarly, I do not know how I would have gotten along without *Rex's Hanger* videos on famous aircraft or Mark Felton's videos on so many military topics. I will confess that in addition to reading several books about the Hundred Years' War, some of the background on Agincourt used in this book was drawn from competing theories about the battle shown on YouTube.

I tend to eat breakfast with various military expert podcasters. There is nothing like watching a talented War College professor give a two-hour presentation on Gettysburg or The Battle of the Marne to take a military buff to the next level—whatever that is. The net effect is like going back to college, only this time, you aren't necessarily stoned for the lecture. I am also deeply indebted to Victor Davis Hanson for his lectures about both ancient and modern warfare.

My love of all things military was greatly facilitated by the museums I have visited over the past fifty years. At the time of this writing, I am just back from visiting the National Naval Aviation Museum in Pensacola, Florida, where I gathered information on airships, World War One bombers, and zeppelins. Lovers of military aircraft should make a pilgrimage to the United States Air Force Museum at Patterson Air Force Base in Ohio. It's huge and mind-bending. The Air and Space Museums that are part of the Smithsonian Institute in Washington, DC, are always overrun with tourists but a good second best. The Owl's Head Transportation Museum in Maine has been a fantastic source of inspiration and information on World War One aircraft where they still fly.

Tank lovers need their museum time too. Reading about tank battles, or even watching good reenactments on screen, is no substitute for being in the same room with one of these battlefield monsters. The Patton Museum at Fort Knox, Kentucky, Aberdeen Proving Ground in Maryland, and the (now closed) AAF Tank Museum in Danville, Virginia, taught me a great deal about armored warfare. Seriously. Go stand in front of a communist T-54 at a tank museum and pretend, for a moment, that you are the Chinese patriot who stood down an entire column of these tanks at Tiananmen Square during the 1989 protests. Consider what it would it be like to get run over by those treads. Imagine dashing up to a tank and planting a bomb on it or throwing a Molotov cocktail inside.

I have visited many battlefields in both the United States and Europe, and I am grateful to the docent guides who put up with stupid questions. Again, one needs to stand where the soldiers stood. In the United States, the must visits include Gettysburg, the Bunker Hill Monument, and The Battle of the Little Big-Horn. Of all the battlefields I have visited, I would most like a return tour of The Airborne Museum at Hartenstein, Holland, where not too far away stands the actual Bridge Too Far.

I do spend some time discussing small arms, particularly machine guns, as well as creatively writing about their use. I must acknowledge my old friend, Ernest Colsmann, for allowing me to fire all of the automatic weapons in his massive personal collection, including many that are featured in this book. These include a plethora of submachine guns, the Lewis gun, an M-2 .50 caliber, and a World War One German anti-tank rifle that loosened my teeth with every shot.

As far as influential reading is concerned, as you will see, the list of authors is extensive. I am very grateful to Alvin and Heidi Toffler for their 1993 work, *War and Anti-War: Survival at the Dawn of the 21st Century.* No other book that I have read on this subject has been more influential.

I am hard-pressed to name all of the prominent military historians that might be cited in this work. The reader should know that I left forty thousand words of hard core tactics, history, and weaponology on the cutting room floor. This leaves a faint trace here and a whiff of history there. There was a hell of a section on the Maginot Line. I discussed Nazi mega weapons and Japanese tank warfare. My editor termed these rabbit holes, or in this case rabbit bunkers, and urged their excision. There are forty-three books stacked up on my desk as I write this section and two dozen more that I might well list for minor contributions. My reading on the Second World War began in high school with Cornelius Ryan's *A Bridge Too Far* (1974) and *The Longest Day* (1959). I am greatly in debt to John Kegan for his works on this conflict, which include the most influential *Six Armies In Normandy* (1994) and *The Face of Battle* (1976), which was my first source for Agincourt material. Rick Atkinson's *Liberation Trilogy*, which begins with *An Army At Dawn: The War in North Africa, 1942–1943* (2002), was essential to this effort. I must also give a shout to Catherine Merridale's *Ivan's War: Life and Death in the Red Army, 1939–1945* (2006) and Joseph Balkoski for his work *Beyond The Beachhead: The 29th Infantry Division in Normandy* (1999). Anyone interested in post-Second World War Europe would do well to read Michael Dobb's *Six Months in 1945: FDR, Stalin, Churchill, and Truman: From World War to Cold War* (2012).

Other authors who flesh out military conflict include Steven Ambrose, Shelby Foote, David Halberstam, Walter Boyne, and Stanley Karnow.

This work examines tanks and their development. Among the most useful books on this theme are *Tank Versus Tank* by Kenneth Macksey (1999) and his *Guderian Creator of the Blitzkrieg* (1975). For a greater understanding of the tank and its influence on the last century, look no further than *Tank* by Patrick Wright (2003). Much of my knowledge of Soviet Cold War Era armored warfare comes from two works written at the height of the Cold War: *Soviet Airland Battle Tactics* by Lt. Colonel William Baxter (1986) and *The Threat: Inside the Soviet Military Machine* by Andrew Cockburn (1983).

As far as aircraft and their military history are concerned, it all began with *Jane's* Military reference books that I read with my toddler son instead of *Green Eggs and Ham*. I was also inspired by narratives about air war from *Sky Battles, Sky Warriors,* edited by Alfred Price (1994), and *Wings of War,* edited by Laddie Lucas (1984). Eric M. Bergerud's *Fire in the Sky: The Air War in the South Pacific* (2000) was of vital importance, as was Malcolm Gladwell's *The Bomber Mafia* (2021). Tony Holmes edited *Dogfight: The Greatest Air Duels in World War Two* (2011), which provided a vast amount of material found herein and may be the best bathroom reading of all time.

Warfare cannot be properly understood without biographical influences. In this area, I must give high praise to Walter Borneman for *Macarthur At War: World War Two in the Pacific* and Peter Caddick-Adam for his *Monty and Rommel Parallel Lives* (2011). *The War Lovers: Roosevelt, Lodge, Hearst and the Rush to Empire, 1898* by Evan Thomas (2010) was also important background for this work. The prize in the biography section goes to Johnathan Jordan for *Brothers*Rivals*Victors: Eisenhower, Patton, Bradley and the Partnership That Drove The Allied Conquest In Europe* (2011).

I must thank my father for teaching me the importance of writing and how to be brave in the face of criticism. My wife deserves even greater accolades for allowing me to stuff our home with military books, artifacts, and relic guns. She happily follows me around museums that do not interest her in the slightest. I am a lucky, lucky man.

Which brings us to the pictures used here in. My personal library and museum "area" is chock full of artifacts and models that cover many of the events and characters portrayed in this book, and it seems only obvious that I present them for your edification. Some I acquired long ago, but others, like the Jagdpanther model and zeppelin badge were built or acquired before I drafted the story so that I might better describe their battles. Many of the miniature soldiers are sold by King and Country toy soldiers. Other die-cast toys and soldiers shown were largely made by Britains, Dinky, Corgi, and Solido toy companies. Models are mostly Tamiya and Airfix kits in 1/72, 1/48, and 1/35 scales. I mixed scales and obviously the toy soldiers are not perfect representations of characters herein, but they speak, in their way, of the story and its themes.

P. R. Hirsh 4/24/25

Bibliography

Ambrose, Stephen E. *Citizen Soldiers: The U.S. Army from the Normandy Beaches to the Surrender of Germany.* London: Simon & Schuster, 2016.

—. *Victors.* Simon & Schuster Ltd., 2016.

—. *Wild Blue.* Simon & Schuster Ltd., 2016.

Ambrose, Stephen E. and Douglas Brinkley. *Rise to Globalism: American Foreign Policy since 1938.* New York: Penguin Books, 2011.

Atkinson, Rick. *An Army at Dawn: Vol. One: The War in North Africa, 1942–1943.* New York: Henry Holt and Co., 2002.

—. *In the Company of Soldiers.* Large Print Press, 2004.

—. *The Long Gray Line.* Picador, 1 Apr. 2010.

Balkoski, Joseph. *Beyond the Beachhead.* Stackpole Books, 4 Aug. 2005.

Baxter, William. *Soviet Airland Battle Tactics.* Presidio, 1986.

Bergerud, Eric M. *Fire in the Sky: The Air War in the South Pacific.* New York, NY: Basic Books, 2009.

Boritt, G. S. and Stephen W. Sears. *Lincoln's Generals.* Lincoln, University of Nebraska Press, 2010.

Borneman, Walter R. *MacArthur at War.* Little, Brown, 10 May 2016.

Boyne, Walter J. *The Two O'Clock War: The 1973 Yom Kippur Conflict and the Airlift That Saved Israel.* New York: Thomas Dunne Books, 2002.

Caddick-Adams, Peter. *Monty and Rommel: Parallel Lives.* Overlook, 2013.

Carius, Otto, and Robert J. Edwards. *Tigers in the Mud: The Combat Career of German Panzer Commander Otto Carius.* Guilford, CT: Stackpole Books, 2020.

Chivers, C. J. *The Gun*. New York: Simon & Schuster Paperbacks, 2011.

Cockburn, Andrew. *The Threat*. Vintage, 1984.

Daniel, Larry J. *Shiloh*. Simon and Schuster, 30 Jun. 2008.

Dennis, Jack Bonnell. *The Nuclear Almanac*. Addison Wesley Publishing Company, 1984.

Dobbs, Michael. *Six Months in 1945: FDR, Stalin, Churchill, and Truman—from World War to Cold War*. London: Arrow Books, 2013.

Evans, Richard J. *The Third Reich at War*. New York, Penguin Press, 2008.

Falls, Cyril. *Great Military Battles*. London: Ferndale Editions, 1981.

Fletcher, David. *The British Tanks, 1915–19*. Crowood Press (UK), 2001.

Foote, Shelby, et al. *The Civil War: A Narrative*. New York: Random House, 2011.

Franks, Tommy. *American Soldier*. Harper Collins, 2004.

Gladwell, Malcolm. *The Bomber Mafia: A Dream, a Temptation, and the Longest Night of the Second World War*. New York: Little, Brown and Company, 27 Apr. 2021.

Hackworth, David H., and Eilhys England. *Steel My Soldiers, Hearts*. New York: Simon & Schuster, 2002.

Halberstam, David. *The Coldest Winter*. Hachette Books, 25 Sep. 2007.

Handbook on German Military Forces. LSU Press, 1990.

Hart, Stephen Ashley. *Colossal Cracks: Montgomery's 21st Army Group in Northwest Europe, 1944–45*. Mechanicsburg, PA: Stackpole Books, 2007.

Hastings, Max. *The Korean War*. New York: Simon & Schuster, 1987.

Hoffschmidt, E. J., and William H. Tantum. *German Tank and Anti-tank*. Paladin Press, 1968.

Hogg, Ian V. *German Secret Weapons of World War II: The Missiles, Rockets, Weapons, and New Technology of the Third Reich*. La Vergne: Skyhorse Publishing, 2016.

Holmes, Tony. *Dogfight*. New York: Chartwell Books, 2013.

Houston, Donald Eugene. *Hell on Wheels: The 2d Armored Division*. Novato, CA: Presidio Press, 1995.

Hoyt, Edwin Palmer. *America's Wars and Military Excursions*. McGraw-Hill Companies, 1987.

Jackson, Robert. *F-86 Sabre*. Smithsonian, 1 Jan. 1994.

Jordan, Jonathan W. *Brothers, Rivals, Victors*. Penguin, 3 Apr. 2012.

Karnow, Stanley. *Vietnam: A History*. New York, NY: Viking, 1991.

Keegan, John. *Six Armies in Normandy: From D-Day to the Liberation of Paris, June 6th–August 25th, 1944*. London: Pimlico, 2004.

—. *The Face of Battle: A Study of Agincourt, Waterloo and the Somme*. London: The Bodley Head, 2014.

Kershaw, Robert J. *It Never Snows in September*. Ian Allen Publishing, 1990.

Lucas, James, and Mazal Holocaust Collection. *The Third Reich*. New York, NY: London, Arms and Armour, 1990.

Lucas, Laddie. *Wings of War*. London: Hutchinson, 1983.

Macksey, Kenneth. *Guderian, Creator of the Blitzkrieg*. Scarborough House, 1976.

—. *Tank versus Tank*. Grub Street, 1999.

Malaparte, Curzio. *The Volga Rises in Europe*. Birlinn, 1957.

McKee, Alexander. *Caen, Anvil of Victory*. London: Souvenir Press, 1964.

Merridale, Catherine. *Ivan's War*. Metropolitan Books, 1 Apr. 2007.

Newark, Tim. *Turning the Tide of War: 50 Battles That Changed the Course of Modern History*. London: Hamlyn, 2006.

Oren, Michael B. *Six Days of War: June 1967 and the Making of the Modern Middle East*. London: Penguin, 2003.

Price, Alfred. *Sky Battles*. Arms and Armor, 1 Jan. 2000.

Regan, Geoffrey. *Great Military Disasters*. Evans, 1987.

Rolston, Les. *Long Time Gone*. Lulu.com, 20 Mar. 2017.

Ryan, Cornelius. *A Bridge Too Far*. London: Coronet, 1975.

Sebestyen, Victor. *1946: The Making of the Modern World*. New York: Vintage Books, A Division of Penguin Random House Llc., 2016.

Sheehan, Neil. *A Bright Shining Lie: John Paul Vann and America in Vietnam*. New York: Vintage Books, A Division of Random House, Inc., 2013.

Sherwood, John Darrell. *Officers in Flight Suits*. NYU Press, 1 Nov. 1998.

Thomas, Evan. *The War Lovers*. Hachette+ORM, 27 Apr. 2010.

Toffler, Alvin, and Heidi Toffler. *War and Anti-War: Making Sense of Today's Global Chaos*. New York: Warner Books, 1995.

Wright, Patrick. *Tank*. United States: Penguin, 2002.

About the Author

P. R. Hirsh is a retired public school English teacher turned college professor who spent twenty-six years teaching students how to write. A University of Richmond graduate, he holds a master's degree in Secondary Education from West Virginia University and completed all the coursework for a doctorate at the same institution before realizing that higher education is no place to be for someone who still believes in classical education. He published his first work of short stories, *The Guns We Left Behind: Tales of Culture and Caliber*, in 2014. P. R. has two sons and resides in Greenbrier, West Virginia, with his wife, Anne, to whom he has been married for thirty-five years in a row, and four goofy dogs.